Welcome to the EVERYTHING® series!

These handy, accessible books give you all you need to tackle a difficult project, gain a new hobby, comprehend a fascinating topic, prepare for an exam, or even brush up on something you learned back in school but have since forgotten.

You can read an *EVERYTHING*® book from cover-to-cover or just pick out the information you want from our four useful boxes: e-facts, e-ssentials, e-alerts, and e-questions. We literally give you everything you need to know on the subject, but throw in a lot of fun stuff along the way, too.

We now have well over 100 *EVERYTHING*® books in print, spanning such wide-ranging topics as weddings, pregnancy, wine, learning guitar, one-pot cooking, managing people, and so much more. When you're done reading them all, you can finally say you know *EVERYTHING*®!

FACTS

Important sound bytes
of information

SSENTIALS

Quick handy tips

ALERT

Urgent warnings

QUESTIONS?

Solutions to
common problems

THE
EVERYTHING
Series

Dear Reader,

When I was growing up in South Florida, hurricanes rolled in every year like clockwork, and every one was exciting. With school closed in advance of the storm, a hurricane was a minivacation, and I welcomed each one as a gift from the weather gods.

Of course, I didn't own a home then.

These days, my fascination with the weather continues, but my enthusiasm for hurricanes is now tempered by the knowledge of how much damage these ocean-going behemoths can cause. In writing this book, I've attempted to show both sides of the weather equation, detailing not only the havoc that severe weather phenomena can wreak, but also their power and beauty. Everything that happens in the atmosphere serves a purpose, although it might not be readily apparent when you're in the middle of a bad storm in any climate.

This book isn't written for the weather professional, but is meant to serve as an introduction to the subject. If your curiosity is piqued and you'd like to pursue some of the topics in more depth, I've included an extensive resource list in the back of the book. I hope my enthusiasm for weather is contagious: If you have to catch something, it might as well be the weather bug.

Sincerely,

THE
EVERYTHING®
WEATHER
BOOK

From daily forecasts to blizzards,
hurricanes, and tornadoes—all you need
to know to be your own meteorologist

Mark Cantrell

Adams Media Corporation
Avon, Massachusetts

Dedication
For Tally

EDITORIAL
Publishing Director: Gary M. Krebs
Managing Editor: Kate McBride
Copy Chief: Laura MacLaughlin
Acquisitions Editor: Bethany Brown
Development Editor: Christel A. Shea
Production Editor: Khrysti Nazzaro

PRODUCTION
Production Director: Susan Beale
Production Manager: Michelle Roy Kelly
Series Designer: Daria Perreault
Cover Design: Paul Beatrice and Frank Rivera
Layout and Graphics: Brooke Camfield,
Colleen Cunningham, Rachael Eiben,
Michelle Roy Kelly, and Daria Perreault

An Everything® Series Book.
Everything® is a registered trademark of Adams Media Corporation.

Published by Adams Media Corporation
57 Littlefield Street, Avon, MA 02322 U.S.A.
www.adamsmedia.com

ISBN: 1-58062-668-8
Printed in the United States of America.

J I H G F E D C B A

Library of Congress Cataloging-in-Publication Data
Cantrell, Mark.
The everything weather book : from daily forecasts to
blizzards, hurricanes, and tornadoes by Mark Cantrell.
p. cm. (An everything series book)
Includes bibliographical references and index.
ISBN 1-58062-668-8
1. Weather–Popular works. I. Title. II. Everything series.
QC981.2 .C39   2002
551.6–dc21   2002004574

This publication is designed to provide accurate and authoritative information with regard to the subject matter covered. It is sold with the understanding that the publisher is not engaged in rendering legal, accounting, or other professional advice. If legal advice or other expert assistance is required, the services of a competent professional person should be sought.

—From a *Declaration of Principles* jointly adopted by a Committee of the
American Bar Association and a Committee of Publishers and Associations

Illustrations by Barry Littmann.
Interior photographs courtesy of the National Oceanic and Atmospheric Administration/Department of Commerce.
Figure 2-1 courtesy of the Franklin D. Roosevelt Library. Figure 19-2 courtesy of The Weather Channel.
Figure 20-1 courtesy of Nick Begich, Earthpulse.com.

This book is available at quantity discounts for bulk purchases.
For information, call 1-800-872-5627.

Visit the entire Everything® series at everything.com

Contents

Acknowledgments

Thanks to Mare for the means, Don for the motivation,
Ceri for the edits, Emily Byrd and Joel Cline for their expertise,
and Mom and Dad for their unwavering love and support.

Introduction

Close your eyes for a moment, and imagine you're standing on the bottom of a deep ocean. Like any ocean, this one has its currents, eddies, and whirlpools—but unlike other seas, you can breathe in this one.

Now open your eyes. You *are* at the bottom of an ocean—a vast sea of air we call our atmosphere.

Since ancient times, the weather has been a source of mystery, awe, and occasionally fear to all of us who live in this ocean of air. From the farmers who depend on rain to water their crops to airline pilots who must fly through it, no one is immune to the weather's effects.

Because of the weather's importance to all of us, billions of dollars and millions of hours have been spent developing ever more sophisticated instruments and methods of measuring and predicting its actions and movements. Yet for all the time invested, forecasting the weather still remains a difficult and frustrating task for meteorologists. Anyone who has had to shovel a "10 percent chance of snow" from their driveway can tell you that.

Weather's unpredictable nature may make it hard to forecast, but it also makes it a fascinating subject. Anyone who has ever looked up at the sky and wondered how clouds form, what causes cold fronts and warm fronts, how tornadoes and hurricanes are born, or why the jet stream gets so much attention on the evening weathercast will appreciate *The Everything® Weather Book*.

You will learn how the same process that produces warm summer showers can also create gigantic supercell thunderstorms that spawn deadly tornadoes. Go flying into the teeth of a monster storm with the Hurricane Hunter squadron, and roam the Great Plains in search of giant dust storms.

You will also explore the debate about whether mankind's influence is changing Earth's climate, and, if it is, what the consequences of that will be in the near future. From snow to rain and back again, everything you need to know about the weather is right here. As the Hurricane Hunters might say, hold on tight—it could be a bumpy ride.

CHAPTER 1

What Is Weather?

Don't knock the weather; nine-tenths of the people couldn't start a conversation if it didn't change once in a while.

—Kin Hubbard, U.S. journalist, humorist

Simply put, weather is what's going on in the atmosphere in any one location at a particular time. Luckily, nothing is as simple as that. Understanding weather allows us to plan our days, our vacations, and our crops. And it's a handy conversation starter.

Why It's a Big Deal

In fact, weather is a complex and dynamic process driven by the Sun; the earth's oceans, rotation, and inclination; and so many other factors that many of its mysteries still remain unexplained. To say that weather is an important factor in everyone's life is a huge understatement. Being prepared for what the weather brings can be as simple as turning on the TV to catch the latest forecast before heading for the beach, or as complicated as examining long-range forecasts to decide which crops to plant. Weather constantly affects people in small ways but can also have major consequences when hurricanes or tornadoes threaten their well-being and livelihoods, or even their lives.

How you view the weather usually depends on *where* you're viewing it from. A spectacular thunderstorm may be exciting to watch from the safety of your living room, but perhaps a bit too exciting from a rowboat in the middle of a lake. A 2-foot snowfall can be a child's wonderland, but not nearly as wonderful for the one who has to clear the car and shovel the driveway. And if you're a contractor working on a hot roof during a sweltering summer, you're not going to have nearly as much fun as the college student on Spring Break lying on a beach sipping a cold drink.

FACTS

During the summer, a stuffy nose and postnasal drip may have you convinced you're suffering from a cold. But the same symptoms may be due to allergies. Remember that colds last an average of three to seven days, while allergic reactions can go on for ten days to several weeks. If you're still miserable after a week, chances are you've got allergies.

The weather can even affect health, especially during extremes in temperature or precipitation. If you're not dressed properly in cold weather, you can fall victim to hypothermia, which occurs when the body's core temperature drops below the point where things function normally. Hypothermia can happen even when the temperature doesn't feel that cold to us, as in the case of swimmers, who can suffer from hypothermia even when the water is relatively warm. The flip side of hypothermia is hyperthermia, where the body's core temperature rises too high. Hyperthermia can cause heat exhaustion or even heat stroke, which can be fatal.

Weather can also affect health in less obvious ways. Long spells of gray winter weather can lead to a condition known as seasonal affective disorder (SAD), a malady that causes depression and a debilitating lack of energy; it's thought to be caused by lower light levels during the winter as the days become shorter and the Sun rises lower in the sky. Many arthritis sufferers complain of worsening symptoms when atmospheric pressure falls, and there is a statistical rise in the number of heart attacks after abrupt weather changes such as passing storm fronts.

The Big Picture

On a larger scale, weather plays a big role in the economic health of every nation on Earth. A timely soaking rain can rescue a crop from ruin, while a sudden torrential cloudburst can wash it away. And farmers aren't the only ones at risk; those who depend on natural gas for heat often watch in dismay as a particularly cold winter sends prices skyward. Hurricanes can drive tourists away from areas that depend on a regular influx of visitors for its livelihood. Even a gentle phenomenon like fog can result in disaster, as the captain of the *Titanic* learned one fateful April night in 1912. And during the Dust Bowl of 1936, one of the hottest and driest summers ever recorded, more than 15,000 people died.

SSENTIALS Scientists look for evidence of ancient hurricanes in a new branch of science called paleotempestology. Evidence of past storms can be found in coral skeletons, sediments from the ocean bottom, and even in caves, where stalactites retain the chemical signatures of abrupt cloudbursts caused by tropical cyclones.

With a growing realization of the weather's importance and so much weather news readily available on TV and the Internet, it's no wonder that interest in the subject is soaring. It seems that almost every day a weather disaster is happening somewhere in the world. Yet it's important to remember that extreme events, from droughts to hurricanes, have been happening for millennia, long before there were cameras to record them or buildings and people to get in their way.

One of the reasons weather is so compelling is because it is universal: Snow falls just as heavily on poor neighborhoods as it does in well-to-do suburbs, and a flash flood can destroy both mansions and shacks with equal force. Weather is the one thing everyone has in common.

FIGURE 1-1:
First-ever tornado photo

(refer to page 280 for more information)

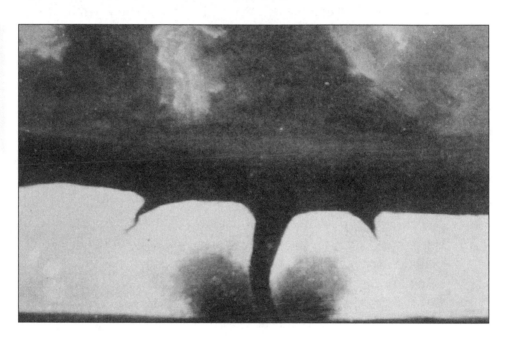

The weather's universal impact was one reason for forming the World Meteorological Organization (WMO). Its 185 member nations are united in not only weather prediction, but also ozone layer depletion studies, air pollution research, climate change–related activities, and research designed to benefit everyone on the planet. From its base in Geneva, Switzerland, the WMO coordinates weather-related research on a global scale, helping to develop new techniques to create more accurate and dependable forecasts worldwide.

The WMO is one of many organizations charged with the responsibility of tracking weather systems and predicting what the atmosphere has in store. Most countries have their own weather agencies that study both current atmospheric conditions and long-range trends that can reveal how the planet may change over time. In the past few years, many scientists have realized that, far from being a static phenomenon, the earth's climate experiences drastic swings, from ice ages to periods of extreme warmth, and back again. Some believe that man's influence is accelerating and magnifying these changes, a topic that will be discussed in more depth later.

Weather Versus Climate

The study of these long-range weather patterns is called climatology. Weather is what's happening locally in the atmosphere right now. Climate is the average, or accumulated, weather for a region over a period of time, including extreme conditions and their frequencies. The longer data is gathered for an area, the more accurately its climate can be measured and its future climate predicted.

Generally, it takes thirty years or more to develop a truly detailed climatological profile for a region. So, if you wanted to find out whether it was going to rain during your trip to Disney World the next day, a climatologist probably couldn't help you. However, he might be able to tell you if the currently landlocked Mouse House might become a beachfront resort in the future.

QUESTIONS?

What is the greenhouse effect?
A greenhouse protects plants by trapping solar energy during cold weather. Because only a small fraction of the Sun's heat ever reaches Earth, the atmosphere acts in much the same way to sustain life. If not for the atmosphere's heat-absorbing effects, the planet's average temperature would hover around –30 degrees F.

Climatologists abound at the National Climatic Data Center (NCDC) in Asheville, North Carolina, where scientists have access to more than 150 years of weather data, with the equivalent of 18 million more pages of information being added each day. With this much information at their disposal, the researchers from the National Oceanic and Atmospheric Administration (NOAA) and other agencies can compare and contrast past climatic conditions to current ones, revealing global climate changes both large and small.

In examining these global patterns, meteorologists have been able to categorize Earth's climates and group them into zones that share similar features. For instance, the Sahara Desert in Africa is nowhere near California's Mojave Desert, yet both share many characteristics. You may tend to think of climates as encompassing huge areas of the earth's surface, but climates can be as small as a few hundred square feet. Such tiny areas of averaged weather are called microclimates, while weather conditions in areas from a few acres to several square miles fall into the category of a mesoclimate. The next step up is the climate of a whole state or country—a macroclimate; long-term weather conditions over the entire globe are called the global climate.

Studies have shown that the global climate is indeed changing, and some feel it's the fault of industries and automobiles that continue to pump huge quantities of particles into the atmosphere. It was once thought that the atmosphere was so vast that nothing could affect it, but it's now understood that it is actually very fragile. Views from orbit show the atmosphere as an impossibly thin, hazy blue line against the background of space. In fact, if you could shrink the earth down to the size of a beach ball, the atmosphere would be about as thin as a human hair.

A Trip Through the Atmosphere

Earth's atmosphere is composed mostly of oxygen and nitrogen, with some carbon dioxide and other trace gases like argon and hydrogen thrown in for variety. Meteorologists divide the atmosphere into several layers, each of which blends seamlessly into the next. Nitrogen makes up around 78 percent of the air we breathe at the surface, with oxygen taking up about 21 percent. Unless you're an astronaut, you spend most of your time in the bottom layer of the atmosphere, called the troposphere, which extends anywhere from 5 to 10 miles up depending on how much of the Sun's energy is reaching the earth at the time.

The Troposphere

In the troposphere, the temperature falls an average of 4 degrees F for every 1,000 feet you climb, a phenomenon called the lapse rate. Eventually the temperature stops falling, meaning you've reached the tropopause and the beginning of the next layer, the stratosphere. Really, you wouldn't want the temperature to fall much lower anyway: At the tropopause, it can dip as low as –70 degrees F. You'd think the temperature would just keep on falling as you leave the troposphere and gain more altitude, but that's not the case.

The Stratosphere

Instead, as you climb up into the stratosphere, the temperature begins to rise again, up to a high of around 40 degrees F. One reason for that is because the stratosphere contains the ozone layer, which acts as a protective blanket to prevent harmful amounts of ultraviolet (UV) solar radiation from reaching the earth's surface (and the people on it) and helps to warm the stratosphere. Even where the amount of ozone is greatest—around 16 miles up—you'll find only about twelve ozone molecules for every million molecules of air, but that's still enough to block out the worst of the UV rays. That's a good thing, because UV radiation is known to cause skin cancer, and can even induce genetic mutations in DNA.

Climbing even higher, you finally reach the edge of the stratosphere, or stratopause, at around 30 miles above the earth's surface. Now you're really getting into nosebleed territory: At this height, the air is much too thin to breathe, and atmospheric pressure is only about 1 millibar. You're now above most of the atmosphere. In fact, without some kind of breathing equipment, you would soon be suffering from a condition known as hypoxia—sometimes called mountain sickness or altitude sickness—as your lungs tried to take in air that isn't there.

The early stages of hypoxia include fatigue, exhaustion, and sleepiness. Soon your vision would begin to dim, your reaction time would become very slow, your breathing would become fast and ragged, and finally your hearing would go. The end stage of hypoxia is death.

Fortunately, you'll probably never find yourself stuck outside 30 miles up, so you can safely continue your imaginary ascent.

The Mesosphere

The mesosphere is the next layer, extending from about 30 to 50 miles high. With very little ozone to provide warmth, the temperature begins to fall again, to a low of about –130 degrees F. It continues to decrease until you reach the mesopause, then begins to rise again as you enter the thermosphere, which extends from 50 to more than 120 miles above the earth.

The Hot Zone

Perhaps "rise" isn't the right word—temperatures in the thermosphere can reach a blistering 2,700 degrees F. The thermosphere gets that hot because it's the first layer of air the Sun's rays hit as they zoom toward Earth. A space shuttle must pass through the thermosphere on its way to and from orbit, so the obvious question is: Why doesn't it burn up? Fortunately, at that height there are so few air molecules that the net amount of heat energy hitting the shuttle isn't enough to destroy it.

QUESTIONS?

Why don't all meteorites burn up in the atmosphere?
Some are just too big or dense for the thermosphere to handle. Thousands of rocks from the size of pebbles down to grains of sand burn up each day, but space rocks larger than about 33 feet in diameter can usually make it to the ground (most often in pieces).

The lack of air molecules would actually make it feel downright cold if you could somehow sit out in the thermosphere for a few moments.

It sounds crazy, but there just wouldn't be enough air molecules to heat up your skin. In his book *Rockets, Missiles & Space Travel,* the great space scientist Willy Ley explained it this way: "You wouldn't expect a person to be burned to death in a cold barn by the admittedly very hot filament of the light bulb. The temperature is indeed very high, but the quantity is utterly insufficient."

It's a good thing for us that the number of molecules in the thermosphere is still great enough to intercept and destroy most incoming meteorites, however.

The thermosphere also contains most of the ionosphere, so-called because energy from the Sun smacks into molecules at that height and separates them into ions, which carry a positive charge, and free electrons, which are negatively charged. Many years ago, it was discovered that this layer reflects radio waves, especially at night, allowing the transmission of signals beyond the curvature of the earth for hundreds of miles or more. This principle allows ham radio operators to receive broadcasts from faraway countries, although the effect is not always predictable.

As an example of uncontrolled warming, scientists point to Venus, a planet nearly the same size as Earth but with a much more hostile atmosphere. On Venus the "air" is about 96 percent carbon dioxide with a temperature hot enough to melt lead. Scientists say the same conditions may occur on Earth if pollution isn't controlled.

What lies above the thermosphere? If you think the answer is air, think again. The layer above 120 miles' altitude—the exosphere—contains so few molecules that many of them are actually able to escape the earth's gravity and fly off into space. The exosphere is the domain of satellites and space shuttles, a transitional zone between the earth's atmosphere and interplanetary space. The exosphere has no real upper boundary; it just becomes more and more diffuse until it's no longer detectable.

The Problem with Ozone

Most people are passably familiar with the ozone layer, but here's some information to help you understand it in context. Ozone protects you from harm because it can absorb UV radiation. When UV rays strike oxygen molecules in the upper atmosphere, they split into two oxygen (O_2) atoms, which are then free to combine with other oxygen molecules to form ozone (O_3). Now the ozone molecule can act as a protector, intercepting and destroying harmful UV radiation before it can reach Earth. But it's a suicide mission, because the molecule is also destroyed during the encounter. Since the oxygen-to-ozone conversion process is continual, there is usually enough ozone to keep everyone from having a perpetual sunburn, although its levels do fluctuate.

FACTS

Each spring, a large hole (actually a significant thinning) appears in the ozone layer over the Antarctic. Scientists believe the destruction is caused by chlorofluorocarbons (CFCs), and although recent attempts to reduce CFC emissions have been successful, researchers say it will take a long time for the atmosphere to repair itself.

What worries scientists is that ozone can be destroyed by other things besides UV rays. Chlorine from the CFCs used in the refrigeration industry and aerosols, and bromine from the halons used in fire extinguishers are two of the major culprits. Their presence in the air upsets the balance between ozone creation and destruction and leads to a net loss in protective ozone over time. CFCs, which are virtually indestructible and can't even be washed down by rain, hang around in the troposphere for a long time—more than forty years—before finally migrating up into the stratosphere.

The Water Cycle

With a better understanding of the atmosphere, you can see that the air you breathe is a finite resource that needs protection. The same is true of the earth's supply of water: A lack of either resource would mean disaster for everyone. Fortunately, down here in the lower atmosphere, water is generally plentiful.

FIGURE 1-2:
Altocumulus
clouds

(refer to page
280 for more
information)

What Goes Up . . .

Most of the moisture in the atmosphere—about 90 percent comes from the oceans. Water is constantly recycled from the ocean into the air and back through a process called the water cycle. At any one time, the oceans contain about 97 percent of the earth's water; the atmosphere contains only about 0.001 percent, and landmasses and ice hold the remainder. Still, if that seemingly tiny amount of atmospheric water vapor suddenly turned into rain, it would cover the entire Earth with an inch of water.

About 121,000 cubic miles of water evaporate from the earth's surface each year, with around 86 percent of that coming from the oceans. The evaporation occurs due to the Sun's heating of the sea surface. Warm air can hold a lot of moisture (think of steam), so some of the ocean surface converts to water vapor and is drawn up into the air.

Evaporation occurs anywhere there is water, from lakes and rivers to storm drains and birdbaths. Plants even give off water through a process called transpiration, as they ooze small droplets of moisture from the undersides of their leaves. All of this warm water vapor begins to rise, joining billions of other water molecules in a dizzying ascent into the troposphere.

FACTS

Water can absorb a lot of heat before it begins to heat up itself. That's why water makes such a good coolant for automobile radiators, and why oceans prevent abrupt seasonal changes. Instead, winter comes on gradually as oceans slowly release their stored heat into the atmosphere, and summer takes awhile to set in as the sea begins to reabsorb heat.

. . . Must Come Down

Eventually the vapor reaches cooler layers and condenses around small particles of dust, pollen, or pollution. As the condensation process continues, the droplets become too big for the wind to support and they begin a plunge toward the surface. Not all the precipitation reaches the ground, however; some of it evaporates directly back into the atmosphere on its way. What's left finally reaches the ground in the form of rain, snow, hail, or sleet, often ruining picnics or closing schools in the process.

If the precipitation falls in the ocean, the cycle is ready to begin again right away, and that's exactly what happens to the majority of raindrops and snowflakes. After all, oceans cover more than 70 percent of the earth's surface, making them a big target. When it rains or snows over land, however, the cycle takes a little more time to complete.

Most water reaching the surface runs off into ditches and streams where it finds its way back into lakes or the ocean, but some water seeps into the ground, percolating down until it is either trapped or it encounters a horizontal flow deep under the surface. The seeping water goes with the flow until it encounters a large underground reservoir known as an aquifer. Most aquifers eventually drain off into streams, which carry the water to rivers and canals and back to the sea. Then, of course, the whole cycle begins anew.

CHAPTER 2

Weather in History

The greater the difficulty, the more glory in surmounting it. Skillful pilots gain their reputation from storms and tempests.

—Epicurus

It's great to be able to turn on the TV or hop on the Web and check the radar picture, get the latest forecast, and know what your day will bring weatherwise. But imagine climbing into a time machine and visiting an ancient civilization that had none of the advanced forecasting methods you take for granted.

Weather Way Back When

Some think of ancient people as primitive, yet they did their best to understand and predict the weather. Lacking modern scientific instruments, early civilizations simply observed nature and kept records of the seasons. Although superstition and prevailing cultural beliefs suppressed weather science for centuries, it's amazing how often ancient weather observers got it right.

Even before Aristotle, ancient people understood how important the Sun was for growing their crops, which explains why many ancient cultures worshiped sun gods. In Mesopotamia, the Babylonians counted on the weather gods Hadad and Marduk to bring them good harvests. The Hittites left the weather-producing chores to their primary deity, Teshub, while in Greece, a violent thunderstorm meant that weather god Zeus was throwing a thunderbolt tantrum.

As far back as 1800 B.C., Hindus in India counted on their weather god, Indra, who also carried a lightning bolt, to command the weather from his perch atop a large white elephant. And in Scandinavia, Norse god Thor protected farmers and serfs from weather disasters while wielding his mighty hammer against his enemies.

Early Forecasts

Around 580 B.C., a philosopher named Thales of Miletus is said to have issued the very first seasonal crop forecast based on past olive harvests. According to legend, Thales was so confident of his forecast that he reserved the use of all the olive presses in his area before the harvest, and made a tidy profit leasing them back to farmers when the bumper crop arrived.

The first real effort to gather all known weather information into one place was accomplished by the philosopher Aristotle around 350 B.C. In his essay *Meteorologica,* the philosopher correctly guessed that the Sun put large masses of air into motion, and that water vapor could condense into clouds. But Aristotle was hamstrung by his era's notion that everything was made of four elements: fire, water, air, and earth, and his futile attempts to force those elements to agree with the realities of nature were his undoing. The other fallacy of his time was the belief that the earth was the center of the universe, which made it impossible to correctly explain the origin of the seasons.

The ancient Etruscans of northern Italy relied on natural phenomena to predict the weather. Soothsayers would examine the songs and flight paths of birds, the temperature, the direction of the wind, and other signs, and would issue prophecies based on their findings. With no other forecasting services available, these diviners were in great demand by both governments and private citizens.

Naming a Science

Resolving the earth's proper place in the universe would have to wait. In the meantime, Aristotle believed that everything that happened could be explained logically, and he got people thinking about the forces that drive the weather.

Aristotle's largest contribution was probably the term "meteorology," which we still use today. The word comes from the Greek *meteoros*, which means "high in the sky." In Aristotle's day, anything falling from or appearing in the sky (like rain or clouds) was called a meteor.

Some people still depend on folklore for weather safety, but many of the beliefs that have been passed down through generations are misconceptions. For instance, some still insist the major danger from a hurricane is the wind, when most victims actually die in storm-spawned flooding.

Aristotle's pupil Theophrastus picked up his teacher's work, writing a journal called *The Book of Signs* that noted how nature can often be used to forecast the weather. He also established a link between the weather and certain kinds of illnesses, and was the first person in recorded history to identify sunspots.

For the next 2,000 years or so, the science of meteorology went dormant. Without accurate instruments to predict developing weather conditions or even measure the basic elements, weather forecasters leaned on folklore or nature for advice on planting crops and avoiding weather disasters.

A Weather Renaissance

Things started falling into place in the sixteenth century when Nicolaus Copernicus appeared on the scene. In 1530, he presented the theory that the Sun, not the earth, was at the center of the universe. Although still incorrect, his theory at least made room for an explanation of the seasons, and he correctly deduced that the earth rotated on its axis once a day and made the long trip around the Sun once each year. This was a scandalous and shocking idea at the time, because it suggested that man was just a part of nature, instead of being superior to it.

Leonardo da Vinci was another sixteenth-century scientist who was fascinated by the weather. He noticed that a ball of wool weighed more on a rainy day than on a dry one, and further experiments led to his invention of the hygrometer, a device to measure the amount of water suspended in the air. Da Vinci wasn't content to measure the air's water content; he also invented the anemometer, which measures wind speed.

QUESTIONS?

Can a cricket be a thermometer?
Because crickets are cold-blooded, their metabolic rate is sensitive to temperature. As the temperature goes up, the rate of chirping generally increases with it. Counting the number of chirps in fifteen seconds and dividing by forty should give you a number close to the current temperature.

Now the air's moisture level and speed could be measured, but for most of the sixteenth century, no one could tell you how hot it was, because there were no thermometers yet. Enter Galileo Galilei, who remedied the thermometer shortage in 1593.

Galileo called his invention a thermoscope. It consisted of a long-necked glass bottle that was placed, upside down, into a vessel containing water. When the bottle was heated slightly, usually by the warmth of the experimenter's hands, the air inside expanded and the water was pushed downward. When the bottle cooled, the air contracted and the water rose back up into the neck of the bottle. Unfortunately, the thermoscope had no degree markings and was useless for determining temperature, but it paved the way for the more accurate versions to come.

The Pressure Intensifies

Now one could tell how humid it was and how fast the wind was blowing, and could get a vague idea of the temperature. But what about the air pressure?

Evangelista Torricelli, a student of Galileo's, created the first mercury barometer to measure atmospheric pressure in 1644, completing the list of instruments needed to develop an accurate weather forecast. However, it would be a long time before these primitive instruments would be of much use; the next few centuries would be spent burning brain cells and midnight oil revising and refining these instruments into the tools used by modern forecasters.

One contributor was a French mathematician, Blaise Pascal, who theorized that if air had weight, it should exert less and less pressure the higher you went. In 1648, he convinced his brother-in-law, armed with one of Torricelli's barometers, to climb almost 5,000 feet up a mountain. Sure enough, the higher he went, the lower the mercury sank.

ESSENTIALS   Aristotle's contention that "nature abhors a vacuum" was accepted without question until Torricelli created one inside his mercury barometer. Catholic Jesuits, alarmed by this breach of faith, theorized that the mercury was being held up by invisible threads, but by then there was no stopping the weather revolution.

The first recorded weather observations in the New World were made by a minister named John Campanius Holm in 1644 and 1645. Some people consider Holm, who lived in the Colony of New Sweden near Wilmington, Delaware, to be America's first weatherman. In fact, the National Weather Service gives an award in his name to outstanding volunteer weather observers each year.

Opposing Scales

Have you ever wondered why the United States uses a method of measuring temperature that's different from the one used by the rest of the world? Blame Daniel Gabriel Fahrenheit, a German instrument maker who, in 1714, came up with the temperature scale that bears his name. He based his system on the difference between the freezing point of water and his own body temperature. Sound arbitrary and confusing? Indeed. (See Chapter 7 for a much more thorough explanation.)

Not content to leave well enough alone, Swedish astronomer Anders Celsius, no doubt believing Fahrenheit must have been running a high fever when he came up with his scale, proposed another method. He divided the freezing and boiling points of water into equal degrees, which he called the centesimal system. Celsius decided the boiling point of water would be 0 degrees, and the freezing point would be 100 degrees. That must not have made any more sense at that time than it does now, because after his death, the scale was turned upside down, creating the measuring system still used today.

SSENTIALS The Fahrenheit scale is considered antiquated by scientists, who use the Celsius scale instead and wish everyone else would, too. Old habits die hard—it'll probably be some time yet before everyone's on the same page temperaturewise.

In 1793, Englishman John Dalton wrote a book called *Meteorological Observations and Essays* in which he advanced the theory that rain is caused by a drop in temperature, not air pressure. Taking the next step, he realized in 1802 that temperature actually affects the amount of water vapor the air can hold, a concept now called relative humidity.

Weather and War

Looking back through the history of warfare, it's evident that weather has played no small part in effecting both victories and defeats. The winter of 1777–1778 was no exception, and General George Washington's Continental Army learned that the weather can be more deadly than any mortal enemy.

After being defeated by the British Army in two major conflicts, Washington's troops marched to Valley Forge, Pennsylvania, 25 miles northwest of Philadelphia, in December 1777. The army of about 11,000 men had little to eat and inadequate clothing, and lived in tents while they set to work building huts in which to weather the coming winter.

By all accounts, that winter was unusually severe. Conditions got so bad that Washington wrote at one point, "For some days past there has been little less than a famine in the camp. . . . Naked and starving as they are, we cannot enough admire the incomparable patience and fidelity of the soldiery, that they have not been, ere this, excited by their suffering to a general mutiny and desertion."

Forging a Victory

Although a few soldiers did desert, the ones who stayed were fiercely loyal to Washington. By the spring of 1778, nearly a fourth of the soldiers had died of smallpox, typhoid fever, malnutrition, and exposure to the severe cold, but the remaining troops had been hardened by the experience. In May 1778, word came of the new alliance between France and the United States, and the worst was over. Valley Forge marked the turning point in the war, and soon Washington and his men were chasing the British from Philadelphia.

FACTS

The winter of 1780 was one of the worst on record. On the coast of Delaware's Delmarva Peninsula, ice formations towered 20 feet high, and the Potomac River froze over so solidly that it was possible to walk across it.

Had the British attacked Washington and his army in the dead of winter, they would have scored an easy victory against the weak and weary American troops. Although the winter was exceptionally severe and the cause of much suffering for the Colonial soldiers, it probably prevented the defeat of the Republic.

The French helped save the day at Valley Forge, but ended up with problems of their own a few years later during Napoleon's invasion of Russia and one of the largest weather-assisted routs in history.

Weather: Russia's Secret Weapon

In 1812, Napoleon controlled nearly all of Europe and had set his sights on Russia as his next conquest. In June of that year, he crossed the Russian border with 600,000 troops and more than 50,000 horses, planning to march all the way to Moscow, living off the land along the way. The Russians had other ideas: As they retreated before the advancing French horde, they burned fields and destroyed houses, leaving little for the French to eat. Dry, hot conditions prevailed all the way to Moscow, and upon arriving there on September 14, the exhausted French troops found the city all but abandoned, its supplies depleted and much of its shelter destroyed. More than 20,000 troops had died of disease and exhaustion on the way, but the worst still lay ahead: Winter was coming.

In the middle of October, with no offer of surrender from the tsar, Napoleon finally ordered a retreat. He had waited too long. As the weary troops turned toward home, an early and unusually cold air mass descended over them, and the weakest soldiers began to die.

 **SSENTIALS**

The weather has been Russia's ally in repelling foreign invaders throughout recorded history. In 1242, the pope sent German Teutonic Knights to take control of Russia and convert its people to Roman Catholicism. But Russian troops were more accustomed to the severe winter conditions and defeated the Germans on the frozen channel between the Peipus and Pskov Lakes in what became known as the "massacre on the ice."

Suddenly the weather turned warmer again, and roads that had been frozen solid turned into muddy quagmires overnight. Streams and rivers that had been solid ice were now raging torrents, slowing the retreating troops even more. Then as quickly as the warm weather had arrived, it was replaced by an even colder air mass, and thousands more died in the driving snow and subzero temperatures.

In early December, Napoleon's troops finally crossed back over the border into Poland, but of the 600,000 fighting men who had invaded Russia just six months earlier, fewer than 100,000 remained. Half a million people had died in the Russian winter's icy embrace.

Dots, Dashes, and Data

In 1837, Samuel F. B. Morse perfected the telegraph, making near-instantaneous access to weather data a possibility. Although the machines had first been proposed in 1753 and built in 1774, early models required twenty-six individual wires to function, one for each letter of the alphabet. Morse knew he could do better, and set his sights on a telegraph that used only one wire to transmit information. Morse was a shameless self-promoter, which may have had something to do with the telegraph's rapid acceptance. On May 24, 1844, Morse gave a public demonstration of his device, sending a message from Washington to Baltimore that read, "What hath God wrought?"

FACTS

By 1854, just ten years after Morse introduced his device, there were already 23,000 miles of telegraph wire strung across the United States, a kind of early Internet that almost instantly made the Pony Express and carrier pigeons obsolete.

The following year, Joseph Henry, secretary of the newly established Smithsonian Institution, foresaw the telegraph's importance as a forecasting tool, suggesting that conditions at one observing location could be transmitted to another to warn of approaching bad weather. He proposed ". . . a system of observation which shall extend as far as possible over the North American continent. . . . The Citizens of the United States are now scattered over every part of the southern and western portions of North America, and the extended lines of the telegraph will furnish a ready means of warning the more northern and eastern observers to be on the watch from the first appearance of an advancing storm."

Making It Official

The telegraph came into its own during the Civil War, when it became a tactical tool in military operations. After the war, the government began looking for peacetime uses for the technology. In 1870, President Ulysses S. Grant signed a resolution directing "the Secretary of War to take observations at military stations and to warn of storms on the Great Lakes and on the Atlantic and Gulf Coasts," effectively creating a branch of the Department of War's Signal Service Corps that would someday become the U.S. National Weather Service. In 1890, the U.S. Weather Bureau was created, and moved from the Signal Corps to the Department of Agriculture at the request of President Benjamin Harrison.

During the Spanish-American War of 1898, President William McKinley ordered the establishment of the first hurricane warning network, admitting that he was more afraid of hurricanes than he was of the entire Spanish Navy. Soon after, hurricane warning stations were built throughout the West Indies, with network headquarters in Kingston, Jamaica. The forecast center, which was later moved to Havana, Cuba, in 1899, was charged with the responsibility of providing early hurricane warnings to the coastal regions of the United States, as well as Mexico, South America, and even ships at sea.

Turning the Corner

As the nineteenth century drew to a close, big changes were in the works for the science of weather prediction. The Weather Bureau received a letter from two brothers who owned a bicycle shop in Dayton, Ohio, asking for the location of the windiest places in the country. When Orville and Wilbur Wright scanned the list, the small fishing village of Kitty Hawk on North Carolina's Outer Banks looked promising due to its almost constant onshore breezes, and in 1903 they flew the first heavier-than-air powered aircraft there, launching the Age of Flight. By the very next year the government was using Wright Flyers for atmospheric research.

FACTS

The first government-issued aviation route forecast was issued by the U.S. Weather Bureau on December 1, 1918. The Wright Brothers' first flight had sparked a widespread interest in airplanes, but it wasn't until America's entry into World War I in April 1917 that the need for accurate, up-to-date aviation weather information became a high priority.

By 1912, the Weather Bureau employed more than 2,000 people, but they weren't really meteorologists. If you were a weather station attendant at the time, your job consisted of watching your instruments and recording their measurements, launching weather balloons, and reporting your findings back to Washington. Training was usually done on the job after a short course to familiarize you with the instruments, as there were no formal meteorological schools yet.

Back to the Front

In 1918, a Norwegian scientist named Vilhelm Bjerknes, the son of a hydrologist, presented his theory that weather is most active at the boundaries of clashing warm and cold air masses. Bjerknes named these areas "fronts," likening them to the battlegrounds of World War I, which were still fresh in everyone's mind. His research convinced him that large-scale motions in the atmosphere behaved very much like their counterparts in the sea, and actually influenced each other in the process. Bjerknes was the first to suggest that any atmospheric behavior could be explained, or even predicted, by mathematics. Proof of that concept would come only after the development of high-speed computers in the decades to come.

In 1919, Charles Franklin Brooks of the Blue Hill Observatory in Milton, Massachusetts, founded the American Meteorological Society (AMS), an organization of weather professionals. Made up mostly of weather observers from the Signal Corps and the Weather Bureau, the society was only about 600 strong at its inception, but its ranks would swell considerably during and after World War II because so many recruits would be trained in meteorology to support the war effort.

Balloons had been used since the early 1900s for atmospheric observation, but until the 1930s, their instruments had to be retrieved to extract the data. The balloon would rise until the drop in air pressure caused it to burst, after which it fell to the ground to await rescue and analysis. The disadvantages of this method of research were obvious, and attaching the balloon to a tether didn't work well either because the balloon couldn't ascend high enough into the atmosphere to be of use. Airplanes couldn't climb much higher but were still used to gather data on conditions in the lower atmosphere.

Meteorologists finally gained easier access to the upper atmosphere in the late 1930s with the development of the radiosonde, a device that could beam data from the balloon directly to observers. With a range of up to 15 miles in altitude and more than 200 miles' distance, radiosondes could transmit constant information on air pressure, temperature, cloud composition, and other factors. The first official Weather Bureau radiosonde soundings were taken at East Boston, Massachusetts, in 1937, and almost immediately replaced aircraft observations, since balloons could go much higher and there was no pilot to worry about.

Weathering World War II

The radiosonde arrived just in time to help forecasters during World War II, and weather science took a quantum leap during the war years as battlefield commanders used every means at their disposal to gain the upper hand. During the war, the Weather Bureau entered an unprecedented period of growth as Allied commanders depended more and more on weather forecasts to plan maneuvers. Coast Guard cutters were positioned at strategic locations in the Atlantic, taking regular radiosonde and surface measurements and transmitting them to convoys.

**SSENTIALS** On December 6, 1941, military codebreakers discovered that Japan planned to sever diplomatic relations with the United States the following day. A warning message to Honolulu was disrupted by bad weather, and the message was finally delivered to army headquarters by bicycle just as the first bombs began to fall on Pearl Harbor.

From the very first battle marking America's involvement in World War II, weather played a major role. On November 26, 1941, a fleet of four aircraft carriers and several other ships under the command of Admiral Isoroku Yamamoto steamed away from Japan toward Oahu, twelve days and 4,000 miles away.

Most of the trip was very difficult, with high seas and cold, stormy winter weather, but the rough conditions helped the huge fleet avoid detection. When the ships finally anchored 220 miles north of Oahu on December 7, 1941, and prepared to launch a surprise attack on the U.S. naval base at Pearl Harbor, America's entry into the war was certain.

The Allies Strike Back

For the next four months, most of the news coming from the Pacific theater was negative, with defeats at Bataan and Corregidor disheartening the American public and military alike. On April 18, 1942, commander Jimmy Doolittle and his squadron of sixteen B-25 bombers took off from the deck of the brand new aircraft carrier *Hornet* and turned toward Tokyo, more than 700 miles away.

Forced to take off early after the fleet was sighted by a Japanese patrol boat, the B-25s lumbered off the deck of the *Hornet* in a light rain, still 200 miles from their intended launch point. The B-25s had been stripped of any unnecessary equipment in order to carry more fuel, but on the way to Japan, they encountered a 20 mile-per-hour headwind that accelerated their fuel consumption. Arriving over Tokyo, the Raiders loosed volleys of 500-pound bombs on war-industry targets and then turned north along the coast toward China, where they hoped to find refuge.

It soon became obvious that the bombers wouldn't have enough fuel to make it to the Chinese airfields due to the headwinds they had encountered earlier. The situation got even worse when they encountered fog over the East China Sea, followed by a hard rain. With visibility near zero, navigators were forced to rely on dead reckoning to chart their course.

Suddenly, the winds shifted and the bomber crews found themselves being propelled by a strong tailwind. Still unable to see through the storm and low on fuel, most of the planes were forced to ditch in the ocean. In the end, all sixteen B-25s were lost, seven men were injured, and three were killed. Eight crew members were taken prisoner by the Japanese, and only four of them survived the war. But the raid not only gave American morale a huge boost after several crushing defeats, it also dealt a shattering blow to Japanese pride.

The Ploesti Raid

In the summer of 1943, Operation Tidal Wave was launched from a Libyan airfield against Nazi-held oil refineries in Ploesti, Romania. Once again the weather would have a marked influence on the outcome. To reach the target and return, the mission's 179 B-24 bombers would have to fly more than 2,400 miles in eighteen hours. The flight over the Mediterranean was uneventful, with beautiful weather and unlimited visibility. Then, on reaching land, the bombers encountered a bank of huge cumulus clouds over the 9,000-foot peaks of the Pindis Mountains. Flying blindly through the clouds at 12,000 feet, the planes became separated into two groups, neither one aware of the position of the other.

Because one bomber group arrived over the target well in advance of the second, the late arrivals suffered heavy casualties since the Germans had been alerted to their presence. Although most of the planes were able to drop their bombs, many important targets were missed in the confusion. Of the 179 planes in the mission, only 99 returned to base, and 58 of the surviving planes suffered severe combat damage.

The Beginning of the End

Although Hitler didn't know it at the time, the end of the Third Reich began with the Allies' Operation Overlord, a culmination of years of planning that aimed for nothing less than the invasion of Europe and the end of the führer's stranglehold on the embattled continent. Under the command of General Dwight D. Eisenhower, five beaches along the coast of France near Normandy were chosen as landing sites, and thousands of troops that had been in training for the mission for up to two years were moved into position.

FIGURE 2-1:
D-Day troops wade ashore

(refer to page 280 for more information)

But before the giant operation could begin, several conditions had to be met in order to boost its chances for success. Low tide should coincide with the breaking dawn, giving the Allies the maximum amount of beach to work with. There should be a rising full Moon to support airborne operations, and a minimum visibility of 3 miles so naval gunners could see their targets. Winds should not exceed 8 to 12 miles per hour onshore, or 13 to 18 miles per hour offshore. No more than 60 percent of the sky should be covered by clouds, and they could not be lower than 3,000 feet.

If Operation Overlord hadn't taken advantage of the temporary break in the weather on June 6, the invasion might never have happened. Just a few days later, one of the worst June storms in English Channel history pounded the beaches, lasting for a full five days. Artificial harbors that had been created by the invaders at critical landing zones were completely destroyed by gigantic waves.

Given these stringent requirements, forecasters estimated that there might be only three days in the entire month of June that would be suitable. Finally, June 5 was chosen as D-Day, but after the troop ships and landing craft were loaded with men and supplies on the fourth, a storm system moved in over England, and with high winds whipping across the English Channel and clouds hovering only 500 feet above its churning waves, Eisenhower was forced to delay the invasion.

FIGURE 2-2:
German
V-2 Rocket

(refer to page 280 for more information)

On the night of June 4, Eisenhower's chief meteorological adviser, James Stagg, informed him that there might be a temporary break in the weather on the sixth, and the general uttered the fateful words "Okay, we'll go," throwing the formidable Allied invasion machine into gear. Six thousand landing craft and other ships left British ports on their way toward France, along with the 822 gliders and other aircraft that would transport Allied soldiers behind enemy lines. The first wave would be followed by 13,000 bombers, sent in to soften Axis positions in advance of the invading forces. This time the weather cooperated, and although Allied losses were heavy, especially at well-defended Omaha Beach, the invaders soon controlled the coast of Normandy and began the long push toward Berlin.

The Final Countdown

Just as weather had influenced the first major attack of World War II, Pearl Harbor, the atmosphere intervened again in the last one: the mission to drop the atomic bomb that ended the war. The honor of ending the war was held not by the *Enola Gay,* the B-29 Superfortress that leveled Hiroshima, but by another B-29, *Bockscar,* which bombed Nagasaki. Although the *Enola Gay*'s mission was aided by clear skies over its target, *Bockscar* wasn't as lucky.

In fact, the residents of Kokura, on the northeast corner of the Japanese island of Kyushu, had the weather to thank for sparing their lives on August 9, 1944, when *Bockscar* took to the air. President Truman had offered to spare Japan further agony after Hiroshima's destruction three days earlier, but promised that, "if they do not now accept our terms, they may expect a rain of ruin from the air the likes of which has never been seen on this earth."

With no response from the emperor, Kokura was selected as the next primary target because of its automatic weapons factories. Two weather observation planes were dispatched to the city an hour before the scheduled bombing, since the bombardier would need a clear sightline to the target. Reports indicated there would be only a 30 percent cloud cover over Kokura, but when *Bockscar* arrived, the crew found the entire city socked in under a thick layer of clouds. Had the weather been more accommodating, the bomb would no doubt have killed a young Kokura college student named Tetsuya Fujita, who would later became famous for developing a tornado damage scale that still bears his name.

ALERT

World War II marked the last use of nuclear weapons in wartime, but scientists warn that a nuclear war could destroy the ozone layer and inject enough dust and other debris into the atmosphere to trigger a new ice age.

Frustrated, the crew turned toward their secondary target, Nagasaki, a major shipbuilding center. When they arrived, they found that it, too, was mostly buried under clouds. Against orders, the crew decided to bomb by radar rather than return to its base in Okinawa and attempt to land with a fully armed atomic bomb on board. In the last twenty seconds of the bombing run, the bombardier sighted the target through a break in the clouds and released the bomb. Fifty seconds later, at 11:02 A.M., the crew experienced a white-hot flash followed by a violent shock wave. Riding in an observation plane, *New York Times* science reporter William L. Laurence described the scene in his book *Dawn over Zero*:

> *Even as we watched, a giant mushroom came shooting out of the top to 45,000 feet, a mushroom top that was even more alive than the pillar, seething and boiling in a white fury of creamy foam, a thousand geysers rolled into one. It kept struggling in an elemental fury, like a creature in the act of breaking the bonds that held it down.*

Five days after the attack, the Japanese announced their acceptance of the Allies' terms of unconditional surrender.

The weather has been at the center of many major turning points throughout recorded history, and has been the single constant in all of mankind's conflicts. In the near future, it's quite possible that advances in weather-control technology will allow people to use weather as a weapon (see Chapter 20).

CHAPTER 3

The Ups and Downs of Clouds and Precipitation

Nature is a mutable cloud which is always and never the same.

—Ralph Waldo Emerson

Look! Up in the sky! It's a bird! It's a plane! It's—well, it's hard to tell behind all those clouds. These giant puffs of water vapor come in a dizzying array of shapes and sizes, from flat and boring to huge, dark, and forbidding, and they're capable of spawning some of the worst weather on Earth.

The Basics

From the ground most clouds look fairly substantial, but if you've ever flown through fluffy fair-weather clouds in an airplane, you know there's not much to them. They're found at all levels of the troposphere, from way up around 60,000 feet down to ground level. Aside from adding interest to a plain blue sky, clouds produce the precipitation that's necessary for survival.

FACTS

In 1803, an English naturalist named Luke Howard classified clouds into four basic groups: stratus, cumulus, nimbus, and cirrus. Roughly translated in Latin, they mean, respectively, "layer," "heap," "rain," and "wispy hair." In 1887, scientists Abercrombie and Hildebrandsson expanded on Howard's system, subcategorizing clouds by height, which is an identification method still in use today.

The High Frontier

The air in the upper troposphere is very dry and cold, so water vapor at high altitudes can't remain in a liquid state for long. Clouds that form there are made of ice crystals and are usually very wispy. High clouds appear white because they're not thick enough to block the Sun. Cirrus is the most common type of cloud found at these rarified heights of 20,000 to 60,000 feet.

You might think a cirrus cloud's upturned "tail" points in the direction of the prevailing wind, but the opposite is true. As the ice crystals that form the tail begin to fall, they encounter a level where wind speed or direction suddenly changes, and the cloud gets pulled like taffy (or cotton candy) into a long, thin streamer.

Cirrus clouds can spread out until they cover the entire sky, forming a thin layer called cirrostratus. You can see right through cirrostratus clouds, and because they're composed of ice crystals, you'll often see a halo where the Sun or Moon peeks through their wispy veil. Because they often form in advance of an approaching cold front or storm, cirrostratus can mean rain in the next twelve to twenty-four hours.

ESSENTIALS   Sometimes known as "Mares' tails," cirrus clouds often resemble thin filaments of white hair as they're stretched out by high-level winds. Cirrus clouds generally move from west to east and often predict an approaching low-pressure system, which is a good hint to go find an umbrella.

One of the most beautiful cloud types is cirrocumulus, which forms a series of small rounded patches or puffs that often extend across the sky in long rows. Because of their regular, repetitive pattern, cirrocumulus clouds can resemble the scales of a fish, which is why a sky full of cirrocumulus is also called a "mackerel sky."

Stuck in the Middle

Forming at an altitude of 6,500 to 26,000 feet, clouds in the troposphere's middle levels can be composed of either water or ice, or a combination of the two. Midlevel cloud types are easy to remember because the most common ones always begin with the prefix "alto-." The two main middle cloud types are altocumulus and altostratus.

Altostratus clouds are either gray or blue-gray, are often thick enough to blot out the Sun, and can blanket hundreds of miles of sky. Sometimes altostratus does allow a glimpse of the Sun through, but it's a dim view, like looking through tracing paper. Altostratus clouds are often confused with cirrostratus, but there's an easy way to tell them apart: If you look at the ground and don't see a shadow, it's probably altostratus. Also, altostratus clouds don't produce halos. This type of cloud often means you're in for an extended, steady rain in the near future.

Altocumulus clouds have a distinctive patchy or puffy pattern like cirrocumulus. They're composed mostly of water rather than ice, though, so they often appear gray instead of white. The individual puffs are also larger than cirrocumulus and sometimes form little cottony "castles" in the sky, meaning it won't be long before it will probably—guess what—rain!

The Real Lowdown

Low-level clouds form below 6,500 feet, and at that height are almost always made of water droplets unless it's winter. Stratus clouds are arguably the most boring clouds in existence; they usually cover the whole sky in a uniform gray cloak, sometimes completely blotting out the Sun. You won't generally see much rain falling from stratus clouds, although there can be some light drizzle or mist. They usually form during stable atmospheric conditions when a large, moist air mass rises slowly to a level where it can condense.

QUESTIONS?

What weather do nimbostratus clouds predict?
If you're wondering that, you're too late: It's probably already raining or snowing with nimbostratus over the neighborhood. If you looked up "gloomy" in the dictionary, there should be a picture of a nimbostratus cloud there.

On the other hand, nimbostratus is a dark gray cloud that forms when a front of warm, moist air meets a mass of relatively cool air. When you're under a nimbostratus layer, you often can't even see the cloud itself because of the rain and the thick mist formed by evaporation. If the air becomes saturated enough, another layer of ragged, swift clouds called scud can form below the nimbostratus. When you see this type of cloud coming, you might as well settle in with a good book or find an old movie marathon on TV, because it's probably going to rain or snow for quite a while.

Stratocumulus clouds are similar to altocumulus, but they're found at lower altitudes and their individual cells are bigger. They don't produce much rain and often form when cumulus clouds spread out across the sky and begin to merge. Stratocumulus clouds generally appear in patches, and you can often see blue sky between them.

From Fair to Middling—to Monster

Cumulus clouds are often thought of as fair-weather clouds, and they usually are—but they can grow into something far more ominous, as you'll see. Cumulus clouds look like big balls of white or light gray cotton drifting across the sky, usually have a flat base, and don't generate much precipitation in their young, puffy phase. They most often form when the morning Sun heats up the earth's surface and fills the sky with hundreds of popcorn-like clouds floating serenely over your head.

As the day progresses and it gets hotter, cumulus clouds can begin to blossom upward, now resembling a cauliflower more than a cotton ball. Called cumulus congestus, these towering pillars of water vapor are the raw material of the most dangerous cloud of all—the cumulonimbus.

FIGURE 3-1:
Ocean
thunderstorms

(refer to page
280 for more
information)

As the 300-pound gorilla of the cloud kingdom, cumulonimbus gets a lot of respect. These are the giant thunderstorm clouds that can produce lightning, hailstorms, and tornadoes. On color weather radar, cumulonimbus cells glow bright red, a warning that their tops have grown high into the atmosphere and severe weather is on its way. Violent updrafts within the storm, which can reach speeds of 100 miles per hour or more, keep it growing ever higher into the troposphere. If the monster cloud has enough energy, it will continue upward until reaching the tropopause or even break through to the stratosphere, where it will begin to flatten and form an anvil shape.

Cumulonimbus can also become nurseries for other types of clouds. When a thunderstorm grows all the way up to the troposphere, it's in cirrus territory, and the tops or anvils of cumulonimbus can shear off and become cirrus or cirrostratus clouds, often being swept hundreds of miles downwind as an early warning of approaching storms.

How Low Can They Go?

Nimbostratus is included in the low-level cloud category because thunderstorms always begin near the earth's surface. But the winner in the lowest-cloud-ever category has to be fog, which is a cloud that forms right at ground level. Actually, fog is nothing more than a stratus cloud you can walk through, although driving through a thick one isn't recommended unless your car is equipped with radar.

Fog that forms near sources of pollution (like industrial cities) tends to be thicker than ordinary fog since it contains so many more small particles for the water vapor to bond with. Unfortunately, these particles often include noxious chemicals that create acid fog, a concoction that can cause serious respiratory distress and other health problems.

Fog usually forms at night when a low layer of moist air is cooled by the ground, creating a surface cloud called radiation fog (caused by cool air radiating from the surface). A light breeze can actually cause the fog to become thicker, as it brings more warm air in contact with the cooler ground. Since warm air rises and cool air falls, you'll most often find the heaviest fog in the lowest-lying areas, especially near sources of moisture like lakes and streams. Fog can hang around long after the Sun comes up, because evaporation of the dew that formed the night before adds even more moisture to the air, replacing the fog that has burned off as the morning Sun warms the ground.

FIGURE 3-2:
San Francisco fog

(refer to page 280 for more information)

Of course, fog doesn't really burn—if it did, San Francisco would have been a cinder a long time ago. Rather, the Sun's light and heat eventually penetrate the upper, middle, and finally the lower layers of a fog bank, causing more and more evaporation until the fog is gone.

You can create your own fog in the wintertime just by breathing. The little cloud formed when you exhale into cold air is an example of steam fog, which is formed when warm water and cold air meet. If you've seen small wisps of steam rising from a lake or pond after a cold front passes, you've seen steam fog.

Fog on a Roll

Speaking of San Francisco, have you ever wondered why it always seems to be foggy there in the summertime? A different kind of fog, called advection fog, is responsible. Prevailing westerly winds off the Pacific Ocean carry sea moisture toward land. When it encounters the colder waters near the coast, it condenses into fog and "rolls in," under and around the Golden Gate Bridge. Unlike radiation fog, the fog formed from the advection process always involves the movement of air, as the fog is formed in once place and moves to another.

Building the Perfect Cloud

Believe it or not, there would be no clouds at all if it weren't for dirt. That's right—if all the microscopic dust, dirt, ash, and salt were somehow vacuumed out of the atmosphere, every day would be a great beach day. Of course, that would cause other problems.

Although there's usually plenty of water vapor in the atmosphere, it could never condense without these tiny particles—called condensation nuclei—because of the high surface tension of each vapor droplet. Condensation nuclei are so small that a volume of air the size of your index finger contains anywhere from 1,000 to 150,000 of them, but they make the perfect seed for a cloud droplet. Some of these specks, such as salt particles, bond easily with vapor and are called "hygroscopic," or water seeking. Ever notice how difficult it is to get salt out of a shaker when the air is humid? Those salt particles love their moisture. On the other hand, other atmospheric bits are "hydrophobic," or water repelling, like particles from petroleum byproducts, and resist binding with water vapor even when the humidity is more than 100 percent.

So now you know a cloud's dirty little secret. Put condensation nuclei and water vapor together, and voila—instant cloud, right? Well, as usual, there's a bit more to it than that. You also have to have air that's (a) rising, (b) expanding, and (c) cooling.

Boiling up a Cloud

If you've ever watched a pot of spaghetti cooking, you've probably noticed that it seems to circulate in the pot even if you don't stir it. Through a process called convection, the hot water carries the spaghetti toward the surface. When it cools slightly, more hot water rises to take its place, circulating the noodles over and over.

With cloud formation, the Sun heats the earth's surface, causing it to radiate warmth. Any area that heats more rapidly than its surroundings, such as deserts or large areas of asphalt or concrete, can create a bubble of warm air that rises into the sky, mixing with the cooler, drier air around it. When this happens, the warm air expands and cools, and if this process continues, the air bubble will begin to fall back toward the surface again, just like spaghetti circulating in the pot. But if more warm air arrives from underneath, it will keep growing until it reaches the saturation point and condenses, making a fluffy little cumulus cloud.

When the cloud gets big enough to cast a sizable shadow, it starts to cut off its own heat engine as the ground below it cools. This throws a monkey wrench into the whole convection process, and the cloud begins to show ragged edges as the wind moves it along, causing it to eventually dissipate. But now the ground is free to heat up again, and soon another bubble floats skyward, ready to make yet another cumulus cloud. That's why you'll often see one cloud after another form around the same spot on a sunny afternoon.

Equilibrium and Instability

Of course, when the atmosphere is unstable, even more interesting things can happen. When meteorologists use the word "stable," they're talking about the atmosphere being in balance. Air that's in a state of balance, or equilibrium, holds true to Newton's First Law of Motion: When it's at rest, it tends to remain at rest, and resists any upward or downward movement. In other words, it doesn't like to be pushed around. So if an air mass encounters surrounding air that's cooler or warmer, and quickly adapts to that temperature, the air mass is said to be stable.

On the other hand, the atmosphere becomes unstable when there's a big difference in temperature between the upper and lower layers, or between warm and cold air masses. Generally speaking, a rising air mass will become unstable. Because warm air rises, instability usually results from the warming of surface air. If air at ground level is warm and moist and upper levels are cold and dry, a process called convective instability can occur, causing a rapid, often violent, cloud growth that can produce severe thunderstorms and tornadoes quicker than you can say, "Run for the basement!"

Growing Pains

Let's take a closer look at a cumulus cloud as it grows up to become a towering cumulonimbus. You've seen how cumulus clouds form and dissipate in a stable environment, but when the air above is cooler than the layers below, more and more heat is released inside the cloud as it rises and its vapor condenses. Rain droplets and ice particles begin to form and are churned and swirled by the turbulence from the rising air. Strong updrafts form in the cloud's core, causing it to grow even faster. The rain and ice particles surge upward, getting larger and larger as they merge with other specks of moisture, creating a swirling mass of rain and ice within the cloud. And even with all this activity, no rain is falling yet, because the cloud is putting all its energy into the growth stage.

SSENTIALS

There are nearly 1,800 thunderstorms occurring worldwide at any moment, although most last an average of only thirty minutes. Out of the 100,000 or so storms that occur each year in the United States, only about 10 percent are classified as severe, but even small storms can create heavy rain and dangerous lightning.

In the next phase, called the mature stage, the raindrops and ice crystals get too large to be supported by the updraft and start to fall. This creates downdrafts within the cloud, and a pitched battle between falling and rising air begins. With updrafts still raging at speeds of up to 6,000 feet per minute, the severe turbulence causes a tremendous amount of friction in the cloud, and jagged lightning bolts begin to stab outward and downward as the storm mushrooms up toward the stratosphere. As the rain-cooled downdrafts reach the ground, they spread out horizontally into a gust front. Rain and hail begin to hammer cars, trees, and buildings, and those unlucky enough to be caught outside in the storm's path run for cover. The monster cloud's top reaches the jet stream, and strong winds begin to pull it into a long anvil shape.

ESSENTIALS

The main part of the storm's life cycle, from its beginnings as a harmless little cumulus cloud to its maturity as a towering storm, happens in less than an hour.

As the gust front spreads out underneath the storm, it cuts off the cloud's supply of warm air. Eventually, the storm's downward-moving air currents gain the upper hand, and the cloud's growth slows and finally stops. Soon the internal updrafts cease completely, and downdrafts are all that's left, carrying the rest of the cloud's moisture to the ground as rain, often for several more hours.

Super-sized Storms

If thunderstorms are the 300-pound gorilla of weather, supercells are the King Kongs. Although fewer than one in eighty thunderstorms develop into supercells, the ones that do are extremely dangerous and can be unpredictable. Supercells are the storms that most often produce tornadoes, making them the targets of storm chasers during springtime on the Great Plains.

Supercells feed off wind shear, which is the effect caused by winds blowing at different directions and speeds at different atmospheric levels. Wind shear actually tilts the storm, causing the cooler air descending inside to be pushed completely out of the cloud. Warm moist air is still free to surge in, however, and without the cooler air to act as a stabilizer, the storm's consumption of warm air becomes a feeding frenzy, creating a strong, rotating updraft within the storm called a mesocyclone—the first stage of a tornado.

Because of the strong vertical wind shear inside a developing supercell (where updrafts can reach speeds of 150 miles an hour!), the updrafts and downdrafts can actually wrap around each other, creating an extremely volatile environment. These violent currents can keep hail suspended for so long that it can reach the size of grapefruit or larger before finally escaping the storm and plummeting to earth.

ALERT

Unlike standard thunderstorms, supercells don't die easily once they get going, and can last as long as six hours, creating havoc wherever they go. They can spawn deadly tornadoes, damaging hail, and intense wind caused by violent downbursts, and are not a weather phenomenon to take lightly.

The National Weather Service gives supercells special attention, using radar to peer deep into their cores to catch early signs of developing tornadoes, which cause a characteristic "hook echo." When a severe thunderstorm or tornado warning is given for your area, believe it and take cover as soon as possible.

Rain: It's Not Just for Parades Anymore

Rain from supercells falls at the extreme end of the precipitation bell curve, but rainfall levels can vary from the cloudbursts that often accompany these huge storms all the way down to a mere trace. To meteorologists, a trace of rain is only .01 inches or less—just a thin film at the bottom of the rain gauge. Mist, a fine form of fog, just hangs in the air without falling, so isn't considered rain. The next largest droplet is drizzle, which measures a tiny .02 inches in diameter.

QUESTIONS?

Why is drizzle so light?
Drizzle usually falls from stratus clouds, and much of it evaporates before reaching the ground, making it seem light. Rain that vaporizes in the atmosphere is called virga.

None of the preceding water particles are in the rain domain yet, though. According to the folks at the National Weather Service, if you want to be a raindrop, you have to be at least $\frac{1}{50}$ of an inch across—just this side of drizzle. Of course, you can be larger, but after your girth reaches $\frac{1}{4}$ of an inch or more, you're likely to be torn apart by wind resistance as you fall.

Just as the size of raindrops can vary from small to large, a rainfall's volume can either be light or heavy, determined by how much is falling over a given period of time (usually measured by the hour). In a brief rain shower, the amounts will generally be small. Heavy rain, however, falls at the rate of .30 inches an hour, and rain falling at that rate or higher doesn't take long to generate flash-flood warnings. When heavyrain hits your area, stay tuned to local television and radio stations for bulletins, and don't venture out onto the highway unless it's absolutely necessary. Flash floods will be explained later, but for now, remember that it takes less than a foot of swiftly flowing water to push an automobile off the road, and less than two feet to turn one into a leaky boat.

Flash floods are especially dangerous in hilly or mountainous terrain, where gravity sends water rapidly downhill before it can be absorbed into the ground. Where there is little ground cover or the soil is already saturated, flash floods can trigger devastating mudslides.

Because rain forms around suspended particles in the atmosphere and takes many of them with it when it falls, the air is usually cleaner and clearer after a rainstorm. As usual, however, there's a downside: If the rain formed around particles of acidic pollution, acid rain is the result. Pollutants like nitrogen oxides and sulfur turn into nitric and sulfuric acids when they interact with sunlight. These acids, when carried into the ground by precipitation, can denude forests, contaminate water supplies, and leach vital components out of the soil. Scientists have found that rain in Europe and North America is now ten times as acidic as it once was. Stay tuned for more on acid rain in a later chapter.

You've Got Hail

If ever there was a weather event designed to convince you Chicken Little might have been right, it's hail. While heavy rain can limit visibility and soak you to the skin, a hailstorm is capable of breaking windshields, decimating crops, and even injuring livestock. If it wasn't for updrafts, hail would never grow very large, and golf ball–sized and larger specimens would be unheard of. But as ice particles fall through a cumulonimbus cloud, they inevitably encounter strong vertical winds and get swirled skyward again, picking up extra layers of supercooled water droplets as they zoom above the freezing level.

FIGURE 3-3:
Hailstone or ice bomb?

(refer to page 280 for more information)

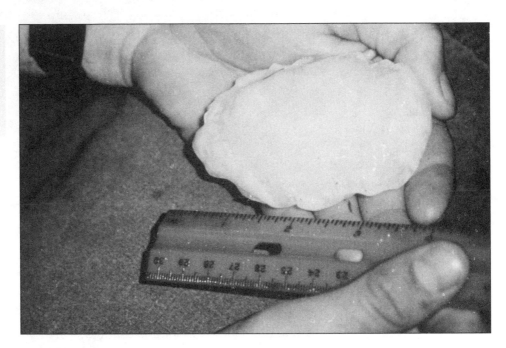

If the updrafts are strong enough, like those in a supercell, the developing hailstones ride a wild roller coaster of wind as they spin up and around inside the storm, growing larger by the minute. Finally some become so big that they overcome the updraft's power and begin to drop toward the ground at speeds of up to 120 miles an hour, denting cars and raising insurance rates wherever they fall.

SSENTIALS

Most hail is relatively small—around 2 inches in diameter or less—but on September 3, 1970, the great-granddaddy of all hailstones fell on Coffeyville, Kansas. It was over 5.6 inches across and weighed almost 2 pounds. Never mind an umbrella—with hail that size, you'd need a bomb shelter.

If you cut a hailstone in half, you can see the multiple layers of ice that mark its journey through the thunderstorm. Generally, the larger the hailstone, the more severe the updrafts were in the storm it came from.

D'oh! Snow

Snow forms from tiny particles of ice suspended in clouds up above the freezing level. As the particles form, they arrange themselves into hexagonal shapes due to the molecular structure of water, which is why simple snow crystals always have six points. Snowflakes that fall through a layer of slightly warmer air, however, can bind with other flakes to form very large, intricate structures that look like beautiful silver jewelry under a microscope.

Much of the rain that falls in the summer actually begins as snow and ice high in the tops of cumulonimbus clouds. In the wintertime the freezing level is much lower, and if you live in a snow-prone state, you're aware that snowflakes can easily make it all the way to the ground, where they gather with billions of their friends for an impromptu party on your lawn.

SSENTIALS

A whiteout occurs when the clouds from which snow is falling take on a bright, uniformly white appearance; the light reflected off the snow is about the same as the light coming through the clouds, making objects in the storm very difficult to see.

If you're a skier, you might just hop on a plane for Aspen at that point—let Nature have her way. Skiers prefer the kind of snow that forms in temperatures that are well below freezing: dry and powdery. When snow forms at temperatures closer to the freezing mark of 32 degrees F, it tends to be stickier and turns into slush more easily, making travel of any kind a miserable experience.

FIGURE 3-4:
Too much
snow

(refer to page 280 for more information)

Snow flurries usually fall from cumulus clouds and provide a light dusting of crystals that don't cause much trouble for commuters. Snow squalls, on the other hand, are brief but very intense snowstorms that are the equivalent of a summer downpour. They arrive with little warning, and their intense driving winds often create near-whiteout conditions in a matter of minutes.

Not Your Average Snowstorm

Wind-driven snow officially becomes a blizzard when below-freezing temperatures are accompanied by winds of more than 35 miles per hour and visibility down to 500 feet or less. In a severe blizzard, winds exceed 45 miles per hour, visibility is limited to a quarter mile or less, and temperatures plunge to 10 degrees F or lower. Blizzards can pile snow into gigantic drifts that can make travel impossible. During the great blizzard of 1888, known as "The Great White Hurricane," some snowdrifts were measured as high as 50 feet.

The 1888 blizzard actually led directly to the creation of the New York subway system, as city leaders vowed to prevent the weather from ever bringing the city to such a standstill again. The entire East Coast, from Maine to the Chesapeake Bay, buried in up to 50 inches of snow, was cut off from the rest of the world as telegraph and telephone wires snapped like twigs under the crushing weight of snow and ice. Washington, New York, Philadelphia, and Boston were paralyzed for days. At least 100 sailors were lost at sea, 200 ships ran aground, and, with lifesaving water frozen in pipes and hydrants, raging fires caused more than $25 million in property losses. More than 400 people perished in what became known as the worst snowstorm in American history.

If you follow winter weather on TV, you've probably noticed that cities like Buffalo and Syracuse, New York, seem to get more than their share of snow. This is due to the "lake effect," a condition that occurs when cold air moves over a warmer body of water, in this case the Great Lakes. Unlike the Great Plains, where snowstorms usually move through, release their quota of snow and leave, states to the south and east of the Great Lakes are often dumped on for days after a frontal passage, as cold air flowing south and east over the lakes picks up moisture and warmth from the water's surface and carries it shoreward.

QUESTIONS?

What is a frontal passage?
The movement of the boundary between two air masses over a particular location. Frontal passages are usually accompanied by a change in wind speed and direction, humidity, cloud cover, precipitation, and temperature.

Snow Wonder

As damaging as snow can be, however, it has a gentler side. Since snow doesn't conduct heat very well, dry snow can actually act as an insulator, protecting plants below its surface by preventing the ground from losing all of its warmth. Just as air spaces within a down jacket help insulate you from the cold, tiny gaps between dry snowflakes act as buffer zones against the cold air above. This same effect is what causes snow to absorb sound, making a walk through the woods after a snowfall a quiet, mesmerizing experience.

FACTS

The Great Lakes are able to retain much of their summer warmth well into fall and winter due to their size and depth. When an air mass warmed by its passage over a lake reaches the shore, it is forced to rise rapidly—a process called orographic lifting—and heavy snow and snow squalls are often the result.

Have you ever heard someone say that it's "too cold to snow"? Is it really possible for the temperature to drop so low that snow can no longer form? Well, no. It's true that there may be a lack of snow on cold, still evenings, when high pressure drives away any snow-producing clouds. But while it's true that cold, dry air can't hold as much moisture as warmer air, there is always at least some water vapor present, and where there's vapor, there can be precipitation.

On the flip side, you may have seen snow fall when the temperature at ground level is above freezing. For this to happen, the air aloft must be very dry. As snow begins to fall from clouds above the freezing level, it encounters warmer layers of the atmosphere and starts to melt. But because the air is dry, the melting snow evaporates quickly, cooling the air and making it possible for more flakes to penetrate downward. Eventually some of these flakes can make it to the surface, although they won't last very long in a frozen state.

Sleet and Freezing Rain: What's the Difference?

If these descending, partially melted snowflakes or raindrops fall through a colder layer near the ground, they can refreeze into sleet, which is tiny clear or translucent ice pellets that sound like falling rice when they hit your window.

When the layer of colder surface air is shallow, raindrops falling through it won't have time to freeze and will hit the surface as freezing rain, which spreads out into a thin film of ice as soon as it hits any cold surface. While sleet is relatively harmless, ice storms caused by freezing rain can be killers, as roads become slick with ice, causing auto accidents and bringing even foot traffic to a standstill. Freezing rain can create winter wonderlands by coating trees with a twinkling, crystalline glaze, but it can also bring down telephone and power lines, cutting off communications and creating a severe electrocution hazard.

QUESTIONS?

Aren't sleet and hail the same thing?

Sleet can form only when the weather is very cold, while hail is a warm-weather phenomenon based on heat convection. Hail forms while bouncing around in a thunderstorm, while sleet is created when a snowflake or raindrop refreezes during a winter storm.

Planes are especially vulnerable to ice, which in a freezing rain can build up very quickly and is very difficult to remove. A coating of ice on a plane's wings increases its weight, making it more difficult to gain altitude, but it also disturbs the airflow over the wings and fuselage, making it more difficult for the plane to stay airborne. Airports in ice-prone areas maintain de-icing crews, who spray aircraft with an antifreeze mixture designed to melt ice before it can accumulate to dangerous levels.

The National Center for Atmospheric Research (NCAR) has found that the most dangerous icing forms when planes fly through supercooled drizzle in clouds. Although the drops are small, they freeze quickly and form a rough ice layer called rime that decreases lift and increases drag much more than a layer of smooth ice would. The National Weather Service's Aviation Forecasting Center in Kansas City, Missouri, is using supercomputers to develop new forecast maps that will enable pilots to steer clear of icy drizzle aloft.

Down at ground level, however, even a good forecast isn't enough. In January of 1998, a severe ice storm hit the northeastern United States and Canada, causing forty-four deaths. In some places more than 3 inches of freezing rain fell, coating trees, buildings, and cars with ice more than an inch thick. In the aftermath, 500,000 people were without power in the United States, including more than 80 percent of the population of Maine. Things were even worse in Canada, where more than 3 million people lost electricity. Damage estimates for both countries totaled $4.5 billion.

FACTS

On January 13, 1982, an Air Florida 737 took off in a blizzard in Washington, D.C. The plane had been de-iced at the gate but was forced to wait for sixteen other planes to depart, and the crew apparently forgot to activate the 737's own anti-icing system. The plane crashed onto the Fourteenth Street Bridge over the Potomac River less than a minute after takeoff. Only five people survived.

Hard to believe that so much mayhem can be caused by something as insubstantial as a cloud, isn't it? But wind is even more tenuous, yet when combined with clouds, it can whip the atmosphere into one really impressive storm. How does wind get started, anyway? Read on.

CHAPTER 4
Air in Motion

There is no good arguing with the inevitable. The only argument available with an east wind is to put on your overcoat.

—James Russell Lowell

Wind is the vehicle air uses to get from one place to another. Although you can't see it, wind obviously exerts force since it powers tall sailing ships and spins the blades of windmills. But what creates wind, and why is it in such a darned hurry sometimes?

The Pressure's On

To understand why air moves, it helps to understand air pressure, which is the amount of force that moving air exerts on an object. There are several ways of measuring atmospheric pressure, the most common being inches of mercury, which we use in the United States, and millibars, the metric equivalent.

If you could somehow isolate a 1-inch-square column of the atmosphere, from the surface all the way to the top of the troposphere, it would weigh just about 14.7 pounds, so meteorologists say that air pressure at sea level is 14.7 pounds per square inch, or psi. That translates to 29.92 inches of mercury (abbreviated as Hg, the symbol for mercury on the periodic table of elements) or 1013.25 millibars. In case you're wondering (or happen to be a Vulcan), 1 millibar is equal to 0.02953 inches of mercury.

QUESTIONS?

Why do people swallow when air pressure changes?
Swallowing helps equalize the pressure between your inner ear and the atmosphere by letting some air out through your Eustachian tubes, which connect the inner ears to the throat.

With nearly 15 pounds of pressure pushing against every square inch of your body, you'd think it would be hard to even take a breath. Fortunately, nature does its best to stay in balance, and there is just as much pressure pushing outward in each cell of your body as there is outside pushing inward, showing how well we've adapted to living on the surface of this planet. But what if you're not on the surface, but up higher where air pressure is less, as you find when climbing a mountain or flying in a plane? As you climb higher, the pressure in your inner ear becomes greater than the pressure outside, and you start to feel that 14.7 pounds trying to get out.

Weighing the Air

Atmospheric pressure is measured using a barometer, either liquid filled (which is where the inches-of-mercury method comes from) or metal based. Although you'll hear your local TV weatherperson use the term "inches of mercury" a lot, liquid barometers are rarely used these days; the aneroid barometer, which uses variations in the shape of a metal cell to measure air pressure, is now much more common, as are newer electronic models.

Unlike temperature, air pressure decreases the higher you go in the atmosphere. (You'd think temperature would go down with altitude, and it does to a certain point. But then it goes up again before coming back down. It isn't what you'd expect, is it?) The only thing keeping all of Earth's air from leaking out into space is gravity, which pulls air molecules toward the earth's surface. Air at ground level is under more pressure because of the weight of all the air above it, so the higher you go, the less pressure you'll find. At a height of 3½ miles, air pressure is only half what it is at the surface, so at this altitude you're above half of all the air molecules in the atmosphere.

Highs and Lows Make Wind

When warm air rises, it relieves the air beneath it of some of that burden and creates an area of low pressure. But if that same air mass rises and cools, it sinks and creates a high-pressure area, descending and pressing down on the air below it. Because the atmosphere is always trying to keep itself in balance, and because low-pressure systems are actually partial vacuums, air moves from high-pressure systems to areas of low pressure, producing wind.

The difference in air pressure between air masses is called a pressure gradient, and the higher the gradient, the faster the winds will blow. Because the earth is rotating, those winds turn to the right in the Northern Hemisphere and to the left in the Southern, following a path first discovered in 1835 by Gaspard-Gustave de Coriolis, a French engineer and mathematician. Coriolis applied the element of rotation to Newton's Laws of Motion, describing how a free-floating object near the earth's surface appears to curve as the globe rotates beneath it. You can duplicate the Coriolis effect by having someone turn a globe while you try to draw a straight line on it from north to south with a piece of chalk: What you'll end up with is a curved line.

Putting a Spin on the Weather

The Coriolis effect is what imparts rotation to weather systems, although its force is too weak to make water flowing down a bathtub drain move either clockwise or counterclockwise, despite popular notions. It affects any moving object not attached to the earth's surface, from space shuttles to artillery shells. In World War II, German scientists developed a giant cannon that was capable of shelling Paris, some 70 miles away. It had a barrel 120 feet long, and the whole thing weighed 138 tons. It took 550 pounds of explosives to hurl its huge shells, which gained an altitude of 24 miles before beginning their fall toward France. If the projectile was fired directly toward Paris, it would land a mile to the right due to the Coriolis effect, so the Germans had to employ not just gunners but also mathematicians to make shells land on target.

You've probably seen weather maps with swirled lines that sometimes look like fingerprints. These lines are called isobars, and they connect locations with equal air pressure. Multiple isobars usually form a target shape, and in the middle you'll find a capital *H* or *L*—a high- or low-pressure area. Because high-pressure areas contain air that is sinking toward the surface, they're usually associated with fair weather, while low-pressure systems, which contain rising air, are more unstable and often mean a dose of rain, snow, or worse. Remember that air is being pushed out of high-pressure systems as it hits the surface and spreads out, while lows tend to suck in air at the surface and pile it up into clouds and storms.

Isobars and Wind Speed

Because lows turn counterclockwise and highs clockwise in the Northern Hemisphere, you can look at an isobar map and tell which way the wind is blowing. Wind blows parallel to isobars above the surface, and the closer together the lines are, the faster the wind speed. In a hurricane, isobars are so tightly packed they almost merge together.

However, down at ground level, the friction caused by air blowing over objects such as mountains, trees, dogs, and people slows down the wind and partially cancels out the Coriolis effect, allowing air to cross isobars as it flows toward low-pressure areas. The section of atmosphere below around 3,300 feet is called the friction layer for that reason.

FACTS

Gas giant planets like Jupiter and Saturn have zonal flow features that can persist for decades, due to the planets' rapid rotation. Due to their long-lasting nature, scientists have given them names: The bright regions are called zones, and the dark regions are known as belts. Jupiter is also home to the largest storm in the solar system: the Great Red Spot.

The isobar maps you see on TV and in the newspaper are called constant height charts because they show equal areas of air pressure at a single height, such as sea level. Another type of map that meteorologists often use is called a constant pressure chart, because it connects areas with the same air pressure whether they're found at the surface or higher in the atmosphere. On a constant pressure chart, meteorologists pick a pressure and show you at which altitude that pressure can be found in different locations.

If you were able to ride along a line on a constant pressure chart, you'd rise and fall as you curved around a low or a high, because air pressure varies by height depending on air temperature and other factors. So if you think of isobars on a constant height chart as narrow speedways around lows or highs, the contour lines on a constant pressure chart are more like roller coasters.

What's Up

While surface maps tell us what the weather is like outside our windows, upper-air maps can tell forecasters what kind of weather we may be experiencing in the near future. With nothing to slow them down, winds aloft are almost always blowing faster then air flowing along at ground level. Winds in the upper atmosphere generally blow from west to east, creating a zonal flow where the wind follows the lines of latitude that wrap around the earth horizontally. In a zonal flow, storm systems follow the course of least resistance, making a beeline across the country as fast as the wind will carry them. Because temperatures don't differ much within a zonal flow, they don't usually bring severe weather.

So what happens when something comes along to disturb the air's nice straight course? Something like a large mass of cold air moving down from Canada, or a big sticky bubble of hot air floating northward from the Gulf of Mexico? Then we have a meridional flow, so-called because those systems move roughly north or south along meridians, the lines that mark off longitude. A meridional flow indicates that air masses from the north and south are mixing, and that can mean stormy weather as areas of differing temperatures battle it out for air superiority.

High-Flying Currents

The Introduction mentioned rivers in the earth's atmosphere, and the jet stream is the biggest of them all. It's not even close to being a stream—it's more like an Amazon of flowing air. The jet stream, found anywhere from 6 to 9 miles up in the atmosphere, separates, transports, and steers the giant air masses created by meridional flows as it snakes its way across the country and around the world.

The jet stream's speed ranges from around 75 to 200 miles per hour, but it can reach even higher speeds in jet streaks, faster-moving areas embedded in the main stream. Flying the wrong way through a jet streak can ruin a pilot's whole day.

Swedish-born meteorologist and Weather Bureau employee Carl-Gustaf Arvid Rossby first proposed the jet stream's existence in 1939, and the U.S. Air Corps's experiences proved that it was the cause of the B-29s' problems. Rossby also discovered that eddies can form in the jet stream, becoming stronger and more powerful until they break up into cells that can be quite long lasting. His namesake Rossby waves have since been discovered in the oceans and even on Mars.

Where the jet stream takes a dive south, a trough is formed; where it moves northward, it forms a ridge. Although local TV forecasters refer to "the" jet stream, there are actually two constantly moving rivers of air in each hemisphere, the polar and subtropical jets. The polar jet, usually found around 60 degrees latitude, is the one most relevant to the United States, marking the boundary between warmer air at lower latitudes and colder Canadian air to the north.

FACTS

In the new high-flying B-29 Superfortresses with pressurized crew compartments, World War II bomber crews were surprised to find that on some missions they were able to reach their targets much faster than planned, but the return trip took longer. In some cases, B-29s on bombing runs encountered so much wind resistance that they almost hovered in one spot.

When a big bubble of frigid high-pressure air surges southward into the United States, the boundary between cold and warm air becomes a battleground, causing severe weather in the form of midlatitude cyclones to break out all along its length. This boundary, marking the leading edge of a cold air mass, is a cold front. Conversely, warm fronts occur when large masses of warm, moist air ride up over the top of cooler air, often causing long periods of rain.

ALERT

Jet streams can shift suddenly, bringing abrupt changes in weather with them. When the polar jet plunges deep into the South, it can cause widespread crop damage. On December 24, 1989, a dip in the jet stream brought 33 degree F temperatures to Miami and virtually destroyed central Florida's citrus crop.

The subtropical jet stream hangs around at 30 degrees latitude and during the summer is barely detectable. Though the subtropical jet is much weaker than its polar cousin, at times it can advance northward over the continent and bring moist, unstable air to the upper levels of the atmo-sphere. In winter the polar and subtropical jet streams can even merge into one, and the resulting superjet creates extremely strong storms.

Seasonal Jet Streams

The subtropical and polar jets remain fairly constant in the atmosphere, but there are other types of jet streams that come and go during the seasons. One is the tropical easterly jet stream, which appears over Asia, India, and Africa during the summer and is associated with the monsoon season. This jet is thought to be generated by warm air moving over large landmasses.

Can you imagine a jet stream that forms only at night? That's the polar night jet stream, which forms in the upper stratosphere at the earth's poles. The night stream results from a steep pressure gradient between polar and tropical air.

ESSENTIALS

Earth is on a budget—a heat budget. The atmosphere constantly tries to balance the heat it absorbs with the warmth being radiated back into space. Jet streams, tropical storms, hurricanes, and ocean currents all combine to spread the heat around, keeping Earth's budget in balance.

The low-level jet stream also forms mainly at night and is found over the Midwest. Both of these fast-moving air streams form when there's a temperature inversion near the surface, meaning that a stable layer of cold air at the surface has warmer air flowing quickly over it, like a drop of oil sliding on Teflon. Winds in a low-level jet can reach speeds of more than 50 miles per hour around 1,000 feet up, although a ground observer might feel only a slight breeze. Just east of the Rocky Mountains, low-level jets funneling warm, moist air up from the Gulf of Mexico into the country's interior can spawn huge nocturnal thunderstorms called Mesoscale Convective Complexes (MCCs). One theory states that low-level jet streams form near the Rockies due to pressure and temperature imbalances caused by the sloping terrain.

Jet streams have a huge effect on our daily weather, and once meteorologists were aware of their existence and learned how to predict their movements, they could look upstream and be able to tell with much more accuracy what the weather would be like in the future. Pilots also learned to take advantage of the jet stream, riding its currents on westbound routes and avoiding it when flying east.

FACTS

The Rocky Mountains have a major effect on the country's weather, acting as a huge dam between eastern and western air masses. One computer-modeling study showed that MCCs develop when rain-cooled air pours down the mountains into a warmer moist air mass on the Great Plains, forcing it to rise and spawning a giant thunderstorm complex.

Meteorogically, jet streams have a much more important purpose: They act as conveyer belts, carrying warm air into the upper latitudes and cool air southward. This heat transfer process is just one way the earth maintains a measure of balance in its atmosphere.

Mixing It Up

Frontal systems are the catalysts of the atmosphere, always bringing a change in the weather as one air mass does its best to shove another one out of the way. Because they mark the boundaries of air masses with differing temperatures, humidity levels, and densities, you can usually find clouds and precipitation at these interfaces, unless the air masses are fairly similar in nature.

As mentioned earlier, warm fronts mark the leading edge of an advancing mass of warmer air where it encounters an area that's colder. The warm air rises over the top of the cold air and begins to cool, and when it reaches the condensation point, clouds and rain form, often far in advance of the actual front. The first sign that a warm front is approaching is often the appearance of cirrus clouds. Those are followed by lower clouds like altostratus and finally a thick layer of stratus or nimbostratus clouds, which can generate a lot of rain and fairly strong winds.

If you could cut a warm front down the middle and view the cross section from the side, you'd notice that it looks like a giant wedge in the sky, with the thinner portion riding over the cooler air. Cirrus clouds are found at the thin end, with the actual front and its clouds and rain at the other. Because of its gentle slope, warm fronts create a gradual change in the weather that can stick around for a day or more, and its rains tend to be less strong but longer lasting than a cold front's. On a weather map, a warm front is marked by a line with a series of rounded bumps that face in the direction the front is moving, and are red on color charts.

QUESTIONS?

What's the difference between a front and a dryline?
While warm fronts and cold fronts mark the boundary between air of different temperatures, a dryline separates an area of warm, dry air from warm, moist air. Drylines are also called dew-point fronts.

Pushy Weather

In contrast, a cold front, usually associated with low-pressure systems, can move in like a linebacker, bullying the warmer air out of its way. Unlike the gentler warm fronts, their colder cousins often bring violent disturbances as they tunnel underneath the warmer air, forcing it rapidly upward and causing a sudden and intense instability in the atmosphere. If the temperature difference between the two air masses is considerable, clouds form rapidly along the front, often growing into towering cumulonimbus in very short order. These clouds form a very well defined line as they rampage across the countryside, bringing a dose of torrential rain, hail, and general unpleasantness to all in their path.

ESSENTIALS

The wind-chill factor is a number that tells you how cold it feels at a particular temperature and humidity level. The method of computing wind chill was recently changed to more accurately reflect real conditions, using wind speeds at 5 feet in height rather than the old 33 feet. Now, the wind-chill factor also takes into account the danger of frostbite.

After the front passes, the temperature can suddenly drop as much as 40 degrees F in just a few hours, and the humidity usually lessens as well. A cross section of a cold front would show a curved bubble of cold air pushing relentlessly underneath a warmer layer. Cold fronts usually move toward the east or south, but occasionally one will make its way westward near the northeast coast, driven by a high-pressure area over Canada. Because it's arriving from the "wrong" direction, these oddball fronts are called back-door cold fronts. On a weather map, cold fronts are depicted as lines with sharp triangles pointing in their direction of motion, and are blue if the map is in color.

FACTS

Some cold fronts are worse than others. In the spring and fall, there may not be much difference in temperature between the air on either side of a cold front. But on January 23, 1916, in Browning, Montana, the temperature plunged from 44 degrees F to -56 degrees F in less than twenty-four hours after a frontal passage—a world's record for the fastest, deepest temperature drop.

Sometimes a cold front catches up to a warm front, creating a hybrid called an occluded front. There are two types of occluded fronts: warm and cold. A cold occlusion occurs when the air behind the occluded front is colder than the air ahead of it. The cold occlusion acts like a cold front, as the cold air behind the front pushes underneath the cool air ahead of it.

A warm occlusion occurs when the air behind the occluded front is warmer than the air ahead of it. The warm occlusion acts like a warm front, since the cool air behind the front, which is lighter than the cold air ahead, passes over the top of the cold air. On a map, an occluded front is shown as a line that contains the symbols for both warm and cold fronts, again pointing in the direction of motion. On a color map, an occluded front is purple.

Faltering Fronts

What if a front loses its way and grinds to a halt, like a befuddled driver forced to stop and consult a road map? That's a stationary front, a line that marks the spot where two air masses have fought each other to a draw. That doesn't mean a lack of weather, however. Clouds and rain can still be active on the northern side of the front, and because it's not moving, bad weather can persist for days, causing flooding and general consternation. Stationary fronts often dissipate over time, but if one starts moving again, it turns back into whichever front is more active. Weather maps show stationary fronts as alternating segments of cold and warm fronts, with the half-round warm-front symbols pointing toward the warm air and the cold-front spikes aiming toward the cold side of the front. Stationary fronts alternate red and blue on a color map.

Small disturbances called frontal lows, caused by upper-level air flows or the jet stream's influence, can form on the frontal boundary. If a front is stationary far enough south over the Gulf of Mexico or the Atlantic Ocean, a frontal low can turn into a tropical depression, tropical storm, or hurricane.

Fronts stall out because the upper-level winds that have been pushing them along change direction. If wind that has been blowing behind the front suddenly starts flowing along it instead, the front loses momentum and finally stops.

Making Waves

Frontal lows are also known as wave cyclones, because the intersection between the warm front and the cold front begins to resemble a wave on a weather map as the cyclone develops. The cold front moves southward as the warm front pushes northward, wrapping around the central low-pressure system. As warm, moist air is drawn around the eastern side of the center and cold, dry air toward the west, the wave cyclone gains intensity, fueled by heat generated by condensation in the rapidly rising air.

How intense can a wave cyclone become? You've probably heard about "The Storm of the Century," a cyclone that started as a wave along a cold front near Texas in March 1993. It then developed into a snowstorm and moved up the East Coast, burying everything in its path. When the final toll was taken, the storm had left more than $3 billion in damage as it passed and had killed 270 people. One hundred million people in twenty-six states had been affected, just about half of the population of the United States—and all from a wave that formed on a cold front.

Making a Mass

Fronts are just the leading edges of much larger air masses, which can cover thousands of square miles. In an air mass, temperatures and moisture levels are similar across the entire length, breadth, and depth of this huge parcel of atmosphere. Because air masses move, creating fronts at their forward edges, they bring the weather conditions from their point of origin to other regions. So, if a large bubble of cold air slides across the Canadian border into the United States (completely ignoring Customs, no doubt) and runs into warmer air, it simply shoves the warm air aside, and Ohio or Indiana will now have the same weather Ontario was experiencing twenty-four hours earlier.

Air masses like to form in source regions that feature large areas of high pressure, and meteorologists categorize them by the region where they were created. An air mass formed in a tropical area earns the designation *T*, while a polar air mass gets tagged with a capital *P*. Those forming over land get a lowercase *c* (for continental), while air masses originating over water get an *m* (for maritime). There are also arctic *(A)* and equatorial *(E)* air masses.

Mixing and Matching Air Masses

Those designations can be mixed and matched to nail down an air mass's nature, and there are other tags that can be used when more detail is needed. If an air mass is moving over a warmer surface, the letter *k* is used, and if the underlying surface is colder, a *w* is added to the designation. That naming system covers any kind of air mass that might form in any environment, anywhere in the world. When a meteorologist sees the letter combination "mPk," he knows it refers to a polar air mass that originated over water and is currently moving over a warmer surface. You'd probably just say it's cold and damp.

Maritime Tropical (mT) air masses, not surprisingly, contain a great deal of moisture. In the winter, they can move northward from the Gulf of Mexico, bringing mild weather to the United States's midsection. In the summer, they cause thunderstorms to form, although they usually die out by nightfall.

Maritime Polar (mP) air also contains a lot of moisture, and mainly affects the Pacific coast of the United States. As they encounter the coast and the mountains farther inland, these systems give up much of their water as rain and snow. Because of the moderating effect caused by moving over water, mP masses aren't nearly as cold as cP air.

Jetting in from the Continent

Continental Polar (cP) and Continental Arctic (cA) air masses bring loads of cold, dry air with them, and are responsible for the worst winter weather over the United States. Because they originate over Alaska and Canada, there is little moisture in them, and when the jet stream carries them deep into the heartland, long-standing low-temperature records can be broken.

Continental Tropical (cT) air masses, which form in Mexico and the American Southwest, bring hot, dry weather. Driven by a stable high-pressure system, cT air can move into an area like the Midwest and stay for a prolonged visit, causing severe droughts.

SSENTIALS The word "synoptic" comes from the Greek *synoptikos,* which means "a general view of a whole." Because early weather data collection sites were so far apart, the only available view of the entire country's weather was a synopsis, or summary, of the nation's current conditions.

All of these air masses occur on a large scale—called the synoptic scale—and each is easily identifiable on a weather map of the continental United States. But other wind patterns occur on a much smaller scale. Swirls and eddies of all kinds constantly whirl around us, embedded in the larger air masses that regularly cruise by.

Economies of Scale

Eddies that occur on a very small scale affect a limited area such as a single block or a back yard. Many of these eddies are caused by wind running into solid objects such as trees, buildings, cars, and mailboxes, which break a straight breeze into a swirling pattern called mechanical turbulence. These swirls become visible when they pick up light objects on the ground, like that big pile of leaves you just finished raking up. Local wind features like these are called microscale winds, the smallest scale of motion measured by meteorologists.

It's strange, but low, low down—within about .01 millimeter off the ground—there's almost never any wind at all, no matter how fast the breeze is blowing above. To get picked up and moved, a particle has to be taller than the .01 millimeter limit, and as these larger particles are picked up and blown around, they can knock other bits into the air, creating dust devils and even dust storms.

All these small disturbances tend to slow down the layers of air above them, too. With no obstacles to cause any friction, the air from treetop level up to around 3,300 feet is often moving much faster, sometimes twice as fast, as at the surface. The area where turbulence interacts with smooth-flowing air is called the boundary layer, or friction layer.

When the Sun heats the ground and those bubbles of warm air begin to rise (as described in Chapter 3), thermal turbulence adds to the general atmospheric mixing caused by mechanical turbulence, and the lower atmosphere can get fairly unstable. As the afternoon progresses, these turbulent eddies grow stronger, producing strong, gusty winds down at the surface.

Deadly Eddies

When these swirls form high in the atmosphere, they give airline pilots and their passengers yet another thing to worry about. Where winds suddenly change direction, they produce a dangerous condition called wind shear, which can cause an aircraft to quickly gain or lose a great deal of altitude without warning. At lower altitudes, that can be deadly. Below a height of around 2,000 feet, with a commercial airliner on final approach, the pilot is forced to reduce speed and has very little time to react to violent changes in wind speed or direction.

On August 2, 1985, a Delta L-1011 was on final approach to Dallas/Fort Worth International Airport when it was hit by a violent downdraft caused by wind shear. Unable to gain altitude, the pilot lost control of the plane, which collided with several objects on the ground before crashing into a water tank near the runway. One hundred thirty-three people were killed and thirty-one injured in the crash, which brought a public outcry for more sophisticated methods of detecting wind shear. After the crash, the Federal Aviation Administration undertook a large-scale project to modernize equipment at major airports, including wind shear detectors and improved Doppler radar.

ESSENTIALS

Wind shear can now be detected with a technology called LIDAR (Light Detection and Ranging), which uses a laser instead of radar's microwave beam. Dust and other small particles in the atmosphere reflect the laser, and their image appears on a monitor, providing instant data on wind speed and direction.

In the Dallas incident, controllers might have been alerted to the turbulence by the presence of a small thunderstorm nearby if more had been known about wind shear at the time. But another type of wind shear, clear-air turbulence, often gives no visible clue to its existence until the plane is in its grip. On December 28, 1997, United Airlines Flight 826 from Tokyo to Honolulu ran into a pocket of clear-air turbulence 5 miles up. The plane started to shake, and then unexpectedly dropped one hundred feet. Oxygen masks deployed, and anyone not wearing their seat belts flew up and crashed against the ceiling of the cabin. The plane made it back to Japan for an emergency landing, but eighty-three people were injured and one passenger was killed in the incident.

To prevent this kind of accident, NASA has begun a program called SCATCAT (Severe Clear-Air Turbulence Colliding with Air Traffic) that will try to find new ways of detecting turbulence before it can cause a disaster.

Wind and Water

While microscale winds occur in a relatively small area, mesoscale systems can encompass from fifty to several hundred square miles. If you've ever been to the beach in the afternoon, you've experienced one of the more common examples of a mesoscale system known as the sea breeze, which you'll find anywhere there's a boundary between sea and land. Because the land heats up more quickly than the ocean, during the day the air over land areas rises and expands from the Sun's heat, creating a weak thermal low-pressure system. The cooler air over the water begins to flow into this low, refreshing beachgoers with a cooling breeze.

FIGURE 4-1:
High winds
at sea

(refer to page 280 for more information)

At night it's the other way around: The land cools off more rapidly than the water, producing a weak high-pressure system. Since air flows from highs toward lows, the sea breeze turns into a land breeze, flowing back toward the ocean.

A Wind by Any Other Name

Mesoscale winds are known by many names according to their type, location, and season. For instance, the warm, dry wind that flows down the eastern slopes of the Rocky Mountains is called a Chinook. Strong westerly winds blow over the Rockies and fall down the eastern slopes, and the air gets compressed and heated as it descends. Because the wind loses most of its moisture on the western, windward side of the mountains, it brings dry, warmer air to the eastern valleys.

A monsoon is a wind that blows one way in the summer and the other way in winter, such as the winds found in the Indian Ocean. Like sea breezes, monsoon winds are a result of the land's ability to warm more rapidly than the sea. During the summertime, the Asian continent is heated until it's much warmer than the ocean to its south. The resulting pressure gradient causes air to flow from the Indian Ocean up into India, where it can cause heavy rain and severe flooding. In the winter, Arctic air and radiational cooling over land reverse the flow, and cold, dry air rushes south toward the sea.

Residents of the Los Angeles Basin are familiar with the hot, dry Santa Ana winds, which flow down from the high desert. When a high-pressure area forms in the Great Basin east of the Sierra Mountains, it forces air downslope, causing it to compress and heat up at the rate of about 5 degrees F for every 1,000 feet it falls. Because Santa Ana winds bring extremely dry air, they also bring a higher likelihood of wildfires in the affected areas.

ALERT

Nor'easters can do some real damage when a high-pressure system over New England or the northern Atlantic blocks the northern progression of a low-pressure system. As the low stops advancing, its counterclockwise winds meet the high's clockwise gusts, battering the coastline with severe winds.

The Sahara desert is home to the sirocco, another hot, dry wind caused when a low-pressure system forms in the Mediterranean south of Spain and France. A sirocco can blow dust from northern Africa all the way to Europe.

New Englanders call the storms that form off the east coast of the United States and move northward into their territory nor'easters, which begin as low-pressure systems over warm Gulf Stream waters. They usually form between October and April, and as they move up the coast and encounter frigid Arctic air flowing down from Canada, instability increases and the chance for heavy snow and gale-force winds is great. Most nor'easters don't turn into major storms, but the ones that do live in memory and folklore for generations.

Coastal residents from Maine to the Philippines have learned to live with the storms that are part of life at the sea's edge, but the ocean's effects don't stop at the shoreline. In fact, the earth's seas influence the global climate more than any other factor.

Chapter 5

Weather and the Oceans

In all my experience, I have never been in any accident . . . or any sort worth speaking about.
　　　　　　　　　　—E. J. Smith, Captain, RMS *Titanic*

Not only are the oceans capable of sinking large ocean liners, but they also team up with the atmosphere to create long-standing climate conditions all over the globe. This power makes them the biggest influence of all on the earth's weather and climate.

Rivers in the Sea

Knowing that giant rivers of air meander through the atmosphere, it probably wouldn't surprise you to find that the oceans have their own streams and eddies as well. Prevailing winds get surface waters moving along with them, and the effect transfers down through the ocean layers, creating currents that span entire seas. Even deeper currents are caused by the water's density. The sea is denser at greater depths because cold water is heavier than warmer water due to the fact that the molecules in frigid water have been squeezed closer together. Seawater also contains salt, which makes it heavier than fresh water.

FACTS

On average, seawater is about 1,000 times denser than air. The division between cold water deep in the ocean and warmer water above is called the thermocline, and it varies in depth depending on a number of factors including prevailing winds and underwater currents.

In the 1500s, Juan Ponce de Leon, who had arrived in the New World on Columbus's second voyage, discovered that his ship was unable to make headway while sailing south from Saint Augustine, even though the wind was behind him. Unaware of it at the time, the explorer was trying to sail against the Gulf Stream, part of a vast river of water that circles the entire Atlantic Ocean. Later, conquistadors learned to take advantage of this current by riding it to a point where prevailing winds could carry them back to Spain.

Gently down the Stream

The Gulf Stream originates, fittingly enough, with the strong currents flowing into the Gulf of Mexico from the Caribbean, then moves eastward through the Florida Straits between Florida and Cuba, where it's called the Florida Current. It then joins the Antilles Current and flows north along the southeastern coast of the United States at an average rate of about 4 miles an hour. At this point it's about 50 miles wide.

FIGURE 5-1:
Oceans harbor undersea rivers

(refer to page 280 for more information)

When the Gulf Stream encounters North Carolina's east coast at Cape Hatteras, it begins to turn eastward, eventually running into the Labrador Current off Newfoundland, creating heavy layers of fog over the ocean. The Gulf Stream has now lost much of its warmth and becomes the North Atlantic Current, which crosses the Atlantic on prevailing southwest winds and begins to turn south near the coast of Europe. There, it joins with the Canary Current to form the North Equatorial Current. Now the cycle begins again as the North Equatorial Current heads west toward the United States again.

In the Gulf of Mexico, the Gulf Stream is only 50 miles wide and surges along at 3 miles per hour, making it one of the strongest currents known. But in the North Atlantic, it slows to only 1 mile per hour and splits into several smaller currents that total several hundred miles in width. At this point, the current moves 500 times more water per second than the Amazon River. The frigid North Atlantic causes the moving water to sink, creating a deep current that keeps the Gulf Stream moving in its constant circular journey.

Ben Franklin: Oceanographer

The Gulf Stream has been a target of intense scientific research ever since its discovery, and one of its first investigators was Ben Franklin, who was Deputy Postmaster General of North America from 1753 to 1774. English postal authorities noticed that American ships were able to carry mail from England to the Colonies much faster than the English ships, in some cases several weeks faster, and they wrote to Franklin for possible explanations.

FIGURE 5-2:
Ocean mapping from space

(refer to page 280 for more information)

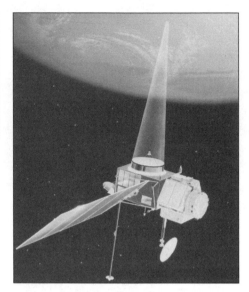

Franklin was no seaman, so he asked his cousin Timothy Folger, a whaling-ship captain from Nantucket, if he had any idea. Folger let Franklin in on the Gulf Stream secret, and drew him a map of its location. Franklin had copies of the map made up and presented them to the British postal authorities, who ignored them. After all, what could a landlubber Colonist statesman possibly know about the ocean?

Undeterred, Franklin continued to study this strange river of warm water whenever the chance arose, which it did in 1776 when he embarked on a voyage to France to gain support for the American Revolution. He conducted more research on each of his eight voyages across the Atlantic, recording them in his book *Maritime Observations.*

ESSENTIALS

A submarine bearing Franklin's name began exploring the Gulf Stream in the late 1960s. Built in Switzerland for famed oceanographer Jacques Picard and the Grumman Aerospace Corporation, the *Ben Franklin* was involved in deep-water ocean-environment research until its retirement in 1999. It now occupies a place of honor in British Columbia's Vancouver Maritime Museum.

Current Information

The Gulf Stream is only one giant whorl of water, although it's the best known in the United States. There are similar circular currents in the Western Pacific and other oceans. These currents, like the flowing air masses above them, serve to transport heat northward. The earth's oceans absorb about half of all the solar radiation streaming through the atmosphere, creating a huge source of potential energy. If all this energy weren't balanced by the oceans' heat transfer process, there would eventually be a huge temperature difference between southern and northern latitudes, causing dire and far-reaching consequences for the global climate.

SSENTIALS In the middle of the North Atlantic gyre lies a vast ocean-within-an-ocean called the Sargasso Sea. Caught between coastal Atlantic currents, its sluggish waters collect seaweed, driftwood, and other floating debris that are home to a multitude of tiny sea creatures.

The scientific term for these giant circling currents is "gyres"; there are five of them dominating the planet's oceans: the North Pacific, South Pacific, North Atlantic, South Atlantic, and Indian Ocean. Because of the Coriolis effect, the water circling around each gyre tends to deflect to the right, which has the effect of moving the water inward, creating a dome of water at the center of each one. There may be a difference of only a few feet between the height of the dome and the gyre's edge, but that's enough to make the surface water eventually flow back "downhill," where it joins and reinforces the stream's current.

Wandering Flows

Even though the Gulf Stream and other ocean currents are permanent features, you won't always find them in exactly the same place. Not only do they tend to meander a bit, but occasionally an eddy will break away and go spinning off by itself, carrying the characteristics of the region where it formed to other parts of the ocean, just as an air mass does in the atmosphere. Scientists can sample water from one of these large whirlpools and learn where it originated. In fact, in one case small surface eddies from 500 miles off Cape Hatteras were found to have begun in the far eastern Atlantic near Gibraltar, more than 2,500 miles away!

When we think of currents we think horizontally, but there are vertical currents in the ocean, too, known as upwellings. When surface waters are moving away from each other, or diverging, more water from underneath comes up to replace them, usually bringing colder, nutrient-rich water to the surface. Fish go where the food is, so upwelling can make fishing a more rewarding experience while cooling nearby shores in the summertime. Upwelling usually occurs near a coastline, where winds blow surface water away from the shore. When the waters are blown back toward the coast, downwelling can occur, and surface water gets compressed against the shore and sinks toward the bottom.

The El Niño Effect

The oceans have always been known as major influences on the earth's climate, but the extent of the seas' effects wasn't known until the last few years. In the 1800s, fishermen along the coasts of Ecuador and Peru noted that sometimes the ocean would become much warmer offshore around Christmastime, so they named this thermal change El Niño, which in Spanish means "the Christ child."

Normally, cold water upwelling from the depths along the coasts makes for good fishing, since it contains nutrients that attract large colonies of anchovies and other types of fish. But during an El Niño event, fish became scarce due to the warmer water, so the fishermen would take time off to maintain their boats, repair their nets, and spend some quality time at home. Most often their break would last from a few weeks to a month, but at other times these warm periods would last much longer than usual, bringing not only warmer sea temperatures but heavy rains as well, and the South American fishing economy suffered as a result.

In the El Niño year of 1972, Peru's annual anchovy catch weighed in at 4.6 metric tons—but the year before, the total had been 10.3 metric tons. Contrary to what you might think, most anchovies don't end up on pizzas; they're ground into fishmeal and fed to poultry and livestock in many countries, including the United States. With much less fishmeal available, the meat and poultry industries turned to soybeans as an alternative, which drove up the cost of poultry in the United States by more than a third; all because of a big warm pool of water.

Winds between 0 degrees (the Equator) and 30 degrees latitude generally blow from west to east and are called the Tropical Easterlies, or trade winds, since early sailors depended on them to propel their ships. Normally, these prevailing winds blow warm surface water from areas of higher pressure in the eastern Pacific all the way across the ocean, where it piles up in low-pressure areas near the western Pacific landmasses such as Indonesia. The surface waters literally do pile up, actually raising the sea level in those areas.

As you've learned, water follows wind, so some of the cooler water from the coast of South America is pulled westward; as it's dragged along, it warms up from the Sun's energy. Now we have a huge area of warmer water in the western Pacific (containing thirty or forty times more water than all the Great Lakes combined), and cooler water in the eastern regions.

QUESTIONS?

What was the longest-lasting El Niño?
The El Niño that began in 1991 lasted until 1995, about three to four times longer than average. It also brought the worst drought in southern Africa of the twentieth century, affecting nearly 100 million people.

Every few years, the trade winds weaken, and atmospheric pressure starts to rise in the western Pacific while it drops in the eastern Pacific. The trade winds reverse direction, and a giant dome of warm water about 5 feet high, El Niño, begins moving back across the ocean toward South America, where water levels begin to rise. In the western Pacific, the levels are dropping and can actually dip below sea level as the ocean sloshes back toward the east. If you've ever tried to carry a pan full of water very far, you're familiar with the sloshing effect, up one side of the pan and then the other. With all the warm water heading east, there can be torrential rains and flooding in Peru, while on the other side of the ocean, Australia and Indonesia are experiencing droughts. El Niño rides up over colder water near the South American coast, forcing it downward and choking off the supply of fish that many depend upon for their livelihoods.

Oscillating Oceans

When water is sloshing around in a pan it's oscillating, and when the Pacific sloshes back and forth it's called the El Niño-Southern Oscillation, or ENSO. El Niños happen about every two to seven years, on average, and every one is different in both its strength and its effects on the global economy.

With the kind of energy El Niño has, it's not hard to see how these events can cause radical changes in climate across the entire globe. Because the ENSO effect has been recognized for only a relatively brief time, scientists are still building databases that will enable them to try and predict the next one. The Pacific experienced one of the strongest El Niños ever in 1982, and by the time it had faded the following year, nearly 2,000 lives had been lost, hundreds of thousands of people were homeless, and damage estimates were in the $13 billion range.

ALERT

At its strongest, an El Niño wields as much potential energy as half a million hydrogen bombs. Signs of their effects have been discovered in ice-core samples taken high in the Himalayas and in tree rings in Arizona, showing us that on average the earth experiences an El Niño about thirty times per century.

During the 1982 event, Peru was doused with 11 feet of rain in some areas that normally experienced 6 inches or less, while Australia, Indonesia, and Africa were parched by drought. The atmospheric pressure at Darwin, Australia, soared to its highest in 100 years, while in Tahiti the lowest pressure in 50 years was recorded. Scientists began calling the 1982–1983 event the "El Niño of the Century." Of course, the record books were rewritten yet again before the century's end.

In 1997, El Niño spawned a string of deadly tornadoes that ripped through central Florida, while in California, heavy rains washed away homes, undermined buildings and roads, and blacked out power to thousands of residents, triggering a state-of-emergency declaration by the governor.

In South America, so much rain fell in Peru that the country's Piura region gained a new lake 8,000 square miles in size. The rushing waters washed away 1,860 miles of highway in the massive floods and mudslides that accompanied the downpours. In East Africa, unseasonable flooding wiped out 90 percent of some owners' livestock, as Rift Valley fever swept through Kenya and Somalia. In the coastal regions of South America, hundreds of thousands of pelicans and other seabirds died as their food supply—the fish that were driven away by warmer El Niño waters—went looking for cooler homes. In California, sea lions found their food supply disappearing as well, and with female sea lions unable to produce the normal amount of milk, an estimated 70 percent of their pups died.

Suffering Sea Life

Living coral is extremely sensitive to water temperature extremes,and when it's too hot, as it is during an El Niño, the corals push out the tiny algae inside them that help them stay alive. The algae, called zooxanthellae, is what gives coral its color; without it, coral reefs turn white, and scientists refer to these dead organisms as "bleached" coral. In the 1997 event, more than 97 percent of the coral reefs near the Galapagos Islands died from the heat.

FACTS

The white part of a coral that's left behind after it dies is its skeleton, which is made of calcium carbonate, or limestone. Coral deposits rings of calcium carbonate at different rates during different times of the year, leaving clues about how the coral grew and what conditions were like when the rings were created.

With friends like El Niño, the earth doesn't need enemies, but despite all the damage left in their wake, these occurrences do have a beneficial side. Hurricanes often form near the western coast of Africa in the summer and travel westward across the Atlantic on the prevailing winds. But in an El Niño year, winds blowing from the west shear off the tops of developing tropical systems, nipping them in the bud before they can get cranked up. Scientists have also found that the increased plant growth caused by heavier-than-average rainfall may trigger a drop in carbon dioxide, a so-called greenhouse gas often implicated in the increase of global warming. And the warmer weather conditions El Niño brought in 1997 resulted in a 10 percent drop in heating bills for many.

El Niños' Flip Side

When an El Niño finally loosens its grip on the Pacific, conditions sometimes shift into reverse and a La Niña (the girl child) event begins. Conditions during a La Niña are the opposite of an El Niño: Areas that were flooded dry out, and instead of fewer hurricanes, stronger and more frequent storms ply the south Atlantic and the Caribbean.

During a La Niña, also called El Viejo (old man) or the anti–El Niño, high pressure near Tahiti and low pressure over Australia strengthen the trade winds, causing surface waters near Peru to blow out to sea. As they depart, cold water from deep in the ocean rises to take their place, and the Pacific's surface temperature begins to drop.

ESSENTIALS

No two ENSOs are exactly alike, so statistics tell you only the likelihood of a certain condition, not what causes it. That's where climate modeling, creating a virtual world using simulated weather conditions, comes into play. Data from actual weather analysis is fed in, and analysts can see how close the results are to actual observations.

La Niñas don't form quite as often—only about every two to ten years—but their effects on the United States can be just as important as El Niños'. Because the jet stream is diverted into a more serpentine flow during a La Niña year, winter temperatures are warmer than normal in the Southeast and cooler and wetter than normal in the Northwest. La Niña can cause droughts in the American Southwest while bringing much colder weather to the upper Midwestern states. Although it doesn't usually cause as many problems as El Niño, La Niña's effects can last much longer.

As the implications of ENSO have become more obvious, research into the phenomenon and attempts to predict it have gone into overdrive. The 1997 event was the first one ever to be successfully predicted, when NOAA announced in April of that year the possibility that a strong El Niño would soon form. We now know it to be the strongest ENSO event in recorded history.

Meteorologists use several tools to predict future atmospheric conditions, including El Niños and La Niñas. One is statistical analysis, where scientists examine past weather records to uncover trends that might give them clues to future conditions. So, analysts can compile statistics and compare conditions in, say, the eastern Pacific during El Niño years, combine them with statistics on conditions in the western Pacific, and use the results to determine what usually happens in those areas during a warm ENSO event.

Predicting ENSO Predicaments

In 1997, for the very first time, meteorologists used climate modeling to forecast El Niño, and came up with a prediction that was more accurate than one obtained by statistical analysis. This is an extremely important development for industries, such as agriculture, that depend on the weather. One reason the 1982–1983 El Niño was so devastating to crops is that it wasn't predicted or even recognized until it was well under way.

FIGURE 5-3:
El Niño fore-
casts help
fisherman

(refer to page
280 for more
information)

After that experience, the Peruvian government undertook a program to predict future ENSO events, realizing their country would be ground zero for every climatic fluctuation. After the system was developed, a forecast for the upcoming growing season was released to the minister of agriculture, indicating that it would be a good year with near-normal rainfall. Sure enough, the forecast was correct, and the government began releasing its predictions each year in November, giving farmers a heads-up on what to plant. If an El Niño is forecast, they can plant water-loving crops like rice, and if La Niña is coming, something more drought-tolerant like cotton can be substituted.

In the United States, the forecasting picture is much rosier than it was in the 1980s. Recognizing that ENSO knows no boundaries, the United States and France teamed up to launch TOPEX/Poseidon, a satellite system that uses a sophisticated radar altimeter to measure sea levels with an accuracy of within 4 inches. The satellite emits a radar beam that bounces off the ocean surface and returns; by measuring how long it takes to come back, the distance to the surface and hence the sea level can be determined. Its follow-up program, a satellite called Jason-1, is hoped to be accurate to within less than 1 inch. As sea levels rise in some places and fall in others when an ENSO event is beginning, much earlier warnings will be available to farmers, governments, and the general public, and loss of life and property will be minimized.

FACTS

TOPEX/Poseidon doesn't measure the height of waves, but of large variations in sea level caused by both wind and thermal upwelling. You may think of the sea level as a constant, but it's really just an average; oceans are masses of peaks and valleys, with a constant dynamic interaction between them.

One reason the 1997 El Niño was successfully predicted is the existence of weather-monitoring tools like the Tropical Atmosphere Ocean Array (TAO). A joint venture of the United States, France, Japan, Korea, and Taiwan, TAO is a series of about seventy ocean buoys placed in the Pacific that constantly gather data on water and air temperature and other factors and then beam them to polar-orbiting weather satellites passing overhead.

Taking the Long View

ENSO might be the least of our worries. In 1996, weather researchers at the University of Washington uncovered a weather pattern that lasts for decades, not just ENSO's year or two at a time. It's called the Pacific Decadel Oscillation (PDO) and is still the subject of much debate in the scientific community—even among those who discovered it.

According to the theory, the Pacific flip-flops back and forth between warm and cold phases every twenty or thirty years. The warm phase is marked by an abnormally warm area of water near the Americas, with much cooler water around the Pacific Rim from Australia to Japan. The warm phase behaves like a weak El Niño, but its effects are much more long lasting.

Because the warm phase of the PDO mimics a La Niña, which brings increased hurricane activity in the Atlantic and encourages tropical systems to move westward, Dr. William Gray of the University of Colorado believes the Atlantic may be entering a period of greater hurricane frequency.

The PDO's warm phase begins as waters around the Asian Rim warm up while sea temperatures near the west coast of the United States cool off, leading to the same kinds of conditions found in a La Niña. While ENSO's effects are mostly concentrated around the equator, the PDO is thought to affect the midlatitudes where most of the population of the United States lives.

Because it was only recently recognized, the nature and causes of the PDO are not yet fully understood, but because the Pacific Ocean covers more than a third of the earth's surface, long-term changes there are usually felt all over the world. As more data is collected in the coming years, forecasts will become increasingly accurate, and no doubt even more atmospheric anomalies will be discovered.

CHAPTER 6
Seasons and the Sun

The cold and darkness of winter, with the naked deformity of every object on which we turn our eyes, make us rejoice at the succeeding season.

—Samuel Johnson

What if the Sun didn't exist? Well, forecasters wouldn't have to worry about issuing sunrise and sunset times, for one thing. But, of course, there wouldn't be any forecasters, or much of anything else, without that big ball of hot gas.

Wishing on a Star

Ancient civilizations knew how important the Sun's light was for growing crops, although they weren't aware that the Sun is just an ordinary star like the ones they saw twinkling in the sky. Actually, they didn't know what stars were either, but that's a story for another book.

What they certainly didn't know is that the Sun is a gigantic thermonuclear furnace that continually fuses hydrogen into helium deep in its core, which releases huge amounts of energy in both visible and invisible wavelengths. The fusion process is very difficult to achieve here on Earth because great pressure and temperature are required, but it's a snap for Old Sol since temperatures at the inner 25 percent of its core (where most of the fusion reactions occur) average around 27,000,000 degrees F. In the heart of the Sun, it's not the humidity; it's the heat.

The Sun's brightness can cause blindness, and it shouldn't be viewed directly unless you're wearing suitable eye protection, or are viewing it through an approved solar filter. Never, ever look at the Sun, even for a moment, without proper eye protection.

Just as with the earth's atmosphere, scientists divide the Sun's layers into zones, none of them a good place to vacation. Energy generated in the Sun's core gradually works its way toward the surface through convection, and on reaching the photosphere, which is the outer luminous layer that we can see from Earth, becomes visible as light.

Layers of Light

The photosphere is the layer that contains sunspots, huge areas of cooler gases that were first discovered by Galileo back in 1610. In this case "cooler" is a relative term—sunspots are only about 3,000 degrees F less than the photosphere's average temperature of 10,000 to 12,000 degrees F, so you'd still need a sunscreen with a rating of at least SPF 1 *million* to get anywhere near one. Sunspots are thought to be caused by magnetic fields deep in the Sun that break the surface, creating dark blotches that are often a sign of increased activity deep in the Sun's interior. Sunspots range in size from roughly Earth-sized to more than twenty times the diameter of our planet.

FACTS

NASA's Solar and Heliospheric Observatory (SOHO) spacecraft recently peered beneath a sunspot using a technique called acoustic tomography, a method similar to ultrasound technology. It found much hotter regions directly below the sunspot that seem to get trapped by magnetic fields, keeping the heat under the surface and making the spot much cooler than its surroundings.

The next layer out is the chromosphere, which is virtually invisible from Earth except during a total solar eclipse, when it can be seen as a narrow red or pink band around the Sun. The chromosphere's temperature is around 14,400 degrees F at the bottom and 36,000 degrees F at the top, so it actually gets hotter as you move away from the Sun. Solar flares originate in the chromosphere, releasing as much energy as a million hydrogen bombs going off at the same time.

The next layer of the Sun's atmosphere is the corona, which is thousands of times fainter than the photosphere and is invisible from Earth except, again, during a total solar eclipse. At that time the corona appears as an elongated, ragged halo around the Sun, with thin white filaments stretching out millions of miles into space like celestial cirrus clouds.

ALERT

Solar eclipses are one of nature's most spectacular shows, as the Moon moves between the earth and the Sun. But for an hour or more before and after the eclipse, only part of the Sun is blocked. During that time, eye protection must be worn, because even a partially eclipsed Sun can permanently burn your retinas.

Consistent with the chromosphere, the corona continues to get hotter as distance from the core increases. Temperature of the corona varies from 2,000,000 degrees F to nearly 4,000,000 degrees F. How does the corona get so hot with a cooler layer below it? Astrophysicists think that huge magnetic bands in the photosphere generate massive amounts of electricity and carry it up into the corona. There are tens of thousands of these magnetic loops scattered around the surface of the Sun, and any one of them could satisfy the country's electrical needs for a 100 years if it could somehow be harnessed. Just imagine: Every inch of the Sun's surface produces 40,000 watts of power each and every moment!

The Wind from the Sun

The corona isn't static; it continually blasts charged particles out into space, creating the heliosphere, an area of the Sun's influence that actually extends out beyond the orbit of Pluto. These particles, collectively called the solar wind, can cause big problems for the Earth when the Sun gets active. The Sun's average distance from the earth is some 93,000,000 miles, but even small changes in its output can have major consequences here, as happens when huge bubbles of plasma erupt in the Sun's outer layers, blowing billions of tons of particles from the Sun's atmosphere in a blast called a Coronal Mass Ejection (CME).

If a CME is directed toward Earth, it will smash into our atmosphere at a million miles an hour, sometimes damaging satellites and causing power and communications disruptions. That's why NOAA and the U.S. Air Force now jointly operate the Space Environment Center, which provides warnings of impending solar explosions.

It's a good thing the earth has a magnetosphere, which deflects most of the particles back into space. But some of the energy from a solar storm can still leak into the atmosphere near the poles where the magnetosphere is weaker, creating the aurora borealis, or northern lights. When appearing over the Southern Hemisphere, the lights are called the aurora australis.

Since the time of Copernicus, most civilized cultures have understood that the earth revolves around the Sun, but the origin of the seasons has often been misunderstood, and even today there are misconceptions about it. When you put your hand close to a stove it gets hot, and when you move it away, it cools. So it would seem that when the earth is closer to the Sun it would be summertime, and when it is farther away, you'd have winter. The earth does indeed get closer and then farther from the Sun during the year because its orbit is slightly elliptical, or oval, but that fact has very little effect on the seasons.

In fact, the earth is closest to the Sun in January, when it's winter in the Northern Hemisphere. In addition, if the seasons were caused by Earth's proximity to the Sun, every country on the planet would experience winter and summer at the same time. But when it's summer in the Southern Hemisphere, it's winter in the Northern. What gives?

The Earth: One Big Tilt-a-Whirl

The reason you get to experience winter, spring, summer, and fall is because the amount of sunlight hitting the earth's surface varies throughout the year, and that's a result of the planet's tilt. The earth rotates around an imaginary axle—its axis—that runs from the North Pole to the South. If you picture the earth's orbit as a flat plane around the Sun, that axis is tilted 23.5 degrees away from that plane, called the plane of the ecliptic, so it's actually leaning to one side. That means that sometimes the Northern Hemisphere is tilted toward the Sun, and sometime the Southern Hemisphere gets more sunlight.

Solar radiation has the most effect on the earth's surface and atmosphere when it's shining straight down. If you shine a flashlight on the middle of a beach ball, you'll notice it makes a round circle, because all the light is focused on that one point. But shine it closer to the top and the beam spreads out into an oval and there's less light shining on any one spot. That's what happens as the earth revolves around the Sun. From June to September, when the Northern Hemisphere is tilted toward the Sun, light shines more directly on it (which is why the Sun seems to be almost straight overhead) and heats up the surface, causing a run on air conditioners. In addition, these days are longer, so the Sun has more time to do its job.

FACTS

If there were Martians, they'd experience even more seasonal variations than Earthlings. Mars's orbit is more eccentric than any other planet (except Pluto), and it's tilted on its axis at a more acute angle. During a Martian winter, a complex carbon dioxide exchange with its polar ice caps causes the planet's atmospheric pressure to drop about 25 percent lower than in summer.

From December to March, with the Northern Hemisphere tilted away from the Sun, there's less light reaching any one place to warm it up, and there's a run on space heaters. Days are shorter, so by the time the Sun has begun to warm up the atmosphere, it's already descending toward the horizon. Also, with sunlight striking the planet at a lower angle, its rays have to penetrate through a lot more atmosphere to get to the surface, and there's a greater chance that some of that light will get scattered by dust particles, reflected by clouds, or absorbed by gasses. Another factor that keeps the surface from heating up in the winter is the presence of ice or snow, which is very reflective and can keep the Sun's energy from ever reaching the ground.

If the earth didn't tilt, the Sun would always shine directly down on the equator and the days and nights would always be the same length: twelve hours. There would be no seasons, and it would be very hot in the equatorial regions. North America would always receive about the same amount of light it gets between September and December, so most of the time it would probably feel like autumn.

Of course, at the equator the temperature *is* pretty much the same all the time, since that region receives the maximum amount of sunlight all year long. But in the midlatitudes where most people live, spring flowers, autumn leaves, summers at the beach, and winter snowball fights give everyone something to look forward to.

Orbits and Oceans

Drawn on a piece of paper, the orbits of Earth and the other planets look like perfect circles, but in truth, none of them is. The earth's orbit is about 2 percent closer to the Sun in January as it is in July, and other planets' orbits are even more out of round, but as mentioned earlier, that small difference isn't enough to affect the seasons very much. The atmosphere receives only about 7 percent more energy when closest to the Sun (perihelion) as it does when farthest away (aphelion). What *does* have an effect is the fact that the earth's landmasses aren't evenly distributed; the Northern Hemisphere has more land; the Southern Hemisphere has more water. Land heats more rapidly than water, so in July when the Sun in shining more directly on landmasses, the temperature of the entire globe is higher than it is in December, when the Sun shines down on the oceans to the south.

QUESTIONS?

Why is the longest day of the year not also the hottest?
Thermal inertia—the tendency of temperatures to remain the same—keeps the land and water from getting instantly hot. Only after several weeks of intense Sun beating down on the earth will the hemisphere start to heat up.

You can see that effect on a smaller scale when you visit the desert in the summertime. During the night, the temperature might get down to 60 degrees F or so, but when the Sun comes up, it can rise to over 100 degrees F. If you're sailing on the ocean, however, the temperature might be only 75 to 80 degrees F. Then, when the Sun goes down, the temperature will fall only a few degrees because water is great at absorbing and retaining heat.

A Quick Tour of the Seasons

If you could push a button and fastforward through an entire year, starting on the first day of summer, you could easily see how each season correlates to the earth's position in its orbit. On June 21, known as the summer solstice, the Sun's rays beat directly down on the Northern Hemisphere. Since the earth is tilted at 23.5 degrees, it shines straight above 23.5 degrees latitude, an imaginary line around the earth called the tropic of Cancer. Some of the cities at this latitude are Calcutta, India; Havana, Cuba; Hong Kong; and Mazatlan, Mexico.

If you're standing on this line on the first day of summer, the Sun is directly overhead, seemingly paused for a moment before beginning to sink lower in the sky each day. (The word "solstice" comes from the Latin word *solstitium,* meaning "sun standing still.") This is also the longest day of the year in the Northern Hemisphere, and from now until December 21 (the winter solstice), the days will get progressively shorter. With the Sun at its highest point, and the days at their longest, common sense would tell you that June should be the hottest month of the year. But due to an effect called thermal inertia, the ocean and landmasses take time to heat up, so the hottest weather usually arrives about six weeks after the summer solstice.

Goodbye Summer

By the time the heat kicks in, you're well on your way to the autumnal equinox on September 22—the first day of fall—when the days and nights are the same length. (The word "equinox" comes from the Latin word *aequinoctium*, meaning "equal night.") The oceans in the Northern Hemisphere are at their warmest and tropical storms and hurricanes begin to form.

ESSENTIALS   The brilliant reds and oranges of fall are actually right there in the leaves all year long, but because the green color of chlorophyll is so dominant, you can't see them until the chlorophyll level decreases. Cooler nights and shorter days reduce the chlorophyll and signal the leaves to begin their yearly show.

The weather has been getting cooler in the Northern Hemisphere, and now the leaves of many trees begin to show their true colors. On the days following the fall equinox, the Sun begins to set at the North Pole, and six long cold months of darkness set in, while at the South Pole the Sun is rising.

Autumn Leaves, Winter Arrives

FIGURE 6-1:
The sun's angle determines temperature

(refer to page 280 for more information)

As the days get shorter and the weather cooler, cold fronts begin to plow southward and some mornings reveal frost on the lawn. As the winter holidays approach, ice and snow can make an appearance, and by the time the first day of winter arrives on December 21, the Sun is shining directly down on the Southern Hemisphere at 23.5 degrees—the tropic of Capricorn and the days are at their shortest.

At the beginning of winter, the Northern Hemisphere is tilted as far back from the Sun as it can get, so the light reaching the ground is dimmer and more diffuse than at any other time of the year. Again the ground and the oceans are slow to give up the heat they've absorbed through the summer and fall, so the coldest weather is still to come.

Welcome to Spring

As heating bills skyrocket and some cities in the North are hit by blizzards and ice storms, everyone gets tired of being indoors and wishes for spring. Then seed and garden catalogs begin to arrive, just making things worse. By March 20, just about everyone north of 35 degrees N has gone stir-crazy, but just in time, the first day of spring arrives. On that date, called the vernal equinox, the days and nights are once again equal in length, and the Sun is directly above the equator.

As the Sun rises higher in the sky each day, the land is warmed and trees begin to leaf out again, hibernating animals wake up and begin to search for food, and many people unearth their treadmills. The days are getting longer, and before you know it, June is here and you're back where you started. Unfortunately, you're also a year older.

Seasons and Circles

In this century, the earth's northern axis points toward Polaris, the North Star. It won't always, though, because the earth's axis wobbles very slowly, about a half a degree per century, like a top just before it stops and falls over. This motion, called precession, causes the planet's axis to describe a giant circle in the sky that takes 23,000 years to complete. So, in about 11,000 years, the earth will be closer to the Sun in July and farther away in December, the opposite of today's situation. In 23,000 years, things will be back the way they are now.

Further complicating the picture is the fact that the earth's 23.5-degree tilt changes over time, too, taking about 43,000 years to run through a full cycle that varies from about 22 to 24.5 degrees. When the angle is smaller, there will be less seasonal variation at middle latitudes; with a larger angle, the variations will be amplified. It's thought that this change in tilt angle is one of the main factors that causes the periodic ice ages that sweep across our planet.

Because the ancients didn't have our knowledge of the solar system and the seasons, the motion of the Sun and stars was a source of mystery, and the annual changes in climate were often incorporated into their worship and ceremonies. Years of observation told early people that by watching where the Sun rose and set for a number of years, they could foretell when crops should be planted, when it was time to prepare for winter, and when to expect the leaves to once again emerge on the trees.

SSENTIALS Archaeologists have found man-made lunar calendars that date back thousands of years. They indicate that Ice Age hunters carved notches and bored holes into sticks, mammoth tusks, and reindeer bones to record the days between each phase of the Moon.

Because the weather was tied to survival, most cultures kept records of its changes and erected monuments that acted as giant seasonal clocks. The most famous of these is Stonehenge, north of Salisbury, England. Although there is still disagreement as to the ancient stone circle's exact purpose, because the structure is aligned with the winter and summer solstices, many feel it functioned as a predictor of the passage of the seasons for the early residents of Britain. On the summer solstice, the longest day of the year in the Northern Hemisphere, the Sun rises directly over a marker called the Heel Stone outside the outer circle of stones, as seen from the center of Stonehenge. Watching the movement of the Sun and Moon through various markers and alignments throughout the monument, observers could have predicted the arrival of each season well in advance.

At Machu Picchu, Peru's "City in the Clouds," the ancient Incas built a "Hitching Post of the Sun" they called the Intihuatana Stone, which was a precise indicator of the date of the winter solstice. The ceremony they performed there was designed to halt the Sun in its northern migration through the sky. Machu Picchu's Temple of the Sun features a window exactly aligned with the sunrise on the summer solstice.

In ancient Mexico, the Mayans built a celestial observatory at Chichen Itza, along with a huge four-sided pyramid with a staircase on each side called El Callisto. Each year during the spring and fall equinoxes, a trick of light and shadow makes it appear as though a giant feathered serpent is descending one of the stairways. In the spring, the serpent's appearance was a signal that it was time to plant corn, the Mayans' staple crop. Thousands of visitors still flock to Chichen Itza each spring to see the spectacle.

The Dating Game

The Egyptians were keen students of the Sun and stars, and around 3,000 B.C. created a calendar very similar to the one used today. Like clockwork, the Nile River would flood each year at about the same time, and Egyptian sky watchers noted that the star Sirius would rise into the sky around that time. The period between appearances was 365.25 days, so the Egyptians based their calendar on that time period and were later copied by Julius Caesar. The Egyptians' extensive knowledge of celestial events can still be seen in the Temple of Amon-Ra at Karnak when Sirius comes up over the horizon. On that spring night, the star shines through a small hole in the temple wall, down a long corridor, and appears as a pinpoint of light on a mural at the far end of the temple!

In the Americas, ancient tribes had their own ways of predicting the seasons. The early residents of Wyoming built a large circle made of stones that seems to point toward the position of the Sun at the summer solstice. The structure, known as the Big Horn Medicine Wheel, lies at an altitude of nearly 10,000 feet in the mountains. It's 245 feet in circumference, with several stone spokes and piles of rock along the rim that point to the spots where the stars Rigel, Aldebaran, and Sirius rise above the horizon. It's no wonder the builders of the wheel were interested in the seasons; at that high a latitude (and altitude!), nomadic or seminomadic people would need advance warning of winter's arrival so they could begin to move south.

Our great-ancestors did the best they could to use the Sun, the Moon, and the stars as predictors of coming climatic conditions, and some succeeded amazingly well. Their early research paved the way for the more sophisticated instruments of forecasting to come. But it's a tribute to their resourcefulness and ingenuity that many of their methods of predicting the seasons still work today.

CHAPTER 7

Measuring and Recording the Weather

The best weather instrument yet devised is a pair of human eyes.

—Harold M. Gibson,
Chief Meteorologist, NYC Weather Bureau

If you were a carpenter who didn't own a tape measure, you'd have a hard time doing your job. That's why meteorology was such a hit-and-miss proposition before the advent of tools to measure heat, humidity, rainfall, and other weather phenomena.

Get a Degree: The Thermometer

When Galileo created a device he called a thermoscope in the early 1600s, it was really just an interesting toy. Galileo's device had no markings to indicate degrees; that task would fall to his friends Santorio Santorio and Gianfrancesco Sagredo, who were the first to apply a crude numerical scale to the thermograph, making it the first official air thermometer. At the same time, similar devices were being developed all over Europe, but each inventor worked independently, so there was no universally agreed-upon scale of measurement.

A few decades later, Amsterdam instrument maker Daniel Gabriel Fahrenheit came along with access to more responsive alcohol thermometers. Still, there was no temperature-measuring scale everyone could agree on. After Fahrenheit invented an even more sensitive thermometer filled with mercury, he decided a universal heat measuring system was needed.

Your mom had her own kind of thermometer: a palm placed on your forehead. Nature has other natural thermometers, too—besides crickets. Rhododendrons, for example, begin to fold their leaves up and inward at around 60 degrees F. The leaves are halfway closed at 30 degrees F, and completely closed when the temperature falls to 20 degrees F.

Fahrenheit filled a container with salt and ice water to obtain the lowest temperature he could and called that point 0 degrees, then measured the temperature of melting ice without the salt and assigned it the value of 30 degrees. His own body temperature was marked at 96 degrees. When he later added the boiling point of water to his scale, at 212 degrees, he changed the melting point of water to 32 degrees so that the scale would balance out at an even 180 degrees between the melting and boiling points of water—the angle of a straight line. On the new scale, body temperature came out to 98.6 degrees.

Hot Competition

Seems pretty confusing, doesn't it? Maybe that's why Swedish astronomer Anders Celsius suggested a simpler system in 1742. His method divided the difference between water's melting and boiling points into one hundred equal parts.

Celsius had observed that snow always began to melt at the same point, noting:

> *I have repeated (the experiment) many times during two yearsin all winter months and all kind of weather, and during different barometric changes, and always found precisely the same point on the thermometer. . . .*

Using the Celsius scale, room temperature is around 25 degrees C, while a hot summer day can reach 30 to 38 degrees C. Water freezes at 0 degrees C and boils at 100 degrees C. What could be easier?

Since there were now two temperature scales to choose from, there was no need to further complicate matters, right? Sir William Thomson, a Scottish mathematician also known as Lord Kelvin, apparently didn't think so. Kelvin wanted to eliminate the need for negative numbers when measuring temperature, so in 1848 he devised a temperature scale that started at the lowest possible temperature, absolute zero. That works out to -273.18 degrees C, or -459 degrees F. His scale is called (surprise!) the Kelvin, or thermodynamic, scale.

FACTS

The Third Law of Thermodynamics prohibits the temperature from reaching absolute zero, even in space. Although there doesn't seem to be an upper limit on heat, the temperature in deep space never gets below 2.7 degrees Kelvin due to background radiation left over from the Big Bang. If it could get that frigid, all motion right down to the atomic level would stop.

The science of measuring temperature has come a long way since then. Bimetal thermometers depend on the expansion and contraction rates of two different metals to move a pointer that indicates temperature. Others measure the high and low temperatures over a given time. Radiometric thermometers measure temperature by reading an object's radiation emission spectrum. Liquid-crystal thermometers change color with the temperature, like a 1970s mood ring. These days, the thermometer you're mostly likely to encounter is electronic, using a device called a thermistor that measures resistance through an internal element.

The Rise and Fall of Barometers

Barometers, too, have changed quite a bit since Pascal's brother-in-law climbed Puy de Dôme with one in 1648. Grand Duke Ferdinand II of Tuscany was the first to notice that barometric pressure dropped during storms, and in 1660, the barometer was used to predict the weather for the first time by Otto von Guericke, mayor of Magdeburg, Germany.

Rumor has it that von Guericke filled his barometer with wine. Since wine is much less dense than mercury, the glass tube had to stand some 34 feet tall—a new record for spirit-filled nonportable weather instruments.

In 1844, the first barometer that didn't use a liquid was patented by Lucien Vidie, a French scientist who based his invention on a small vacuum chamber attached to a pointer that would rise and fall as the atmospheric pressure made the chamber expand and contract. He called his barometer an aneroid, from a Greek word meaning "without water." Vidie's invention is still in use today, as are the mercury-filled variety, but the electronics revolution has helped create a much more advanced version of the barometer.

An electronic barometer uses an electrical sensor to measure minute changes in atmospheric pressure, and sends the readings to a digital display. Originally very expensive, these barometers are now available to home users either as a stand-alone instrument or as part of a home weather station to help you predict coming weather conditions.

Why It's a Bad Hair Day

Of course, the more instruments you have, the more accurate your forecasts will be. One of the most important measurements you can make is how much moisture the air contains. The instrument used to measure humidity is called a hygrometer, invented in 1780 by Horace de Saussure, a Swiss meteorologist and geologist. De Saussure based his invention on the fact that hair becomes longer when the air is humid and shorter when it's dry. He attached small levers to human hairs that measured the change in length, correlating to how much water vapor the air held.

Relative humidity can actually exceed 100 percent. When the temperature drops below the dew point, air can become supersaturated with moisture, raising the humidity to a higher percentage. But the condition is just temporary: The moisture will condense into fog or dew fairly quickly, and the relative humidity will once again be 100 percent.

The hair hygrometer was rather inaccurate, leading to the invention of the sling psychrometer: two thermometers mounted side by side. One is covered with a wick that is moistened with water, while the other is kept dry, and the unit is spun around for a few minutes. Water evaporating from the wet side will cool the thermometer, making it lower than the actual air temperature. The drier the air, the greater the evaporation, and, therefore, the greater the difference between the two temperatures. The difference tells the reader how much water the air can hold versus how much it's currently holding—the relative humidity. The sling psychrometer has largely been replaced by the electronic hygrometer, although you'll still see them in use occasionally.

This is probably a good time to address the dew point. You know it's important because weather forecasters mention it often, but it's rarely well explained. Just remember that the warmer air is, the more water vapor it can hold. When the air can no longer hold anymore water, condensation occurs. When this change happens up in the clouds, it forms rain; on the ground it makes dew. So the dew point is the temperature at which the vapor in the air will begin to condense. For instance, if the current temperature is 80 degrees F and a forecaster says the dew point is 70, you know it has to get ten degrees cooler before dew can form.

Catching the Wind

FIGURE 7-1:
A windrose

(refer to page 280 for more information)

The instrument that tells you how fast the wind is blowing is an anemometer. Leonardo da Vinci usually gets credit for inventing the first one, which he designed around 1500. But the first working model was put together by Robert Hooke in 1667. Hooke's version used a hanging plate of metal hinged at the top; when the wind blew, the plate would swing out at an angle and the wind speed could be read off a scale attached to the side of the instrument. Today's anemometers use three or more cups mounted on a vertical shaft. The speed of the cups' rotation translates directly to wind speed; the data can then be transmitted to an electronic base station that displays the information.

ESSENTIALS

Before 1850, weather vanes were produced by hand, but growing interest in the devices sparked an increase of factories to meet the demand. Most of the major weather vane producers went out of business during the Great Depression, and today their works are in demand as highly sought-after collectibles.

The oldest weather instrument is no doubt the wind vane, which reveals which way the wind is blowing. The earliest known wind vane stood atop the Tower of the Winds in Athens, Greece, which was built to honor the god Triton around 48 B.C. The vane featured the head and torso of a man attached to a fish's tail, and is thought to have been from 4 to 8 feet long.

The Vikings used bronze weather vanes on their ships in the ninth century, and about that time the pope reportedly decreed that every church in Europe should have a rooster on its steeple as a reminder of Luke 22:34, which states that a cock would crow after the disciple Peter had denounced Jesus three times. You'll still see roosters on weather vanes today.

In the digital age, the weather vane has been combined with the anemometer in an instrument called the aerovane, which looks rather like an airplane with no wings. The propeller part measures the wind speed, while the tail keeps the unit pointing into the wind, indicating which way it's blowing. Data on wind velocity and direction are constantly fed to a display unit and recording station.

FIGURE 7-2:
Aerovanes
measure
wind speed

(refer to page
280 for more
information)

Gauging Rainfall

The rain gauge is another important tool in the meteorologist's array of instruments. A modern gauge consists of an outer cylinder, a measuring tube that can record as little as .01 inch of rain, and a funnel. The gauge can directly measure up to 2 inches of rain; when more than that falls, the extra water flows into the outer cylinder. The observer then pours the excess from the outer cylinder back into the measuring tube to determine the total rainfall amount.

Another kind of rain gauge is the tipping bucket type, which tips and empties itself when it has accumulated .01 inches of rain. Immediately another bucket moves into place to continue recording rainfall, and an electronic signal is sent to a recording unit. Rainfall is measured by adding up the number of tips in a given period and multiplying by .01. The advantages are obvious: No one has to go outside and empty the gauge each day, and there is no water lost to evaporation. In a downpour, however, the tipping bucket gauge may not be able to empty fast enough, so its readings can be inaccurate.

Radiosondes and balloons became vital tools in the study and prediction of weather during World War II, and these instruments are still used today. The National Weather Service is undertaking a program to replace its older radiosondes with new units that employ Global Positioning System (GPS) receivers, which will be cheaper and easier to maintain and will deliver much more accurate and reliable data.

If you find a radiosonde, send it back to the National Weather Service for reconditioning (instructions are printed on its side) to save the Weather Service the cost of a new unit. Currently, only about 20 percent of the approximately 75,000 radiosondes released each year are found and returned to the NWS.

Although the balloons used to loft radiosondes haven't changed much since the war, the units themselves have undergone several improvements. Wind speed and direction can be determined by tracking the balloon as it rises, and additional data streams down from the radiosonde to a ground station where it's processed through a computer before being released for distribution. The balloons can ascend to a height of more than 19 miles before they pop; a parachute then gently lowers the equipment to the ground so it can be recovered and flown again.

The Radar Revolution

One of the most important weather instruments developed during the twentieth century grew out of a wartime invention. In the mid-1930s, with the situation in Europe deteriorating rapidly, the director of Britain's Air Ministry asked Robert Watson-Watt, superintendent of a radio department at England's National Physical Laboratory, if there was some way to develop a "death ray" that could shoot down aircraft from a distance. The request resulted not in a death beam but in Watson-Watt's report "Detection and Location of Aircraft by Radio Methods," which detailed how certain radio waves might be reflected off aircraft and back to the origin point, revealing the planes' positions.

Watson-Watt's invention came to be called Radio Detection and Ranging, or radar, and by the beginning of World War II, the coast of England bristled with radar installations. By the end of the war, both the Axis and the Allies would depend on radar just as military commanders do today.

FACTS

Scientist Nikola Tesla was said to have actually invented a death ray in the early 1900s. Tesla was reportedly testing his invention on the night of June 30, 1908, when an owl flew into the beam and was disintegrated. Some scientists think the military may have since actually developed a weapon based on Tesla's idea (see Chapter 20).

Often, radar echoes from large storms would obscure the images of approaching planes on early radar screens, and large areas of rain would show up as a green fog. There must have been an "aha!" moment when a meteorologist first saw those radar echoes. After all the guesswork and ground observations used in the past to track weather systems, radar was a forecaster's dream come true. After the war, surplus radar systems were pressed into service by the U.S. Weather Bureau to track weather systems. Further research led to more powerful radars, which the bureau began to install along the coastline in 1954 as part of a hurricane early warning system.

The surplus radar units served their purpose, but as the years went by and the systems aged, spare parts became scarce and breakdowns were more frequent. Additionally, the old radar units were unable to detect developing tornadoes or accurately measure rainfall amounts. It became obvious that something new was needed.

Dazzling Doppler

In the 1960s, the U.S. Weather Service began experimenting with Doppler radar, which was a big improvement over the older types. During the late 1970s and early 1980s, Doppler radar began to appear at a few television stations, and around that time NOAA and the Department of Commerce joined forces to produce a next-generation radar system—NEXRAD—that would greatly improve severe weather forecasting. NEXRAD used the Doppler effect to spot rotating weather systems that often indicate a tornado is forming.

QUESTIONS?

What is the Doppler effect?
Named after Austrian mathematician and physicist Christian Andreas Doppler, the Doppler effect is the change in wavelengths (of sound or light) between two objects as a result of motion. For example, the change in sound as a motorcycle approaches, then passes, a stationary observer demonstrates the Doppler effect.

Light waves were much too fast to experiment with at the time, but in 1845 Christoph Heinrich Diedrich Buys Ballot, a recent graduate of the Netherlands' University of Utrecht, set out to debunk Doppler's theory with a real-world test using sound waves. Ballot put a group of trumpeters on a train that would pass by a group of listeners. As the train passed with the trumpeters blasting away, the listeners heard the din rising in frequency as the train approached and then dropping as it moved away. On the train, however, the trumpets' pitch stayed the same.

FIGURE 7-3:
A doppler radar facility

(refer to page 280 for more information)

Instead of refuting Doppler's theory, Ballot's experiment proved that the frequency of light or sound depends on the speed of an object's movement in relation to the viewer. The word "frequency" refers to how fast the peaks and valleys of a sound or light wave are moving past an observer. Let's say you're standing at a station watching a train approaching. When the engineer sounds the horn, it will seem to rise in pitch because the speed of the train as it comes toward you is added to the speed those waves are passing by, so they're arriving at your ear closer and closer together. Once the train passes, the distance between the wave peaks is farther apart, so the horn seems to shift to a lower pitch.

In Doppler radar, pulses of microwave radiation are used instead of sound waves, but the effect stays the same. When a Doppler beam is aimed at a storm, the echoes that return are coded by color: areas of precipitation moving toward the radar are shown in one color, while any areas moving in the other direction are displayed in another. The National Weather Service's Weather Surveillance Radar 1988 Doppler (WSR-88D) uses green to indicate rain that's approaching the radar, and paints receding showers in red. When the radar sees green and red in close proximity, it's a sign of rotation within the storm that can indicate a developing tornado.

Doppler radar can identify gust fronts and microbursts as well, something conventional weather radar can't do. Peering deep within storms, the Doppler beam can identify mesocyclones swirling inside, identifying a region that may spawn a tornado and giving much more time to alert those in its path. Since about 30 percent of mesocyclones generate tornadoes and 95 percent produce severe weather, Doppler radar has become a welcome addition to a forecaster's arsenal.

CHAPTER 8

Predicting Chaos

Isn't it interesting that the same people who laugh at science fiction listen to weather forecasts and economists?

—Kelvin Throop III

Most meteorologists will admit that if they had a dollar for every blown forecast, they'd be sipping a tropical drink on some Caribbean island by now. If weather technology is so great, why isn't the science of weather prediction more foolproof?

A Checkered Past

January 2000 had already been an especially snowy month for the residents of Raleigh, North Carolina. Accustomed to an average yearly snowfall of 2 to 4 inches, the city had already seen more than 3 inches accumulate by January 23. That afternoon, the forecast called for an additional 1 to 2 inches over the course of the evening.

By midnight, with snow falling steadily, the forecast was 4 to 6 inches by morning, but after dawn many awoke to find a startling 20 inches of powdery frozen precipitation on their lawns. With thousands of people trapped in their homes and even interstate highways impassable, the governor declared a state of emergency. The North Carolina Department of Transportation's small fleet of snowplows was woefully inadequate to remove the record accumulation, which shattered a 107-year-old record.

 **SSENTIALS**

For generations, country folk have relied on the woolly bear caterpillar (sometimes called the woolly worm) for their winter weather forecasts. According to legend, the little black-and-brown caterpillar can predict the severity of the coming winter by the width of its bands: the wider the brown segment, the milder the winter.

How could a forecast go so spectacularly wrong, especially with the powerful computers and technology now available? There are some very good reasons, but fully understanding them requires an appreciation of how the art and science of weather forecasting has evolved and why it's still an inexact science. Let's start at the beginning.

Homespun Forecasting

Figuring out what the weather is going to do next has always been a challenge, and before there were reliable instruments to predict future conditions, weather watchers relied on nature for clues. Changes in animals and plants, as well as signs in the sky, were often used to predict coming weather, and very often this folksy weather wisdom had some basis in fact.

When early American settlers noticed that birds were going to roost early, they knew that rain or snow was approaching. They also watched flowers such as dandelions, which fold their petals before a storm. If night brought a halo around the Moon, rain was expected. (Now we know that a lunar halo is caused by light shining through the ice crystals of cirrus or cirrostratus clouds that often precede thunderstorms.)

"Red sky at night, sailor's delight; red sky in the morning, sailors take warning." Often a gorgeous sunset is associated with an approaching high pressure system, which generally brings fair weather. Mariners would say, "Mackerel scales and mare's tails make tall ships carry low sails," because the altocumulus of a "mackerel sky" and cirrus clouds come before a cold front, which often causes high winds at the surface. An early red sky was a sign for sailors to lower the sails, because storm winds could shred them or break the mast in two.

Just as modern forecasters can't boast of a 100 percent success rate in their forecasts, folk wisdom often got it wrong. Have you ever heard that "lightning never strikes twice in the same place"? Tell that to the workers in the Empire State Building, which gets hit about twenty-three times a year, on average. In fact, during one especially bad thunderstorm it was struck eight times in twenty-four minutes.

One myth says to open windows on the far side of your house to balance the pressure drop caused by an approaching tornado. In fact, opening windows will only let in the wind, increasing the internal pressure and making it easier for the storm to tear the house apart.

Pretech Troubles

After the development of weather instruments, forecasting became much more accurate. But as late as the mid-1950s, incoming weather data were assembled and plotted on charts by hand. In many cases, forecasts were based on historical records that were compared with current conditions for similarities. Often the results were surprisingly accurate, but human brains were just not up to the task of quickly analyzing the huge quantities of data that were needed to consistently generate accurate forecasts.

Crunching Numbers

In the 1940s, the invention of the electronic computer would mean big things for forecasting. The word "electronic" might seem redundant, but Charles Babbage had designed a mechanical computer he called the "difference engine" as far back as the mid-1800s. In 1943, with most scientific resources being directed toward the war effort, scientists at the Moore School of Electrical Engineering at the University of Pennsylvania began construction on a machine that would, quite literally, change the world.

Dubbed ENIAC (Electronic Numerical Integrator and Computer), the groundbreaking device was designed to compute the trajectories of ballistic artillery shells. ENIAC was a behemoth by today's standards, containing 18,000 vacuum tubes (which broke down at the average rate of one every seven minutes) and 1,500 relay switches. It weighed in at a hefty 30 tons, and could compute fourteen 10-digit multiplications per second. Operators used 6,000 switches and a host of jumper cables to program the beast.

In 1946, while using ENIAC to simulate nuclear explosions, Princeton mathematician John von Neumann realized that the computer might also be used for weather prediction. In 1950, his team produced the first computer-based numerical weather forecast, and while it wasn't an unqualified success, it did show that numerical forecasting was feasible.

Although the house-sized ENIAC was much faster than manual calculations, those early electronic pioneers learned that atmospheric conditions change more rapidly than the early machines could calculate them. The sheer volume of data meant that there was still much room, and need, for improvement.

In 1954, elements of the Navy, Air Force, and Weather Bureau formed the Joint Numerical Weather Prediction Unit in Suitland, Maryland, to further refine numerical forecasting, and in 1955, the unit began issuing regular real-time forecasts. Still, computerized forecasts were not as accurate as the older subjective methods.

Forecasting Takes Off

While computer makers toiled to create faster processors, the science of weather observation and forecasting was about to take its next giant leap. In 1946, with Hitler's V2 rocket attacks on London still a fresh wound, the Army Air Force and the Rand Corporation cosponsored a paper entitled "Preliminary Design for an Experimental World Circling Spaceship." Though mostly concerned with military surveillance, the paper mentioned that such a satellite might also make a good weather reconnaissance platform.

In 1954, the first pictures of a tropical storm were taken from space using a U.S. Navy Aerobee rocket. The spectacular photos galvanized the meteorological community: For the first time a giant weather system could be seen in its entirety. But rockets took time to prepare for launch, were expensive and difficult to recover, and spent very little time over their targets. What was really needed was an observation platform that could stay in space for long periods of time, and the Air Force's World Circling Spaceship was it.

FACTS

NASA had its hands full just getting TIROS 1 off the ground. While still in the planning stages, the satellite went through a succession of proposed launch vehicles until the Thor-Able rocket (a modified intercontinental ballistic missile) was chosen. The first Thor-Able blew up 146 seconds after launch, and the first prototype TIROS spun out of control after reaching orbit.

On April 1, 1960, the recently formed National Aeronautics and Space Administration (NASA) launched the world's first weather satellite atop an Air Force Thor-Able rocket. Weighing only 263 pounds, TIROS 1 (Television and Infrared Observation Satellite) began to return dozens of pictures of the earth and its cloud cover on its very first day in orbit.

Though grainy, those first crude pictures were a snapshot of the future for weather forecasters, who for the first time had an eye in the sky for tracking weather systems like fronts and hurricanes. Orbiting the planet every ninety-nine minutes, TIROS 1 spotted a tropical cyclone in the waters of the South Pacific north of New Zealand nine days after launch, the first storm to be detected by satellite. Until that time, tropical storm prediction relied on ship and aircraft reports that were often spotty and unreliable.

GOES to Show You

Today NOAA operates two satellites called GOES (Geostationary Operational Environmental Satellites); one keeps an eye on weather conditions in North and South America and most of the Atlantic Ocean, and the other monitors part of North America and the Pacific Ocean. Geosynchronous satellites provide an overview of a whole hemisphere's weather conditions since they are capable of imaging the full disk of the earth in one snapshot.

FIGURE 8-1:
Inside TIROS

(refer to page 280 for more information)

FIGURE 8-2:
TIROS
prelaunch
checkout

(refer to page
280 for more
information)

GOES satellites sport two main instruments called an imager and a sounder. The imager measures the amount of energy being radiated from the earth and how much solar energy is being reflected from the surface and atmosphere. The sounder takes the earth's temperature and determines the atmospheric moisture level, as well as surface and cloud top temperatures and ozone levels.

But wait—there's more. GOES is also outfitted with a search-and-rescue transponder and a space environment monitor consisting of a magnetometer, an X-ray sensor, a high-energy proton and alpha detector, and an energetic particles sensor. These instruments allow GOES to report on the state of the solar wind and warn of approaching solar storms caused by CMEs from the Sun. That's a lot of bang for the buck considering GOES started out strictly as a weather satellite.

QUESTIONS?

What is a geosynchronous satellite?
TIROS 1 was slow-orbiting and could only take quick pictures of storms as it passed over them. Geosynchronous satellites, however, are far enough away so that one orbit takes twenty-four hours—or the length of a day. This makes them appear to hover continuously over one spot.

POES for Pictures

NOAA still operates three polar-orbiting satellites (POES) as well; from their closer viewpoint, POES not only monitor and help forecast the weather, but also watch for volcanic eruptions, forest fires, and other surface disturbances. They feature both infrared and UV detectors that can detect and measure the annual ozone hole that forms over Antarctica each year, and can peer through clouds to determine rainfall amounts. POES satellites pour more than 16,000 measurements from all over the globe into NOAA computers each day. And you thought you got a lot of e-mail!

With more powerful satellites being launched and returning more and more data, there was a growing need for faster computers that could handle the load. Once supercomputers arrived on the scene, forecasters finally had a tool that could assemble and make sense out of the huge volume of data that could now be gathered.

FACTS

Supercomputers feature massively parallel architecture, meaning that several different processors are all working on the same problem at once. Each processor has its own operating system and memory and works on one part of a task, although the processors can communicate via internal pathways. This method produces a result much faster than the older technique of single-processor computing.

For centuries, even without computers, astronomers have been able to accurately track the movements of the planets and predict eclipses and other celestial events. But the Moon and the planets orbit in mostly predictable orbits, whereas the weather is a constantly changing phenomenon that often defies prediction. Supercomputers gave weather scientists a more powerful forecasting tool, but—as we know—predicting the weather more than about a week out is still an exercise in futility.

Doing the Math

Forecasting is really educated guesswork because there are so many variables that go into a forecast, and they're always changing. To more fully understand these changes, atmospheric models with a limited set of data were developed in the early days of computing. These models attempted to describe the present state of the temperature, moisture, and pressure in the atmosphere and how those conditions change with the passage of time.

Unfortunately, early weather-predicting computer systems like the IBM 1620 were able to compute at a rate of only 1,000 additions per second, which may sound fast until you consider that today's supercomputers calculate at trillions of operations per second, or about a billion times faster than the early mainframes. Although they gave only a crude approximation of atmospheric conditions, the early systems were the first step in translating a maze of extremely complicated variables into weather predictions.

FIGURE 8-3:
Computers are improving forecasts

(refer to page 280 for more information)

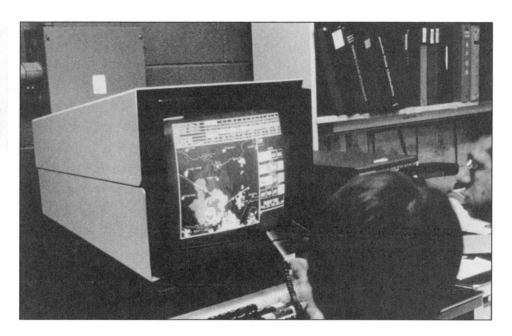

These days, a forecast is a product of six to eight mathematical equa-tions for a given point. Information on air pressure, wind speed, humidity, air density, and the results of surface and upper-air measurements are loaded into a supercomputer, and a program is run that describes the conditions that will occur in a small unit of future time. The program analyzes data for a large number of "grid points," or imaginary squares of various sizes, both at the surface and up to eighteen layers into the atmosphere.

Now the forecaster has a prediction of future conditions for the next ten minutes or so. Using that data as a starting point, the information is fed back into the computer, which does another prediction for the next few minutes until it reaches a desired time in the future, such as twelve, twenty-four, or thirty-six hours from the starting point. The computer can now draw a map called a prognostic chart that shows how all of the lows, highs, and other weather factors will appear at a future time.

As computer models are developed, their accuracy is tracked and small adjustments are made to improve them. Because one model may evolve to be better at forecasting surface low-pressure systems, while another excels at predicting the movement of upper-level air, meteorologists can pick and choose among the many models available, selecting the ones that are more likely to result in a correct forecast.

True Grids

Because computer modeling is accomplished using grid points, and a forecast is drawn using conditions within each grid box, it follows that the smaller the grid the more accurate the forecast will be. Global climate models work with a grid that's about 300 miles square (larger than the state of Iowa). Because it's a three-dimensional box that extends into the upper levels of the atmosphere, with data being plotted at each level, the output of just one grid computation can total hundreds of megabytes. With smaller grids, the data analysis and storage requirements rise exponentially, so global models are still much less accurate than regional ones, although they're useful in determining large-scale climate changes over time.

QUESTIONS?

Will computers eventually replace human forecasters?
Computers are great at performing repetitive tasks, but humans are much better at pattern recognition (identifying a radar hook echo, for example). Both human and computer forecasters will enjoy job security for a long, long time.

Regional grids produce more accurate forecasts than the global variety, but because they're smaller, they're dependable only for a short period; weather from adjacent grids will always intrude before long. And the finer the grid resolution, the more computing power necessary to examine the many data points it contains. With so much raw data, examining and interpreting them become increasingly important.

Although computers are great tools for aiding in the creation of weather forecasts, human interpreters still need to analyze the output from computer models, compare them with past data that have been gathered over a long time period, and determine what changes will improve the model's accuracy. There is simply no substitute for human experience and wisdom.

Climate models depend on a detailed description of a grid point for their accuracy, so each area is modeled differently depending on whether it's over land, ice, or ocean. Land specialists help build models that incorporate topographic features like mountains and rivers, as well as water runoff on the surface and the amount of water in the soil. The models also include forests and other areas of vegetation, because plants reflect less sunlight than land, and their carbon dioxide can affect local air composition.

Oceanographers are called on to use their knowledge of the sea to input factors such as salt content, freshwater runoff, sea ice, ocean temperature, and density into numerical models. Atmospheric scientists input information on the distribution of gases in the air, how solar radiation is affecting air temperatures, and the amount of pollutants like industrial smoke and automobile emissions.

Disorderly Models

With high-tech teamwork and speedy supercomputers combining to create forecasts, why aren't at least short-term forecasts more dependable? The answer lies in the tendency for small atmospheric disturbances to be greatly magnified in time. Meteorologist Edward Lorenz discovered this effect, called chaos theory, in 1963. Lorenz was running a weather-modeling computer program accurate to the sixth decimal place, but after running into a problem, he re-entered the data using a printout, which rounded to three decimals. To his great surprise, the extremely small difference caused by the missing decimal places resulted in a very different processing run.

Utter Chaos

Lorenz described chaos theory as "a system that has two states that look the same on separate occasions, but can develop into states that are noticeably different." A golf ball dropped from the same height above a fixed point would always land on the same spot, he noted, but a piece of paper would not because during its fall it would be acted on by chaotic forces like air movement. Because those forces changed constantly, the path of the paper to the ground could not be predicted with any degree of accuracy.

ESSENTIALS

Lorenz illustrated chaos theory by concocting the "Butterfly effect," which states that the flapping of a butterfly's wings in China could cause tiny atmospheric changes that over a period of time could affect weather patterns in New York City.

This was quite a blow to meteorologists, who realized that even a tiny error in their initial computer input could produce a seriously flawed model. The error would be magnified by time, so that forecasts for longer periods would be increasingly inaccurate. After Lorenz's discovery, some felt that it was pointless to even try to predict the weather, since it was nearly impossible to eliminate every single error from a model's initial input.

It's What You Put into It

Computer models are only a simulation of the atmosphere; they make assumptions about weather conditions that may or may not be accurate. Even though great pains are taken to eliminate models that don't perform well, they are not now, nor will they ever be, perfect. Another problem is inherent in regional models: Errors creep in along their boundaries as weather from nearby grids sneaks in.

With the advent of satellites and radiosondes, many more observation points are now available than in the past, and forecasts have improved as a result. But because of the computational requirements of smaller grids, most models still use data points that are too far apart to accurately predict the movement of small-scale weather systems like thunderstorms.

In addition, many models don't take land features like hills and lakes into account, thereby introducing that first small error that Lorenz showed can be magnified over time into one giant boo-boo.

A New Hope

When you take the effects of chaos into account, is there any real hope that forecasts—especially long-range ones—can be improved? Actually, it's already happening. Ensemble forecasting combines several computational models into one, using a weighted average system. Introducing different weather factors into a model at the outset mimics the effects of chaos, and often results in a more accurate result. Running several of these ensemble models while using a slightly different weight factor each time increases the chances of at least one being correct, and by weeding out the ones that don't work, forecasts can become much more dependable.

Forecasters compare the output of different models and assign a degree of confidence in each one depending on how much faith they have in a particular forecast. In general, the more the models disagree, the less predictable the weather is.

Another way that scientists are improving forecasts is by filling in data gaps that have long existed in certain remote parts of the globe. In much of the Southern Hemisphere, for example, which is mostly covered by vast oceans, gathering atmospheric information in real time has been a challenge. Now a NASA scatterometer, which is able to measure wind speeds from orbit, passes over 90 percent of the world's oceans each day, greatly improving marine forecasts.

Recently, it was discovered that some areas of the earth's surface are responsible for more chaos errors than others, and were dubbed "chaos hot spots." These areas, which cover about 20 percent of the earth's surface, are now the target of intense observation since they seem to cause most of the inaccuracies in current global forecasts. As scientists move from the global to the regional and even local scale, more hot spots will be identified, and forecasts for those areas will improve.

Researchers are now comparing computer models with historical conditions, feeding climatic information for a certain day in the past into the system and running a projection of the weather fifteen or thirty days later. Comparing the results of the projection with the actual conditions that occurred can demonstrate the accuracy of a model.

With the realization that a small atmospheric eddy in one country can affect the weather in another, the WMO began a program called the Global Climate Observing System (GCOS) in 1992. GCOS was designed to improve forecasts by coordinating weather data from all over the globe.

Power to the Prognosticators

Of course, one way to improve forecasts is to throw more computing power at them, and that's just what IBM is doing with its Deep Thunder project. Using the same type of supercomputer as Deep Blue, the system used to defeat Russian chess master Gary Kasparov in May 1997, the company is hoping to substantially reduce the size of a weather-modeling grid and produce a much more accurate local forecast. IBM is currently issuing a daily forecast for New York City using Deep Thunder, creating complex 3-D images that can give forecasters a snapshot of future weather conditions at a glance.

Improved forecasts will help you avoid a cloudy day at the beach and let you know when to bring an umbrella to work, but the implications for businesses could be enormous. It's been estimated that in the airline industry alone, weather-related problems cost up to $269 million a year, and even power companies lose money when bad forecasts cause them to overproduce electricity. Former Secretary of Commerce William Daley has said that "weather is not just an environmental issue, it is a major economic factor. At least one trillion dollars of our economy is weather sensitive."

Even more importantly, accurate and timely forecasts can save lives. From 1988 through 1999, major disasters cost the United States more than $170 billion, and in 1998 alone, weather-related catastrophes did $92 billion in damage worldwide. Clearly, every small step in improving weather prediction is welcome, especially when that weather turns violent.

CHAPTER 9

The Electric Sky

Although lightning often strikes more than once, once is usually sufficient.

—Encyclopedia Britannica

Ever since Zeus threw his first thunderbolt, lightning has been a source of awe and fear. Unlike other weather phenomenon, lightning can strike in a fraction of a second, sometimes without warning, not only injuring people but also creating fires that can destroy homes and businesses.

Danger from the Heavens

There was a light drizzle in Fort Lauderdale, Florida, on the afternoon of September 15, 1983, as Linda Cooper drove to the bank to deposit a check. Remembering that she needed to mail a package, Linda was making her way across the street to the post office when a bolt of lightning struck an ungrounded flagpole, then leaped across the street and struck her in the head.

The next thing Cooper remembers is putting her package down on the post office desk, wondering how she had gotten there. Her skin soon turned a sickly gray, the hair on her arms stood on end, and she was so fatigued she couldn't function. Finally seeking treatment at a hospital, she was kept under constant medical care for six days, and after discharge she continued to suffer from headaches, memory loss, and chronic fatigue.

Incredibly, that rainy September afternoon wasn't Linda Cooper's last run-in with lightning: She was struck two more times, once in 1993 and again in 1994 at her home in Spartanburg, South Carolina. Now Ms. Cooper works to educate others on the dangers of lightning and what can be done to avoid being a victim.

SSENTIALS According to the National Weather Service, your chance of being hit by a lightning bolt over a course of a lifetime is only 1 in 600,000. That's a good thing, because lightning carries a charge of up to one billion volts of electricity carried by a current of 200,000 amperes!

Satellite observation has shown that there are more than 100 flashes of lightning per second all over the globe, or more than 3 million bolts blasting from the more than 40,000 thunderstorms that dot the planet each day. Lightning kills about one hundred Americans each year—more than any other kind of severe weather except floods—yet many of its secrets still remain undiscovered.

The First Lightning Rod Was Named Ben

A bolt of lightning is really just a giant spark that discharges pent-up electrical energy from a cloud into the ground, or from one cloud to another. In Benjamin Franklin's day, charges created by static electricity were already being stored in containers called Leyden jars, a primitive form of capacitor. Lightning wasn't yet linked with electricity, although Franklin suspected a connection between the two.

Franklin had designed an experiment to prove his theory that used what he called a "sentry box," but construction delays caused him to set it aside in favor of using a kite with a conductive string. At the end, he would tie a key followed by a short length of nonconducting silk cord that he would hold in one hand while holding his other hand near the key. Franklin theorized that when lightning struck the kite, a spark would jump from the key to his knuckles.

In 1752, during a Pennsylvania thunderstorm, the most famous kite in history took to the air. Sure enough, a lightning bolt hit the kite and immediately sparks flew from the key to Franklin's hand, proving once and for all that lightning was indeed an electrical phenomenon. It seems a miracle that he wasn't killed on the spot.

ALERT

The year after Franklin's kite flight, Swedish physicist G. W. Richmann constructed a sentry box of his own. Following Franklin's instructions to the letter, he stood in the box during a lightning storm. He was rewarded with a direct strike, which killed him instantly. The moral: Don't try this at home, or anywhere else.

Franklin also invented the lightning rod after discovering that an electrical charge could be drained away by a conducting rod buried in the ground. Eventually, he came up with the idea of putting the rod on a rooftop and connecting it to a wire that would transfer the energy of a lightning bolt directly into the soil, sparing the building from harm. Lightning rods don't "attract" lightning, they just give it a harmless path to take into the ground, which is all it really wants in the first place.

Lightning Illuminated

The most common type of lightning is the cloud-to-cloud type; only about 20 percent of all strikes are directed toward the ground. But the cloud-to-ground variety is the one that affects people more often, so it receives the most study.

For lightning to occur, there have to be areas of opposite electrical charges within a cumulonimbus cloud. How those regions develop and why they separate is one of the undiscovered secrets mentioned earlier, but one theory says that the collisions between small hailstones and ice crystals within a storm cause a positive charge in the upper regions while the lower and middle parts of the cloud gain a negative charge due to the influence of downdrafts and gravity.

Since unlike charges attract each other, the ground below the thunderstorm becomes positively charged, and as the cloud moves it drags this area of positive charge behind it. The resulting electrical field continues to build, but because the air between the cloud and the ground acts as an insulator, there is still no current flowing between them. If you measured the positive charges under the storm at this point (not recommended!), you'd find that protruding structures like radio towers, church steeples, and stubborn golfers have a stronger charge than the ground, making them a much more likely target for lightning.

FACTS

When lightning strikes sand or certain rock, the heat immediately melts and fuses the material it encounters, creating long underground glass tubes called fulgurites. These channels are usually from 0.5 to 2 inches across and can burrow as far as twenty yards into the ground. Fragile fulgurites are difficult to remove from the soil, so large specimens are rare.

Eventually this charge becomes so powerful that it overcomes the air's insulating effect, and a bolt of lightning zaps out of the cloud. It's over in less than a second, but in that time as many as ten separate lightning strokes have been generated. The fact that it looks like one continuous streak is because the human eye can't register the distinct pulses fast enough; instead of separate flashes, your retinas see a flickering effect, because each pulse lasts only a few millionths of a second.

Golfers are much more likely to be struck since their game is played outdoors. Jim Lushine, a nationally recognized expert on lightning and an avid golfer, recommends heading for shelter the minute you hear thunder or see lightning. "You can always hit a mulligan (free stroke) later," says Lushine.

Looking At Lightning in Slo-Mo

Lightning is difficult to study; not only is it extremely short-lived, but nobody wants to get too close to a billion volts of electricity. Imagine for a moment that you could slow down the passage of time, so that microseconds lasted for minutes. You'd be able to clearly see each phase of a lightning bolt as it developed, and what you saw would probably surprise you.

The first thing you'd see in a cloud-to-ground flash is a barely visible streamer of lightning, called a stepped leader, emerging from the cloud. The stepped leader travels the distance of about a city block in a microsecond and then pauses for up to fifty microseconds to decide where to go next. If there's a stronger electrical field in a different direction, the leader will change course and head toward it, creating a crooked appearance. This stop-and-start process continues until the leader gets close to the ground, when it will often branch into several forks.

As it gets closer to the ground, the leader induces a rapid increase in the strength of electrical fields on the ground (around 10 million volts' worth), especially in taller objects. Suddenly another bolt of lightning jumps from the ground up toward the stepped leader, completing a cloud/ground electrical circuit.

Although the stepped leader had to go through the trial-and-error process of finding the best path to the ground, the return stroke doesn't have that limitation. Taking advantage of its prefab pathway, it leaps back toward the cloud with a flash as bright as a million lightbulbs, making the trip all the way up to the cloud and back as many as ten times in a fraction of a second.

The Big Flash-Bang

The pencil-thin bolt instantly heats the air in this corridor to 54,000 degrees F—hotter than the surface of the Sun—and since heated air expands, a shock wave explodes outward from the lightning channel at the speed of sound, creating a blast of thunder. The bright flash caused by the bolt is expanding outward too, but at the speed of light, a million times faster than the thunder. It reaches us almost instantly, while the thunderclap moseys along toward our eardrums at a leisurely 186,000 miles per second or so. If the lightning strike is more than about 15 miles away, you probably won't hear the thunder, since sound waves generally curve upward around thunderstorms.

Just because you're quite a distance from a thunderstorm doesn't mean you should let your guard down. Cumulonimbus clouds can spawn "positive giants," lightning strikes that come from the storm's anvil-shaped head and can blast outward for 20 miles or more.

Most often there will be at least four distinct bolts traveling through the channel before the strike is over. Stepped leaders that form after the first one are called dart leaders, and they're usually less powerful than the initial bolt. If they depart from the original channel on their way back to the ground, dart leaders will give the lightning stroke a forked appearance. If the wind is blowing the lightning channel sideways at high speed, ribbon lightning results, as the moving corridor seems to create a luminous strip in the air.

Shocking Variants

Other forms of lightning include heat lightning, which is just ordinary lightning seen from a great distance, and sheet lightning, which is lightning striking within a cloud or from one cloud to another. When the actual bolt is obscured by the cloud, it lights up the entire structure, momentarily making it look like a huge white sheet.

Sometimes the positive charge that accumulates on flagpoles, ship masts, and other high points doesn't provoke a lightning strike, but instead appears as a halo of sparks or a weird glow around the top of the object. That's called St. Elmo's fire, named after the patron saint of mariners. The effect is caused by charged plasma called a corona discharge, and is similar to the glow given off by a fluorescent light.

Don't Catch This Ball

St. Elmo's Fire isn't really lightning, but at least the basic electrical phenomenon that causes it is understood. Not so with the phenomenon of ball lightning, which continues to confound scientists with its elusive nature. About as far from split-a-tree-in-your-backyard lightning as you can get, ball lightning is a true original. Although it has never been photographed, so many people have reported seeing the phenomenon that there's little doubt of its existence.

QUESTIONS?

What is St. Elmo's Fire?
St. Elmo's Fire occurs when a highly charged electrical field affects a gas. When a high-voltage current is applied to a gas, it pulls the electrons and protons of the gas apart, creating a conductive plasma that glows brightly.

Most observers describe ball lightning as a luminous red, orange, or yellow sphere floating along in the air a few yards or less from the ground, often near a thunderstorm. Some people hear a hissing sound or smell an odor like ozone. The spheres range in size from a few inches to a few feet, although most are in the 4- to 8-inch category and last only a few seconds.

A Close Encounter

Most run-ins with ball lightning are reported, not by UFO theorists, but by average people who are genuinely puzzled about what they've seen. One such viewer was Roger Jennison, a professor in the University of Kent's Department of Electronics, who encountered the phenomenon during a late-night flight from New York to Washington in March 1963. The plane was flying through a thunderstorm when it was suddenly surrounded by a loud, bright electrical discharge. Jennison later related his experience:

> *Some seconds later, a glowing sphere some 20cm in diameter emerged from the pilot's cabin and passed down the aircraft's central aisle. . . . The ball moved on a straight course the whole length of the aisle 75cm above the floor at a velocity relative to the aircraft of about 1.5 ms-1. It was blue-white in colour and its optical output amounted to about 5 to 10 Watts. Interestingly, no heat was felt when it passed close by and the limb darkening (like that of the Sun) gave it an almost solid appearance, indicating that it was optically opaque. No asymmetry could be seen in any dimension so it was impossible to determine whether or not it was spinning.*

Theories on the nature of ball lightning are a dime a dozen, ranging from plasma suspended in a magnetic field to swamp gas ignited by a lightning strike. One recent theory supposes that when lightning strikes certain types of soils, the ground can vaporize, creating hot gasses that "burp" out of the soil and then condense into tiny, electricity-conducting wires that form a glowing sphere.

The Celestial Fairyland

Recently even more exotic forms of lightning have been discovered above thunderstorms. Faint flickers of light from the tops of storms had been reported for more than a century—some observers said it looked as though the tops of clouds were on fire—but verification was difficult until the right instruments were developed. In fact, some Air Force pilots had seen the phenomenon for years but were reluctant to report lightning that went the "wrong" way. In 1989, researchers videotaped a pulse of light leaping from the top of a thunderstorm toward the heavens. With no idea what they were seeing, they dubbed it a "sprite."

Snapshot of a Sprite

In 1994, a group of scientists from the University of Minnesota in a high-flying NASA jet were testing a low-light camera normally used to image the aurora borealis. While orbiting high over a thunderstorm, they pointed the camera at the distant horizon and quite accidentally captured the first color images of a sprite. The pictures revealed a large red puff rising from the storm, appearing just as a powerful lightning bolt exploded below. The sprite, which had a surprisingly delicate structure, rose some 60 miles toward space before dissipating.

What could account for the existence of something that looked like a huge red jellyfish high in the atmosphere? That's still being debated, but scientists do know a few things about sprites:

- They appear only during very large thunderstorms.
- They're usually brightest about 40 miles up in the atmosphere.
- They last only about ten milliseconds.
- They appear only after reverse, or positive, cloud-to-ground lightning.
- They almost always appear in groups.

Elves and Blue Jets

With the discovery of sprites, many more observers turned their attention to the lofty heights of severe thunderstorms, and soon some other strange effects were discovered. Narrow beams of blue light were spotted over some clouds, although they were even rarer than sprites. Named "blue jets" by their discoverers, these narrow cone-shaped columns seem to leap from the top of a thunderstorm and soar high into the stratosphere at more than 300 times the speed of sound. They're much rarer than sprites, but a bit more long-lived; they are visible to the naked eye at night.

Shortly after the discovery of blue jets, scientists at Stanford University announced that they had spotted an even stranger light in the heavens: a red halo that seemed to do the impossible by propagating outward from a thunderstorm to an altitude of about 40 to 60 miles high at a velocity faster than the speed of light. But it wasn't yet time for Einstein to roll over in his grave; further research showed that no single particle was moving that fast. The phenomenon, dubbed "elves," was caused by air molecules firing in rapid sequence after being stimulated by the lightning pulse, like chase lights around a movie marquee. Their causes are still being investigated.

One theory on the origin of elves says that the electromagnetic pulse caused by a lightning strike can rise and expand through the cloud like a balloon, finally breaking free above the storm, where it causes charged particles to glow red. Others say they could be caused by storm-produced gamma rays that were recently detected by NASA's Compton Gamma Ray Observatory satellite.

Bolts, Blazes, and Blackouts

Each year, lightning starts around 10,000 forest fires in the United States alone, laying waste to more than $50 million worth of timber. The National Lightning Safety Institute estimates that the total cost of lightning strikes, including damage to both property and people, may total upward of $4 billion to $5 billion per year. A strike near your home can shred your trees, shut off your power, and cook your appliances, but a large, well-placed bolt can knock out power to an entire city.

Brownouts and blackouts can wreak havoc with your electronic devices, and a lightning strike can destroy them. A surge protector for each device is imperative, but an even better bet is an uninterruptible power supply (UPS), which can allow you to shut your computer down after a power problem without losing data.

On the night of July 13, 1977, a line of thunderstorms formed to the north of New York City. The sound of air conditioners running at full blast nearly drowned out their rumble as New Yorkers sought relief from the heat. Shortly after 8:30, powerful lightning strikes hit two high-voltage power lines, starting a chain of events that knocked out the city's power grid and plunged the Big Apple into darkness. During what became known as "The Night of Terror," 3,776 people were arrested for looting and other crimes, and the fire department fought 1,037 blazes. One Bronx dealership was robbed of fifty cars in a single evening. Thousands were trapped in darkened elevators and subway cars. Both Kennedy International Airport and LaGuardia were closed, and hospitals were forced to resort to emer-gency generators for power.

With so much at stake, the federal government assisted in financing a national lightning data service that eventually grew into the National Lightning Detection Network (NLDN). Consisting of a web of magnetic direction finders scattered across the country, the NLDN can instantly triangulate the location of a cloud-to-ground lightning strike and transmit that information to the Network Control Center, where it appears on an electronic map of the United States. Warnings can now be issued for storms with especially violent electrical activity.

Lightning and Rocket Science

Today, lightning research is being conducted on multiple fronts. Taking a page from Ben Franklin's book, NASA now launches sounding rockets attached to long copper wires into thunderstorms to study lightning close up. When the rocket is hit by a lightning bolt, the wire is vaporized, but not before relaying data about the strike to a computer. Modified U-2 spy planes have also been used to study cloud-to-cloud lightning in its own neighborhood, thousands of feet above the surface of the earth. The planes bristle with instruments like infrared, visible, and microwave scanners; lasers; spectrometers; and electric field antennas that give researchers a snapshot of thunderstorm conditions.

NASA has experimented with space-based lightning detection systems that show promise in not only providing early warning of severe thunderstorms but even of tornado formation. Researchers at NASA's Global Hydrology and Climate Center have observed that although supercell thunderstorms have a much higher rate of lightning strikes than ordinary storms, just before a tornado forms, lightning rates drop rapidly. It's hoped that by studying lightning from space, tornado warnings can be issued earlier while at the same time reducing the number of false alarms.

CHAPTER 10

From Floods to Drought

A little and a little, collected together, become a great deal; the heap in the barn consists of single grains, and drop and drop makes an inundation.

—Saadi

Because the atmosphere is always trying to keep itself in balance, there's usually enough rain to keep farmers and gardeners happy but not enough to cause problems for the rest of the population. Occasionally, however, that balance is interrupted, and the result is often tragic.

Why Floods Happen

Flash floods remain difficult to predict because they're a result of rapidly changing conditions. They can be caused not only by sudden cloudbursts but also by quickly melting snow or ice and the collapse of natural or manmade dams. The seeds of disaster can be sown on what seems to be a perfect day.

Floods caused by several days of rainfall or melting snow give plenty of notice, but their effects can be much more damaging and widespread. Many rivers flood on a regular basis and have done so for centuries, but as people build homes on their banks and floodplains, placing themselves directly in harm's way, the loss of lives and property becomes inevitable— another reason why floods are America's number one weather-related killers.

FACTS

According to Sierra Club statistics, current state and federal laws allow developers to build in 100-year floodplains if they elevate the home or business 1 foot above the 100-year level. But many of the state's floodplain maps are more than ten years out of date, and much of the current flooding is occurring outside the mapped 100-year floodplain.

Population growth calls for more housing. With wetlands being drained for developments, rivers being channeled, and levees being built, flooding rivers will crest at a higher elevation. Urban development covers large areas with pavement and concrete, so water that was once able to soak into the ground over time now rushes directly into streams and rivers. When you throw an approaching hurricane or tropical storm into the mix, it's time to look for higher ground.

Floyd's Fury

In mid-September 1999, a small tropical disturbance moving west across the Atlantic grew into a 600-mile-wide hurricane and tore through the Bahamas with winds of 155 miles per hour. Florida residents jammed grocery stores and home improvement warehouses as Hurricane Floyd bore down on the peninsula, but the Sunshine State was spared at the last minute as the storm turned north. Not so lucky was the Atlantic seaboard, which bore the full brunt of Floyd as the hurricane surged inland at Cape Fear, North Carolina.

FIGURE 10-1:
Floods: perennial hazards

(refer to page 280 for more information)

Fortunately, Floyd had weakened in its trip up the coast, and by the time it made landfall, the highest winds were around 110 miles per hour. High winds caused some damage along the coastline, but the worst was yet to come. Hurricane Dennis had lingered off the North Carolina coast only a week before, pounding the eastern part of the state with wind and rain, and the ground was saturated with water. In Rocky Mount, Dennis had dropped 5 inches of rain, and Floyd deposited another 16.18 inches on top of that. In less than a week, many areas of the state received more rainfall than they usually saw all year.

Rising Rivers

As the rain continued to fall, already-swollen streams and rivers rose even further, overflowing their banks and spreading out into floodplains that had remained dry for more than a 100 years. The flooding spread eastward as the overflowing tributaries carried huge amounts of water downstream toward the sea, virtually wiping out the small town of Princeville, which had been founded by former slaves in 1865. The town was built on the banks of the Tar River, and when the river crested at an estimated 27 feet (estimated because the measuring gauge was completely submerged at that point), Princeville all but disappeared.

ESSENTIALS

One of Floyd's worst effects was felt in eastern North Carolina, which is home to the majority of the state's hog farms. Each day thousands of tons of hog waste and manure are flushed out of hog houses into open-air cesspools. When these lagoons were flooded, millions of gallons of waste poured out of lagoons into rivers and streams, polluting groundwater and posing a serious health threat.

Many people had to cut holes in their roofs after being trapped in their attics by rising waters, and Coast Guard helicopters were pressed into service to rescue thousands. Pigs and cattle died in droves, trapped in the flood, and county after county was declared a disaster area. Floyd completely destroyed 7,000 homes in North Carolina alone, and left another 17,000 uninhabitable. H. David Bruton, the state's secretary of Health and Human Services, said, "Nothing since the Civil War has been as destructive to families here."

Floyd wasn't through with the East Coast yet. Many rivers in southeastern Virginia broke 100-year records as they rose high above flood stage. The rampaging waters left nearly 300,000 people without power, damaged 5,000 homes, and filled downtown Franklin with 12 feet of muddy, smelly water.

By the time Floyd reached New Jersey, it was a tropical storm with winds of only 60 miles per hour, but its rains had lost none of their punch. The Raritan River Basin in the north-central part of the state received 7 to 11 inches of rain in less than twenty-four hours, and when the river crested on September 17, it set a new record of 42.13 feet, the highest recorded level since 1800. Tens of thousands of utility customers were without power after the storm, and flooded water treatment plants left thousands more without drinking water. The flooding caused electrical short circuits in many places, and fires began to break out, burning out of control as firefighters tried to reach them by boat.

Floyd took a final swipe at the United States in Maine and New Hampshire, where it dumped another 3 to 7 inches of rain before exiting into eastern Canada. The storm killed fifty-seven people, mostly deaths by drowning, and caused damages estimated to be more than $6 billion. More than 2.6 million people were evacuated from their homes ahead of the storm—the largest peacetime evacuation in U.S. history—and ten states were declared major disaster areas in its wake.

Not a Surprise

Hurricane Floyd didn't exactly sneak up on the East Coast. By 1999, satellite and aircraft observation methods were advanced enough to give everyone plenty of warning. Unlike a flash flood, Floyd gave coastal residents several days to make preparations. If that's the case, how could so many people still get caught unaware as floodwaters swept away their homes and families? Weren't any flood warnings issued before the storm?

FACTS

Many of the disaster-relief problems uncovered by Floyd were organizational. The radios in military vehicles called in to help support relief efforts often couldn't communicate with civilian disaster workers', for example, and many rescue units were neither equipped nor trained for flood rescue.

In fact, the Southeast River Forecast Center (SERFC) in Atlanta was predicting 6 to 12 inches of rainfall from Floyd the day before it made landfall in the Carolinas, warning that rivers 80 to 100 miles inland would experience record floods. But the media were concentrating on the coastal regions, broadcasting video of thousands of evacuees heading west as the storm advanced. Kent Frantz of the SERFC remembers, "we tried to tell everyone that the main problem was going to be inland flooding, but no one seemed very interested."

Making Changes

Since Floyd, the Federal Emergency Management Agency (FEMA) has developed an extensive buyout plan that helps move those in flood-prone areas to higher ground, and it encourages others who insist on remaining to raise their homes up on supports.

The National Weather Service began a modernization program designed to identify potential flash floods before they occur. It now maintains thirteen regional River Forecast Centers that keep an eye on developing conditions that could lead to flooding, based on data from remote rain gauges, satellites, and NEXRAD rainfall estimates.

With that information, computers can generate rainfall runoff predictions that tell forecasters how long storm waters will take to reach a river or stream, and how high the floodwaters will be. In addition, the Office of Hydrology at the National Weather Service has developed the Hydrologic Forecast System (WHFS), a collection of computer applications that helps forecasters model and predict flood events.

Natural disasters create a high demand for cleaning and repair, which can attract unscrupulous scam artists. Be sure to check out a contractor's credentials before signing a contract; get several written estimates; and above all, don't pay a large advance sum to a contractor you don't know.

One pattern meteorologists look for in a developing flash flood is where storms with heavy rainfall linger over one area for hours, or move in such a way that a continuous line of storm cells passes repeatedly over the same spot, a pattern called "training." They also watch out for "backbuilding," which occurs when a storm is able to regenerate itself on its back edge as quickly as it moves forward. When this happens, one small area can receive catastrophic amounts of rain in a short time.

The Flip Side of Floods

As damaging as too much water can be, too little can cause just as much trouble. When an area doesn't receive enough rain for an extended period of time, drought conditions result. It may seem strange, but when eastern North Carolina was drowning under hurricane Floyd's flood waters, the western part of the state was suffering from a severe drought.

Most droughts result from fluctuations in large-scale circulation patterns in the atmosphere, and can be directly influenced by the location of high-pressure systems. When large rotating air masses get cut off from the standard airflow moving from west to east across the country, they linger in one place and can block the progress of advancing weather systems, introducing a wholesale change in climate. If these atmospheric roadblocks last for extended periods of time, floods, drought, freezes, and heat waves often become the rule.

Dust in the Wind

Sometimes the effects of a drought can be amplified by human activity. In the 1930s, the Great Plains of the United States began to experience droughts. For years, settlers in the region had been planting wheat and harvesting bountiful crops, but when the dry conditions arrived, they kept on planting and plowing in spite of the diminishing rainfall. With the native grasses mostly gone, high winds whipped huge clouds of dust and soil into the air, in some cases completely burying homes and automobiles in heaps of drifting soil. By May 1934, a cloud of topsoil from the Great Plains blanketed the eastern United States for a distance of some 1,500 miles.

No one who saw it ever forgot the Black Blizzard that occurred on Palm Sunday of 1935. Eyewitnesses described it as a beautiful, peaceful day until late afternoon, when flocks of birds appeared on the horizon, fleeing for their lives. Behind them came a black wall of dust rising 7,000 feet into the air, engulfing everything in its path. With the morning's weather so calm, many people had taken to the roads for leisurely day trips, and as the dust storm engulfed them, motorists collided with each other in the choking darkness, unable to see more than a foot or two ahead. The grit generated so much static electricity as it swirled over the highways that automobile electrical systems shorted out, stalling engines and stranding many drivers in the storm.

Taking refuge indoors, homeowners stuffed rags, sheets, and clothing into cracks under doors and around windows, but the dust got in anyway, coating everything in the house with a thick layer of black dirt. The April 18 edition of the *Ochiltree County Herald* in Perryton, Texas, described the scene:

> *The worst dust storm in the memory of the oldest inhabitants of this section of the country hit Perryton at five o'clock Sunday afternoon, catching hundreds of people away from their homes, at the theatre, on the highways, or on picnic parties. The storm came up suddenly, following a perfect spring day.*
>
> *In just a few minutes after the first bank appeared in the north, the fury of the black blizzard was upon us, turning the bright sunshine of a perfect day into the murky inkiness of the blackest night. Many hurried to storm cellars, remembering the cyclone of July, two years ago, that followed a similar duster.*
>
> *Without question, this storm put the finishing touch of destruction to what faint hopes this area had for a wheat crop. Business houses and homes were literally filled with the fine dirt and silt driven in by this fifty mile an hour gale.*

The next day, Robert Geiger, a correspondent for the *Washington Evening Star,* would name the ongoing drought "The Dust Bowl." It lasted for nearly a decade and excavated an estimated 850 million tons of soil from the Great Plains.

Forecasting Droughts

Droughts are difficult to predict because they're always the end result of many causative factors. Because they develop much more slowly than floods, often droughts aren't identified until they're already under way. Adding to the confusion, there are different ways of measuring droughts:

Meteorological—How much the precipitation amounts differ from normal. Because not every area gets the same amount of rainfall, a drought in one place might not be considered a drought in another.

Agricultural—The amount of moisture in the soil is no longer sufficient to grow a particular crop.

Hydrological—Both surface and underground water supplies are below normal.

Socioeconomic—A lack of water begins to affect people's daily lives.

NOAA researchers examining tree rings and other indicators of historical droughts are learning that large-scale dry weather events tend to occur on a regular basis, and their findings may eventually lead to better ways of forecasting droughts. The bad news is that disasters like the Dust Bowl may not be all that unusual on a climatological scale, and that more severe and longer-lasting droughts could occur at any time. History indicates that the United States might expect a Dust Bowl–sized drought once or twice each century, and that past droughts have been much worse than more recent ones.

ESSENTIALS

With the El Niño/La Niña pattern now identified and successfully forecast, meteorologists are getting better at making the connection between large-scale recurring weather patterns and how they cause droughts, flooding, and other natural disasters.

Like other weather processes, flooding and droughts are just part of Earth's natural water cycle, and sometimes even bring benefits instead of disaster. Floods recharge groundwater supplies and create new land where river deltas wash into the ocean. In ancient Egypt, the Nile River flooded each year, sometimes causing the loss of lives and property. But when the flood waters receded, they deposited a rich, fertile layer of silt full of organic matter that greatly improved farmers' crops.

In the Path of Danger

The problem is less the weather than man's inattention to its cycles. Some of the worst flooding is caused by the tidal surge that precedes a hurricane, yet the construction of beachfront homes and condominiums continues unabated. Homes wiped out by flooding are often rebuilt in the same vulnerable location, even though another future disaster is a virtual certainty. Before hurricane Floyd's dirty floodwaters had fully receded, for example, the residents of Princeville had already decided to rebuild their town on the same spot.

In 1968, the federal government established the National Flood Insurance Program to provide insurance policies to homeowners living in high-risk areas on floodplains and in coastal areas prone to hurricane damage. Critics say that the program encourages people to build in harm's way, since any losses will be reimbursed at little cost to the homeowners. In fact, National Flood Insurance policies allow multiple claims without a premium increase, so more than a third of total payouts have gone to 3 percent of all claimants.

FEMA has been studying the problem and looking for ways to minimize costly multiple payouts. The agency is considering denying flood insurance to homeowners who have filed two or more claims that total more than the value of their home, refuse to elevate their home, refuse to flood-proof their home, or refuse to accept a buyout relocation offer.

The lure of coastal living is a strong one, and FEMA will no doubt have an uphill battle in encouraging less growth there, and in attempting to relocate long-time residents of floodplains. But as long as people continue to place themselves in the path of floods and hurricanes, there will be loss of life and destruction of property. When man pits himself against nature, nature tends to win.

CHAPTER 11

Tornadoes—
The Wicked Wind

The destructive violence of this storm exceeds in its power, fierceness, and grandeur all other phenomena of the atmosphere.

—John Park Finley, early tornado researcher

Packing the fastest winds on Earth, F5 tornadoes are truly terrifying apparitions, but even smaller tornadoes can wreak unbelievable destruction. Incredibly, some people spend significant amounts of money and time trying to get closer to them.

A Chaser's View

On May 30, 1998, storm chasers Martin Lisius and Keith Brown were following a supercell across the rolling hills of South Dakota when they came over a ridge and saw a rapidly moving tornado to the west. With lightning crashing around them, the two men stopped and captured several still pictures and some movies of the twister, which was now nearly a mile wide at its base. As the vortex entered an area of trees, they saw bright flashes of light as power lines and transformers arced and exploded. They didn't realize it at the time, but they were witnessing the destruction of the town of Spencer.

SSENTIALS Some tornadoes catch their victims by surprise: Either the cyclones lack a clear funnel shape or they're obscured by sheets of rain, clouds of dust, or darkness. In addition, there may be more than one funnel in a tornadic system, and in avoiding one, it's possible to run into another.

At the end of the day, the chasers convened at a restaurant in Sioux Falls, exuberant after their successful hunt. As they compared notes on the day's events, a television in the restaurant broadcast a bulletin about the storm. The group grew silent as the news unfolded: The tornado had killed six people, injured more than ⅓ of the town's 320 residents, and destroyed most of its 190 buildings.

After the Storm

As with most tornadoes, the unpredictable forces of nature had spared some, but not others.

"As storm chasers, we live two lives," said Lisius later, "one as scientists, the other as humans. As scientists, we concentrate on the physics and the logistics. We are excited and awed by the power of nature. Violent storms and tornadoes are beautiful to us. Sometimes we forget, if only briefly, that to many others violent weather is a curse. Spencer was destroyed by nature. Simply put, an amazing amount of atmospheric energy came together there for a moment. It was haphazard. Unlike man, weather does not kill by intent."

We're Number One!

The United States has the dubious distinction of being the tornado capital of the world, averaging more than 800 of the killer storms each year. In 1992, a record 1,293 tornadoes formed in America. Although tornadoes have been recorded in every state in the Union, most occur in the "Tornado Alley" states of Oklahoma, Texas, Nebraska, and Kansas, as well as in many southern states. Unlike hurricanes, which satellites can spot in their formative stages over a period of days, tornadoes form quickly, which makes them an extremely dangerous short-term threat.

FACTS

The gentlest type of whirlwind is the dust devil, caused by the Sun heating up the ground at different rates. Air rising faster in one area than in another nearby causes a weak low-pressure system to form, and the air in adjacent areas flows into it, creating a spinning parcel of air that picks up dust, dirt, or leaves in its path.

Also unlike hurricanes, which may last for a week or more, most tornadoes last only a few minutes, and their paths average a mere 4 miles in length. They generally move along the ground at 20 to 50 miles per hour, but a few have been clocked doing more than 70. They're a lot smaller than hurricanes, too, usually only 400 to 500 feet wide, although some monster storms grow to a girth of more than a mile. Tornadoes almost always turn in a counterclockwise direction in the Northern Hemisphere and clockwise in the Southern Hemisphere, but a very few twisters somehow overcome the Coriolis force and rotate in the opposite direction.

Killer Winds

Tornadoes may be smaller than hurricanes, but what they lack in size they make up for in intensity. While a Category Five hurricane, the strongest on Earth, has winds of more than 155 miles per hour, some tornadoes exceed speeds of 300 miles per hour. Add to that the fact that these awe-inspiring funnels can descend from the clouds at a moment's notice, and you have one very dangerous weather phenomenon on your hands.

In 1949, Edward M. Brooks of St. Louis University was examining the data from weather stations situated near the paths of tornadoes when he discovered a link between twisters and mesocyclones, the large rotating air masses found in supercells. In 1953, the first mesocyclone was actually seen on radar at Urbana, Illinois. It appeared as a hook shape, since the radar beam was reflecting off rain that was being drawn into a rotating cylinder of air within the storm. These classic "hook echoes" are still looked for on modern radar screens as evidence of possible tornado formation.

Mr. Tornado

FIGURE 11-1:
Tornado and wall cloud

(refer to page 281 for more information)

The man who really put tornadoes on the map was Dr. Tetsuya "Ted" Fujita, who developed a scale of tornado intensity measurement that's still in use today. Fujita became interested in weather in his native Japan and came to the United States in 1953 to further his research in mesoscale meteorology.

Soon Fujita became interested in the damage caused by tornadoes and began collecting aerial photos of twister debris, hoping to find patterns that would help him understand their internal structure.

In one image, he noted "cycloidal marks," or smaller swirls of damage within the larger path of a tornado that had torn through a cornfield. Fujita deduced that they had come from minitornadoes spinning around the vortex of the main twister. Later observations proved him right.

After years of studying piles of debris and other damage left behind by twisters, Fujita (now known as "Mr. Tornado") developed his famous

F-scale in 1971. The Fujita Scale was based on the damage a tornado would do to "strong frame houses," and although the scientific community took him to task because there was no direct verification of his conclusions, his scale has proved remarkably accurate.

FACTS

After an Eastern Airlines crash in 1975, Fujita examined the flight records of other planes in the area and discovered that some had experienced updrafts while others fought severe downdrafts. His research led him to postulate the existence of microbursts, violent but compact columns of air rushing toward the ground, that can cause planes to crash on landing or takeoff.

Ted Fujita died on November 19, 1998, at the age of seventy-eight, leaving one of the most remarkable legacies in meteorology. He was not always right in every assumption and theory, but unlike many scientists, he never feared being wrong. "Even if I am wrong 50 percent of the time," he once said, "that would still be a tremendous contribution to meteorology." And so it was.

THE FUJITA SCALE		
F-#	DAMAGE	WIND SPEED
F0	Light	Up to 72 mph
F1	Moderate	73 to 112 mph
F2	Considerable	113 to 157 mph
F3	Severe	158 to 206 mph
F4	Devastating	207 to 260 mph
F5	Incredible	Above 261 mph

Recipe for Disaster

Meteorologists know which conditions may spawn a tornado, but the actual birth process within a thunderstorm is still up for debate. The most likely scenario is that a warm, humid layer of air forms near the ground under a layer of colder air in the upper atmosphere. When you have warm air near cooler air, you get an unstable atmosphere, and when there's wind shear between the layers, a rotation forms.

Tornadoes can form in other ways, too: They often spring up within hurricanes, which already contain all the heat, rotation, and moisture that a tornado needs for survival. Tornadoes can even form in the winter during intense storms. Winter tornadoes are most common near the Gulf of Mexico, when warmer air collides with advancing storm systems.

If a layer of hot, dry air becomes established between the warm, humid air below and the cooler air aloft, it forms a boundary called a "convective cap," which keeps the layer near the surface from rising. A convective cap acts like the radiator cap on your car, keeping the atmosphere from boiling over. As solar energy passes through the cap, it heats up the humid air at ground level, which pressurizes the cap like steam in a radiator.

Now add a dryline, or cold front, into the scenario, and the cap can weaken to the point where all that built-up warmth near the surface explodes through the layer of hot air, mixing with the colder air above it to form a supercell, with strong updrafts rotating rapidly upward through the cloud. As the thunderstorm builds higher, a rotating "wall cloud" descends beneath the storm—the direct precursor to a tornado. Some theorists say that a tube of air spinning horizontally near the surface (like a rolling pin) can get picked up by the updrafts at this point, and with the tube now spinning vertically, a funnel cloud forms. Within the funnel is a strong downdraft, which descends toward the ground, creating a tornado.

Gustnadoes and Landspouts

Sometimes small whirlpools of wind form on the leading edges of gust fronts and are called gustnadoes. They're not really tornadoes since they're not connected to the cloud base, but they can still cause damage. On June 9, 1994, a line of strong thunderstorms racing through central

Tennessee spawned a gustnado that passed within 100 yards of the Memphis National Weather Service Forecast Office, causing F1-level damage to houses and apartments nearby. Some gustnadoes have been clocked at speeds of up to 110 miles per hour.

Another type of tornado that doesn't form in a supercell is the landspout, a weak column of spinning winds that usually occurs in Colorado or Florida. Unlike their larger cousins, landspouts don't generally show up on Doppler radar and their life cycles are much shorter than a tornado's. Landspouts usually form beneath building cumulus clouds, and although relatively weak, a few become powerful enough to cause serious damage.

Whirling Water

FIGURE 11-2:
Waterspouts:
Wet tornadoes

(refer to page 281 for more information)

A landspout over water is called—wait for it—a waterspout, and is also one of the weaker types of atmospheric funnels. In this case the word "weaker" is relative, because a few of these seagoing cyclones can spin at speeds of up to 190 miles per hour, although they never reach the 300-miles-per-hour-plus velocity of an F5 tornado. Waterspouts form when moist, humid air is pulled into a rotating updraft over a body of water. Until the rotation reaches a speed of 40 miles per hour or so, the funnel may be invisible, but as moisture begins to condense, a column of spinning water vapor reaches down from the cloud toward the surface. Waterspouts look like they're sucking huge amounts of water into the clouds, but it's really just vapor. Sometimes waterspouts can move inland and become tornadoes.

Seeing It Coming

In the last few years, millions of dollars and thousands of hours have been spent learning how to predict these storms using sophisticated Doppler radar and other electronic methods. But the very first tornado forecast was accomplished back in 1948 without the aid of today's high-tech gadgetry.

On March 20, California native Robert C. Miller, an Air Force captain and meteorologist, was putting together the evening forecast for Tinker Air Force Base in Oklahoma where he was stationed. Miller and a fellow forecaster analyzed the latest weather maps from Washington and concluded it would be a relatively quiet night, with moderately strong winds but no storms, and that's what their 9 P.M. forecast predicted. The two men didn't realize that some of their source data were erroneous until a strong twister tore through the base an hour later, narrowly missing the aircraft hangars and operations center and blowing the windows out of nearly every building on the base.

FIGURE 11-3:
Tornado vs. airplane: Aftermath

(refer to page 281 for more information)

A Second Chance

Five days later, on March 25, Miller was producing the morning charts when he noticed that the day's expected weather conditions would be almost identical to those on the day of the tornado. He alerted General Fred S. Borum, who was by now in charge of the operation. The general ordered Miller to issue a thunderstorm warning, and by 2 P.M. a squall line had formed, just as it had before the last tornado.

"Are you going to issue a tornado forecast?" the general asked. Miller and Fawbush hemmed and hawed, neither relishing the idea of having another blown forecast pinned on him. "We both made abortive efforts at crawling out of such a horrendous decision," said Miller in his memoirs. "We pointed out the infinitesimal possibility of a second tornado striking the same area within twenty years or more, let alone in five days. 'Besides,' we said, 'no one has ever issued an operational tornado forecast.'"

"You are about to set a precedent," said the general.

On the Money

The forecast was composed, typed, and sent to Base Operations. A weather alert was sounded and base personnel flew into action, securing planes in hangars and tying down loose objects. At 5 P.M. a squall line passed through a nearby airport, but with only light rain and some small hail. Dejected, Miller drove home to commiserate with his wife. Later that evening as the couple was listening to the radio, an announcer broke in with an urgent bulletin about a tornado at Tinker Field.

FACTS

Bouyed by their success, the Air Force set up the Severe Weather Warning Center in 1951, and soon the public was clamoring for its own storm warnings. In 1952, the Weather Bureau finally set up its own storm prediction agency, the Weather Bureau Severe Weather Unit, which eventually became the Storm Prediction Center in 1995.

Miller rushed back to the base to find a scene of devastation, with power poles down and debris strewn everywhere. A jubilant Major Fawbush told Miller what he'd missed: "As the line approached the southwest corner of the field, two thunderstorms seemed to join and quickly took on a greenish black hue. They could observe a slow counterclockwise cloud rotation around the point at which the storms merged. Suddenly a large cone shaped cloud bulged down rotating counterclockwise at great speed. At the same time they saw a wing from one of the moth-balled World War II B-29s float lazily upward toward the visible part of the funnel. A second or two later the wing disintegrated, the funnel shot to the ground and the second large tornado in five days began its devastating journey across the base very close to the track of its predecessor."

Introducing Doppler

The tornado left $6 million worth of damage in its wake, and made Fawbush and Miller instant heroes. More importantly, it was a first small step in predicting twister formation. At the time, the only radars available for use by forecasters were World War II vintage units with fuzzy screens and limited range. But the next few decades would bring a flood of new tools to aid in tornado forecasting, including the most valuable of all: Doppler radar.

In 1971, the same year Ted Fujita came up with his tornado-damage scale, Doppler radar was first used to confirm that winds within a hook echo were rotating, giving scientists a picture of a storm's internal mesocyclone—the "smoking gun" that pointed to the origins of tornadoes. In 1973, Doppler radar pinpointed an area in a thunderstorm near Union City, Oklahoma, where winds abruptly changed direction, which turned out to coincide with the occurrence of a violent tornado. For the first time, meteorologists had direct evidence that Doppler radar could spot a twister in its formative stages.

A Closer Look

Doppler is great if a tornado happens to pass by a radar installation, but few twisters are that accommodating. In 1995, NOAA's National Severe Storms Laboratory (NSSL) formed a plan to hunt tornadoes on their own turf, taking the war to the enemy for the first time. The main purpose of Project VORTEX (Verification of the Origins of Rotation in Tornadoes Experiment) was to find out exactly how and under what conditions tornadoes form.

After formulating twenty-two hypotheses for the project to either prove or disprove, Dr. Erik Rasmussen was assigned the role of project director and field coordinator, and several universities were brought on board to aid in the project and analyze the data. Unlike previous efforts to study tornadoes, all the equipment and manpower available would be brought to bear on only one storm at a time, analyzing each twister in exhaustive detail to obtain as much data as possible from different vantage points and with myriad instrument types.

Data gathered by the mobile mesonet included the time and the exact position of the vehicle as determined by a GPS satellite. The temperature, relative humidity, and wind speed were also sampled, while a barometer constantly measured atmospheric pressure. Wind speed could be determined by accounting for the vehicle's direction and speed.

Twelve cars and five vans were outfitted with the latest in sensors designed to measure temperature, humidity, wind speed, and air pressure. The data would be gathered every six seconds and stored for later analysis and comparison. Another van would serve as a traveling command post where the field commander could constantly monitor the position of the other vehicles. The vans were equipped with weather balloons that would transmit upper-air information back to the convoy, which would form a "mobile mesonet" that could cover the tornado from all angles.

A Phalanx of Sensors

The crown jewel of project VORTEX was a mobile Doppler radar unit mounted on a truck that would allow researchers to intercept and study supercells and tornadoes wherever they occurred. This "Doppler on wheels" would become the most important element during the hunt, peering deep inside a supercell's mesocyclone to watch the actual birth of a twister.

Orbiting overhead as the convoy spread out around a storm were NOAA's WP-3D Orion (the same type of aircraft used by the Hurricane

Hunters) and a Lockheed Electra owned by NCAR. The two planes gave the project three-dimensional coverage of any target, using their belly radars to scan horizontally to determine a storm's internal structure, and their tail radar to scan vertically for wind speed information.

FIGURE 11-4:
Doppler on
wheels

(refer to page
281 for more
information)

VORTEX was launched in 1994, which turned out to be one of the slowest years ever for tornadoes in the target area. Even though there were no twisters to study, scientists practiced deploying the mobile mesonet and were able to gather data on several supercell thunderstorms.

A Major Success

Things changed in 1995, when the team was able to intercept nine tornadoes and study them at close range. One tornado that formed near Dimmitt, Texas, became the most intensely examined twister in history. On June 2, after gathering data on a tornado that destroyed part of the town of Friona, Texas, radar showed another mesocyclone forming near Dimmitt. The teams quickly moved into their assigned positions around the developing storm, and just as quickly, a tornado formed south of the town. The team was able to capture high-resolution Doppler data of the debris cloud caused by the tornado, as well as some video footage.

The tornado evolved into a powerful F4, literally sucking the pavement off a stretch of State Highway 86 and snapping telephone poles like matchsticks. Several vehicles were destroyed, and two trucks disappeared completely. Ten miles away, another tornado had formed, so the Electra was able to gather data from only one side of the Dimmitt storm. Even so, the planes were able to document how air flowed through the mesocyclone, and the ground units collected nearly 1,000 automated surface observations near the storm and around 1,000 additional measurements by balloon and other methods.

Some of the findings are:

- Most of the elements that lead to tornadoes are present in one small part of a supercell, allowing scientists to narrow their focus.
- Tornadoes can form rapidly at the beginning of a storm's life, in less than half an hour from the formation of the supercell.
- Before a tornado forms, a large invisible rotating segment of the storm's mesocylone already extends to ground level.

In 1997, a follow-up to the project, called Sub-VORTEX, was conducted, but with fewer vehicles and a tighter focus. Sub-VORTEX used two Doppler radar trucks to look into the same tornado from different angles, forming a two-dimensional image of the storm's interior. As Dr. Rasmussen said, "I think it's safe to say that VORTEX is going to revolutionize our understanding of tornadoes."

Chaser with a Twist

If every supercell thunderstorm produced a tornado, storm chasers would probably more often become storm chasees. Fortunately for Great Plains homeowners, supercell tornadoes are relatively rare. Most people became aware of the storm chasing phenomenon in 1996 with the release of the movie *Twister*. Unfortunately, rather than educating the public about the nature of storm chasing, the film created many misconceptions. In the movie, storm chasers are often less than a few hundred feet from a twister, and the funnels seem to pop up everywhere in rapid succession. But just as films tend to exaggerate the excitement of police work, *Twister* was an overdramatization of what can actually be a boring, frustrating pursuit.

Many storm chasers are also meteorologists, with experience and knowledge of how and where tornadoes are likely to form. Because a chase may require hundreds of miles of driving in a single day, expert chasers will often already be waiting in the area when a supercell forms instead of driving frantically toward it from miles away. Many new chasers wait until a warning has been issued for a particular area to strike out in search of a storm, but by then it's probably too late. In the world of tornado chasing, doing your homework pays off.

Veteran chasers recommend that, before taking to the road in search of tornadoes, budding chasers learn as much as possible about the pursuit first and sign up for one of the many chase tours now offered on the Internet and elsewhere.

Who Are They?

No matter what the danger, there will always be those who pursue these giant storms across the Midwestern flatlands. If you don't have a risk-taking gene, you may wonder what sort of person would risk his or her life for the slim chance of seeing a tornado. A few are scientists who are working under the auspices of a university or professional weather organization. Others are professional chasers who earn their income from the sale of storm photos and video. A very few are thrill seekers who like to put themselves in harm's way for the adrenaline rush.

The majority of chasers are ordinary people with a keen interest in meteorology and a love of nature. Some are fascinated by the mechanics of thunderstorms and supercells, and find a satisfying challenge in predicting their formation and comparing their forecasts with the experts'. Other chasers simply enjoy being outdoors and witnessing formidable weather phenomena. They'll tell you that there's nothing like the experience of watching a distant cumulus cloud grow into a towering thunderstorm, or watching a pitch-black squall line sweep across a golden field of wheat. Still others feel duty-bound to seek out violent weather and report it to the National Weather Service or other authorities, helping to save lives and adding to the growing body of research into severe storms.

ESSENTIALS

If you want to chase tornadoes to get rich, think again. Although some do make a living selling photos and videos, it's only after years of hard work and traveling many, many miles. Others host "tornado tours," but that requires a large investment in what is a very seasonal business.

While spring is the prime season for Great Plains tornadoes, late summer and early fall bring another type of cyclone to life: the tropical kind. While tornadoes can cause severe damage, their paths of destruction are usually confined to a relatively narrow track. Not so the hurricane, which can grow so large that its swirling winds can span entire states.

CHAPTER 12

Hurricanes and Other Tropical Troubles

The skipper he stood beside the helm,
His pipe was in his mouth,
And he watched how the veering flaw did blow
The smoke now West, now South.

Then up and spake an old Sailòr,
Had sailed to the Spanish Main,
"I pray thee, put into yonder port,
For I fear a hurricane."

—From "The Wreck of the Hesperus,"
by Henry Wadsworth Longfellow

Attack of the Cyclones

With hurricanes like Floyd, it's understandable why some view these violent storms as malevolent entities bent on the destruction of humans and their property. It seems inconceivable that something so large and deadly could possibly have a beneficial side. But hurricanes are really just giant heat engines that pick up warmth from the oceans in the warmer latitudes and transport it to the colder climates, helping to balance the earth's warm and cool zones.

SSENTIALS   Tropical disturbances often form when stormy weather over Africa moves offshore near the Cape Verde islands and begins to make its way east across the Atlantic. During the peak of the Atlantic hurricane season in September and October, some of the largest and most dangerous hurricanes form in this region.

When ocean waters are warm, humidity is high, and winds are light, the conditions are right for a hurricane to form, and the tropical Atlantic, the Caribbean, and the Gulf of Mexico provide this atmospheric mix every year from June through November. Hurricanes also need something to set them spinning, a job handled by the Coriolis force created by the earth's rotation. Because the Coriolis force is zero at the equator, storm systems must migrate at least 5 degrees north of it before they can pick up enough spin to become a hurricane.

Most hurricanes—about two-thirds—form between 10 degrees and 20 degrees latitude, along a constant feature called the Intertropical Convergence Zone, or ITCZ. This zone marks the area where northeasterly breezes meet southeasterly trade winds, causing the warm, humid tropical air to rise. As the air rises, it naturally condenses into clouds and rain, which often gather into groups of thunderstorms and move along the ITCZ from east to west.

Mixing the Ingredients

Like tornadoes, hurricanes can form only when a specific set of conditions is in place. Because they feed on heat, hurricanes need water that is at least 80 degrees F from the surface down to a depth of about 150 feet. The atmosphere above a developing storm must be substantially cooler than the surface, allowing the system to develop towering thunderclouds. The midlevel layers of the atmosphere must be saturated with water vapor, adding to the fuel that powers the storm. As noted earlier, hurricanes can't form at the equator, so a developing storm has to be at least 500 miles away from zero latitude to get going, and there must be at least some low-level spin in the atmosphere to get it started.

Unlike tornadoes, which depend on winds blowing in different directions at varying levels of the atmosphere to get them spinning, wind shear is a hurricane's enemy. Many potential hurricanes have been ripped apart by areas of strong wind shear aloft. But once conditions are right and a low-pressure system has developed at the surface, it can become a self-sustaining atmospheric juggernaut.

Although hurricanes usually begin in the tropics, they can wander far from their breeding grounds, bringing their own brand of mischief to northern climates. Many major hurricanes have battered New York City, and one model predicts that a Category Three storm could cause a storm surge of 20 feet at the Statue of Liberty.

As converging winds spin toward the center of the low, they are drawn into its core and rise upward, producing an area of high pressure above the storm. Although the upper air that helped the thunderstorms build initially is much colder than the surface air, it isn't long before the rising, warmer air heats up the air aloft and it begins to flow away from the top of the storm. This provides an exhaust port for the developing system, lowering the pressure at the surface even more and causing large quantities of humid air to be drawn into the rotating cyclone.

Feeding Frenzy

As the storm spins up, a chain reaction begins: More outflow at the top lets more hot air in at the bottom, resulting in faster surface winds pouring in and spiraling up through the storm's center. Until the winds reach 39 miles per hour, the storm is known as a tropical depression, and its main threat is rain and the potential for flooding if it moves over mountainous terrain or stalls over any land mass for an extended period.

FACTS

At this writing, forty storm names have been retired since 1954. Before 1953, a variety of naming schemes was tried, and after that, weather services began using female names for storms. In 1979, the current system of alternating male names with female was adopted.

When wind speeds exceed 39 miles per hour, the system is called a tropical storm and the National Hurricane Center assigns it a name from a list established by the WMO. The Atlantic Basin is assigned six lists of names, with one list being used each year. After six years, the first list is used again. If an especially destructive hurricane develops, its name is retired and no future storm will ever bear that name.

A 'Cane Is Born

A tropical cyclone is known as a tropical storm until its winds reach 73 miles per hour, when it officially becomes a hurricane. At that point, it can be measured on the Saffir-Simpson scale, a method of rating hurricanes developed by Herbert Saffir, an engineer who became interested in how wind causes damage to buildings, and Robert Simpson, who was director of the National Hurricane Center in the 1970s.

The scale rates hurricanes by their wind speed, barometric pressure, storm surge height, and damage potential in categories from One to Five. After Hurricane Floyd in 1999, which caused extensive flooding in eastern North Carolina, a need for an additional scale that would measure the risk of flooding was identified; its creation is still a work in progress.

QUESTIONS?

Has a hurricane ever exceeded a Category Five?
Not lately, but MIT researchers theorize prehistoric hurricanes may have reached 750 miles per hour or more. These "hypercanes" could have formed after asteroid impacts, wiping out whole species.

In the meantime, the categories and their characteristics break down accordingly:

Category One—Wind speeds of 73 to 95 miles per hour. Category One storms are not exactly harmless, but are still the least destructive hurricanes where winds are concerned. Most damage is usually confined to trees, shrubs, and unanchored mobile homes, although flooding can cause much more harm than wind. As the hurricane grows, it forms an eye in the center, a circle of relative calm where the sky may be blue and the winds light. Surrounding this area is an eye wall, a ring of intense thunderstorms that spin around the center of the hurricane.

Category Two—Winds of 96 to 110 miles per hour. The storm surge, a giant dome of water that moves along with the hurricane, can be from 6 to 8 feet above normal, causing coastal areas to flood in advance of the storm. Doors, windows, and roofing materials are all at risk in a Category Two hurricane.

Category Three—Winds range from 111 to 130 miles per hour. This storm kicks it up another notch, flooding low-lying areas near the coast with a storm surge 9 to 12 feet above sea level. The surge can move inland up to 8 miles, requiring some evacuations. At these wind speeds, mobile homes are completely destroyed and even concrete block homes sustain some damage. The foliage of shrubs and trees is blown off, and many trees are uprooted by the wind. Large structures near the beach are battered by floating debris carried by high waves.

Category Four—Winds of 131 to 155 miles per hour. Once a hurricane has this strength, you know it's extremely dangerous. Low-lying areas may be flooded hours before the storm moves ashore, and mass evacuations are necessary. The storm surge can reach a towering

13 to 18 feet above normal, causing major damage to any structures near the shore. The roofs are stripped off some homes and other buildings, and even external walls may fail. Signs, trees, and shrubs are torn from the ground and become flying missiles.

Category Five—Winds are *sustained* at over 155 miles per hour. Thankfully, Category Five storms are rare, but they are among the most treacherous winds on Earth. With a storm surge of more than 18 feet, these hurricanes leave major devastation in their wake. There is extensive damage to even strong buildings, and the complete destruction of others, especially those near the shoreline. Category Four and Five hurricanes making landfall near inhabited areas have caused some of the worst damage and loss of life in our nation's history. One such storm was Hugo, a giant storm that brought the highest storm surge ever recorded on the east coast of the United States—nearly 20 feet above sea level.

Only two Category Five hurricanes struck the U.S. coastline in the entire twentieth century: Camille and the 1935 storm that hit the Florida Keys. During the same period, an average of two major hurricanes every three years made landfall somewhere along the U.S. Gulf or Atlantic Coasts. In all categories, the average was about five hurricanes every three years.

Hugo the Huge

Hugo began as a classic Cape Verde tropical wave, slowly intensifying until it became a hurricane on September 13, 1989, when it was still more than 1,000 miles from the Leeward Islands. By September 15, a NOAA WP-3D Hurricane Hunter aircraft reported that Hugo's winds were screaming at an astounding 190 miles per hour at the 1,500-foot altitude. The turbulence and extreme wind shear damaged one of the plane's engines, which caught fire and was shut down. The plane plummeted from 1,500 to 800 feet before the pilot regained control in the hurricane's relatively calm eye.

FIGURE 12-1:
Hugo
decimated
Charleston

(refer to page
281 for more
information)

Drawing a bead on the Lesser Antilles, the giant storm smashed into the island of Guadeloupe on September 16, destroying half the capital city and killing eleven people. The next day, Hugo plowed through the Virgin Islands, leveling the island of St. Croix before it sideswiped Puerto Rico and headed northwest into the Atlantic as a Category Two storm. Forecasters issued warnings from Florida to North Carolina, and stores along the Atlantic seaboard were soon stripped of bread, milk, plywood, and other items as residents rushed to make last-minute preparations.

FACTS

There are two Hurricane Hunter squadrons, one based at McDill Air Force Base in Tampa, Florida, and the other at Keesler Air Force Base in Biloxi, Mississippi. The NOAA Corps, the nation's smallest uniformed service, flies WP-3D Orion and Gulfstream IV Hurricane Hunter aircraft, while Keesler's Fifty-third Weather Reconnaissance Squadron pilots large four-engine WC-130 transports into the hearts of the giant storms.

By September 20, it was obvious that Hugo was heading for South Carolina. Satellite views of the massive storm showed a giant white pinwheel larger than the states of North and South Carolina combined. Around midnight on September 21, Hugo howled ashore near Charleston, South Carolina, as a Category Four hurricane with sustained winds of up to 138 miles per hour, carving a path of destruction more than 150 miles wide. As roofs were ripped off historic buildings on the waterfront, bridges crashed into the sea, yachts were carried inland by the storm surge, and television towers were snapped like pencils by the screaming winds.

Storm Surge: A Hurricane's Most Deadly Weapon

NOAA estimates than nine out of every ten victims of hurricanes are killed by storm surge. Because hurricanes are huge low-pressure systems, some think the surge is caused by the storm's lower atmospheric pressure raising the sea level. While that effect is real and measurable, it is so small as to be insignificant when a hurricane makes landfall.

The storm surge is caused by the hurricane's winds piling water up ahead of the eye as it moves toward shore. As long as the hurricane is in the open ocean, there is no storm surge to speak of, because water that gets pushed up ahead of the storm has room to flow away. But as the storm approaches the coast, there is no room for the water to escape and it rapidly rises, sometimes in a matter of minutes, into a mountain of water. How high the storm surge will be above average sea level and how much damage it will do depends on several factors. One is wind speed: a Category Four storm will have a higher storm surge and cause much more destruction than a Category Two, for instance.

The storm surge isn't just another wave pushed ahead of a storm; it acts like a gigantic bulldozer that can destroy anything in its path. Think of the storm surge as a moving wall of water weighing millions of tons.

But just as important as the hurricane's wind speed is where you are in respect to the hurricane's eye. If you're behind and above a hurricane looking toward its direction of motion, the front part on the right side will have the highest wind speeds. That's because the hurricane's forward speed is added to the wind speed in that area, called the right front quadrant (RFQ). So, if a hurricane approaching land has sustained winds of 100 miles per hour, and it's moving forward at a speed of 20 miles per hour (a fairly fast-moving hurricane, by the way), winds in the RFQ will be measured by a stationary ground observer at 120 miles per hour. As you might guess, winds on the left side of a hurricane are rotating in the opposite direction, and won't cause as much damage.

Direction Makes a Difference

The storm's angle of attack is a key factor in its impact. Just as in an automobile accident, the highest level of destruction is caused by a hurricane hitting the coastline head-on. If a storm travels up the coast, with its left side brushing the seashore, the most dangerous part of the storm stays offshore and the net effect will be much less damage.

The shapes of the shoreline and the ocean bottom have a great deal to do with a storm surge's magnitude. The worst damage occurs when a developing surge meets a shallow seabed sloping gently to the beach, which is why areas like New Orleans are especially at risk.

The worst-case scenario would be a hurricane arriving onshore at high tide. With the ocean level already at its highest point of the day, the storm surge from a Category Four or Five hurricane can add another 15 or 20 feet of water, with abnormally large waves breaking on top of that. Water weighs around 1,700 pounds per cubic yard, and there are few structures that can stand up to the abuse a high storm surge can produce.

That's what happened during Hugo, when an astronomical high tide and the hurricane's storm surge ganged up on South Carolina beaches with a wall of water some 20 feet high. But the worst storm surge ever experienced in the United States was created by a Category Five hurricane that came ashore near Pass Christian, Mississippi, in 1969.

Camille's Trail of Terror

The storm that would become the second-strongest hurricane ever to strike the United States came to life as a tropical depression near the African coast on August 5, 1969. By the fourteenth, its winds were strong enough to earn it the name tropical storm Camille. By the next day, it was a hurricane with winds of 115 miles per hour, but after passing over Cuba, the storm had weakened considerably.

As the storm moved north into the Gulf of Mexico it stalled, rapidly gaining strength as it fed off the Gulf's warm waters. The National Hurricane Center issued hurricane warnings from Louisiana to the Florida panhandle, but jaded residents had seen many tropical storms and hurricanes come and go over the years and many remained complacent. At the Richelieu Apartments in Pass Christian, many of the residents gathered for a hurricane party as the giant storm lurked offshore.

A Killer Comes Ashore

On August 17, with Camille only 250 miles south of Mobile and churning steadily northward, a U.S. Air Force reconnaissance planewas dispatched into the hurricane, and their findings were stunning, even for seasoned forecasters. Camille's winds were now screaming at an unbelievable 200 miles per hour, and her central pressure was bottoming out at 26.61 inches of mercury. The Hurricane Center hastily doubled its 12-foot storm surge forecast to an unprecedented 24 feet.

Around 10:30 P.M., Camille's eye made landfall, smashing into the coastline with a 24.2-foot storm surge. Boats, barges, automobiles, and even a giant oil storage tank were picked up by the massive dome of water and deposited far inland as Camille scoured the Mississippi shoreline. The Richelieu Apartments were directly in the storm's path. In the book *Storm,* sole survivor Mary Ann Gerlach vividly recalls the sound of windows popping out as the hurricane's relentless winds smashed against them.

"We held our shoulders to the bedroom door to try to keep the water from coming in," Gerlach remembered. "But in about five minutes the bed was floating halfway to the ceiling. You could feel the building swaying like we were in a boat." Gerlach and her husband managed to swim out of their second-story window, but her husband was lost in the dark, swirling water. Gerlach seized a piece of floating debris and held on tight as the storm raged around her.

A minister and his wife had taken refuge at a 100-year-old church that night, but it was smashed by the storm surge and the wife was swept away. In Boothville, Louisiana, five meteorologists planned to ride out the storm in their hurricane-proof weather station, but they hadn't counted on Camille's exceptional surge. After a gust of 107 miles per hour, their anemometer blew away, and as the water continued to rise, it flooded the emergency generator. Trapped in a small building with ocean water lapping at chest level, the men waited through the long night for morning.

The Day After

At first light the next day, southern Mississippi looked like a war zone. Where buildings had once stood, only foundations were left. Mary Ann Gerlach was found clinging to a tree 5 miles from the Richelieu Apartments, which were now only a memory; the storm had claimed twenty-three of the residents. Camille destroyed more than 6,000 homes and nearly 700 businesses on its rampage, and 256 people lost their lives. When all the damages were assessed, the storm had cost the United States $1.4 billion, making it the most expensive disaster in the country's history up until that time.

ESSENTIALS

Hurricane parties had become common in the Gulf Coast region by 1969. They were an opportunity for family and friends to gather and thumb their noses at the weather, and sometimes to consume a great deal of alcohol. Party-crasher Camille showed how deadly that practice can be.

When Camille threatened, 150,000 people were evacuated along the Gulf shore. That sounds like a lot, but a Camille-class hurricane striking land today would cause a much larger exodus, because seaside populations have skyrocketed in the last two decades. Atlantic and Gulf Coast residents are fortunate to have ready access to satellite photos and radar images that can provide them with plenty of warning when a hurricane forms, but the sheer numbers of people who would face evacuation in the event of a major storm would no doubt cause severe problems.

Who's Next?

One American city especially at risk is New Orleans, which sits in a wide, shallow depression that puts the Big Easy below sea level. Nearby Lake Pontchartrain, with its millions of gallons of water, perches 8 feet above the city, although it's surrounded by a 15-foot levee. The nearby Mississippi River is also a threat to the low-lying metropolis, and a 20-foot levee holds the muddy waterway in check. But planners fear that a Category Three or Four hurricane and its storm surge could push Lake Pontchartrain or the Mississippi over its banks and flood the city to a depth of 20 to 30 feet, up to the first three or four stories of downtown buildings.

South Florida is another potential flashpoint, according to Dr. William Gray of Colorado State University, a prominent hurricane expert who has called the state "a sitting duck." No matter where you are in Florida, you're no more than 60 miles from the Atlantic or Gulf of Mexico, and during a mass evacuation, there would simply be no place to go. The danger is compounded in the Florida Keys, which has only one exit route: the Overseas Highway from Key West to Miami.

FACTS

Florida's location makes it an especially easy target for landfalling hurricanes, but the state has been extraordinarily lucky since the 1960s. Donna hit central Florida in 1960 as a Category Two storm, causing $6 million in damage, and Betsy blasted Miami and the Florida Keys in 1965 but it wasn't until Andrew in 1992 that the state experienced a taste of what the new millennium might bring.

Gray, who issues an annual hurricane forecast that has proven remarkably accurate, has been sounding the warning for several years, pointing out that the 1990s ushered in an era of increased hurricane activity and the potential for much more damage that may last for as long as thirty years. Given this forecast, Gray predicts that Florida, which he says has been "lucky" recently, will suffer ten times the economic losses in the next thirty-five years than it experienced during the previous thirty-five.

FIGURE 12-2:
Severe hurricanes: They're coming

(refer to page 281 for more information)

The reason: overbuilding along the coast, a phenomenon that's not limited to just the Sunshine State. Neil Frank, former director of the National Hurricane Center, put the problem in a nutshell: "While I was at the Hurricane Center, there was only a 10 percent improvement in forecast error in twenty-five years. At the same time, the coastal areas were just exploding in population. The increase in population is far surpassing any small improvement we are realizing in our ability to forecast hurricanes."

Not much can be done to prevent people from willingly putting themselves in harm's way, so the burden of providing hurricane warnings and instructions falls to forecasters and emergency managers. In the era of weather satellites, hurricanes and tropical storms can no longer escape detection as they once did; tropical weather systems are now tracked from the moment a disturbance forms.

So why aren't they always right?

Twists of Fate

Hurricanes are affected by a multitude of variables as they churn through the ocean, not just at the surface, but all the way to the top of the storm, passing through several atmospheric layers. Conditions in each layer can change suddenly and dramatically, causing a hurricane to suddenly weaken or to rapidly intensify. Aircraft observations are taken at several points within the storm, but at widely spaced intervals when a storm is well offshore. Along with other input, those few data points are used to predict the storm's future.

FIGURE 12-3:
Which way
will they go?

(refer to page 281 for more information)

This is where chaos theory comes into play. You'll remember that if the initial data fed into a computer model aren't perfect, the results of its calculations will become increasingly incorrect as a weather system's movements are plotted over time. That's why the Hurricane Center issues strike probabilities for hurricanes, based on the best current forecast track and factoring in prior errors. If this sounds like a big crapshoot, you're not far off. In trying to stay one step ahead of a hurricane, forecasters really have their work cut out for them.

As you might suspect, the closer a hurricane is to landfall, the more accurate its forecast track will be. But for hurricanes meandering offshore with no clear direction, forecasting is dicier. The Hurricane Center has been criticized in the past for issuing hurricane warnings that resulted in evacuations, but with no landfall occurring.

FACTS

Some hurricanes simply defy prediction. In 1999, hurricane Dennis flirted with the East Coast from Florida to North Carolina for days. After blowing through the Bahamas, the storm headed north and stalled off Cape Hatteras. After meandering around for a week, Dennis finally made landfall on the Outer Banks as a tropical storm.

During the approach of hurricane Floyd in 1999, 1.3 million Floridians were urged to leave their homes, many of whom ended up gridlocked on interstate highways for hours. But Floyd turned north and made landfall on the North Carolina coast, leaving some to grumble that the warnings were unnecessary.

A Necessary Hassle

Erring on the side of caution makes sense. It's estimated that Tampa, a city considered to be a prime hurricane risk, would take ten to seventeen hours to evacuate, and many of the roads out of the city are subject to flooding. In low-lying New Orleans, emergency managers plan to begin evacuations seventy-two hours before a hurricane's predicted landfall despite the high probability of a forecasting error. In Key West, hurricane shelters close when a hurricane greater than Category Two is approaching, and residents and tourists alike must make for the mainland over a two-lane highway subject to auto accidents and bridge trouble.

Forecasters do their best to balance the discomfort and inconvenience of a hurricane evacuation against the possible loss of life if they failed to evacuate. They're not always right, but they have no doubt saved many lives by moving people out of the paths of dangerous storms. Where hurricanes are concerned, "better safe than sorry" are words to live by.

Where the Action Is

The Atlantic Ocean is the most familiar hurricane source for U.S. residents, but there are other areas where tropical cyclone formation is common. There are seven "basins" where they occur:

- Atlantic Basin
- Australian/Southwest Pacific Basin
- North Indian Basin
- Northeast Pacific Basin
- Northwest Pacific Basin
- Southeast Indian/Australian Basin
- Southwest Indian Basin

In Mexico, hurricanes are known as El Cordonazo, while those that form in the Indian Ocean and Bay of Bengal are called cyclones. Typhoons originate in the western Pacific, while Australians must endure the Willy-willy's winds. In Haiti, hurricanes are Tainos, while in the

Phillipines they're Baguios. Whatever their names, hurricanes are best avoided if possible.

Unless, of course, you're a hurricane chaser.

Close to the Action

This relatively new pastime ratchets the tornado-chasing hobby up a level, as chasers endeavor to put themselves as close to a landfalling hurricane as possible. Unlike the Hurricane Hunter squadron, which tracks down the storms for scientific reasons, many follow hurricanes to photograph or videotape them for later sale, while others chase them for the sheer rush they get from being so close to an unstoppable force of nature. Some chasers spend their springs in Tornado Alley and their summers following the paths of hurricanes.

As with tornadoes, hurricane chasing is inherently dangerous and should not be attempted without a thorough knowledge of these storms and their power and preferably a tour or two with a professional storm chaser. Unlike most tornadoes, hurricanes cause widespread damage, and roads may remain impassable for days after a strong storm.

Whether you're chasing hurricanes or trying to avoid them, the most important element in your plan should be thorough preparation. The best ways to plan for, and stay safe in, violent weather are featured in a later chapter. Until then—be careful out there.

CHAPTER 13
Raining Fire

Then the Rabbit filled the paddle with hot coals and throw them up into the air and shouted, "It's raining fire! It's raining fire!" The hot coals fell all around the Otter and he jumped up. "To the water!" cried the Rabbit, and the Otter ran and jumped into the river, and he has lived in the water ever since.

—Cherokee children's story

Since the beginning of time, mountains spewing fire have transformed the earth, and wreaked havoc on animal life. Luckily, with advancing technology, scientists can now monitor and predict volcanic activity with better accuracy.

The Angry Saint

The pristine, snow-covered summit of Mount St. Helens had been living up to its Indian name *Louwala-Clough,* or "smoking mountain," for two months when dawn broke on May 18, 1980. The volcano that some called "America's Mount Fuji" had been rumbling and emitting steam for so long that many nearby residents had nearly stopped hearing it. But at 8:32 that morning, a magnitude 5.1 earthquake centered a mile beneath the mountain caused its entire north flank to collapse.

A huge avalanche of melting ice, earth, and debris raced downslope at speeds of up to 180 miles per hour, and without the burden of its outer shell, gas and steam that had built up to tremendous pressure within the mountain caused it to literally explode in a lateral blast that was heard hundreds of miles away.

Moving horizontally at nearly 670 miles per hour, just below the speed of sound, a hellish steamroller of magma, ash, and volcanic debris destroyed everything in its path to a distance of 19 miles from the mountain.

Following the lateral explosion, a plume of ash and steam launched skyward, reaching an altitude of 12 miles in ten minutes, finally punching through the stratosphere where it began to spread out. Around the remains of the mountain, lightning forked through the thick, swirling ash, starting forest fires. By noon, the cities of Yakima and Spokane were covered in a thick blanket of gray, choking ash. Before it was over, fifty-seven people were dead.

FACTS

Once dust and ash are injected into the upper atmosphere by an eruption, the debris can remain suspended there for years. Fortunately, the eruption of Mount St. Helens had no significant effect on global climate, due largely to the fact that most of its force was directed sideways instead of upward.

Scenes of the eruption of Mount St. Helens burned themselves into the national consciousness, and the explosion was the largest in the recorded history of the United States. But there have been far larger explosions, and their effect on the atmosphere has been much greater.

The Big Blasts

Television crews usually focus on spectacular fountains and streams of lava when covering erupting volcanoes, and no one will argue that they make compelling subjects. Volcanoes can eject lava bombs—blobs of magma the size of coconuts or larger—which are just as hazardous as they sound, and pyroclastic flows, which are avalanches of hot ash, pumice, and melted rock that can race down a mountainside at 100 miles per hour. But those effects are confined to a small area around the eruption. Far greater and more widespread are the effects of ash and other particles flung into the stratosphere by these exploding mountains.

The Cascade Range of the Pacific Northwest is home to more than a dozen potentially active volcanoes, including Mount St. Helens, and most of them tend to erupt explosively. The U.S. Geological Survey has set up a Volcano Hazards Program to watch these potential trouble spots, since some, like Mt. Hood, are close to major cities.

During the twentieth century, two volcanoes had a huge impact on Earth's climate: El Chichon in Mexico and Mount Pinatubo in the Philippines. The Mexican volcano spewed 120 tons of material into the atmosphere, and Pinatubo disgorged a stunning 310 tons, laden with caustic chemicals such as sulfur dioxide and hydrogen chloride, which can damage Earth's ozone layer.

As sulfur particles from volcanic eruptions drift in the upper atmosphere, they combine with water vapor, and as the particles are bombarded with sunlight, they mutate into sulfuric acid, which forms a hazy layer that reflects solar radiation back into space. With less solar energy reaching the surface, temperatures begin to drop. After the eruption of Mount Pinatubo, average global temperatures fell 1.5 degrees F.

A link between volcanic eruptions and global climate change was first established after the eruption of Krakatau, in the Sunda Strait between Java and Sumatra. The volcano, also known as Krakatoa, exploded in 1883 with a blast said to have been the loudest sound ever heard on Earth.

Ten times more powerful than Mount St. Helens, Krakatau's eruption caused tsunamis, giant waves more than 100 feet high that killed more than 36,000 people, and instantly vaporized two-thirds of the volcano. Its dust cloud covered 2 million square miles, lowering global temperatures for five years. The blast set off seismometers all over the world, and for the first time, scientists were able to gather observations from widely spaced locations in order to study the explosion.

FACTS

Accounts of Krakatau's aftermath include tales of brilliant sunsets that could be seen all over the world for weeks after the eruption, caused by the enormous quantity of ash pumped into the stratosphere by the blast. The sky became so bright in New York and Connecticut that some residents thought their cities were ablaze and called local fire departments.

The Mother of All Eruptions

Even Krakatau wasn't the largest volcanic eruption in recorded history: Sixty-eight years earlier, a volcano named Tambora exploded in Indonesia, spewing 150 times more ash into the upper atmosphere than Mount St. Helens did in 1980. The column of dust, ash, and debris rose to a height of 28 miles before collapsing on itself, causing devastating pyroclastic flows to sweep down to the ocean. Around 10,000 people died in the explosion and its immediate aftermath, but Tambora wasn't through causing misery.

In the months to come, thousands more would die on nearby islands as epidemics and famine swept through their midst. As the unimaginably huge cloud of ash spread farther across the globe, it began to trigger climate changes far and wide. In China, the skies above Hainan Island went black, obliterating the Sun and destroying crops and trees.

By the next year, known as "the year without a summer," economic losses were piling up as far away as North America. In June 1816, severe frosts killed Northeast farmers' crops as they repeatedly tried to replant. In Vermont, foot-long icicles hung from the trees while ice an inch thick covered ponds and lakes. Newly shorn sheep died by the thousands, and so did migratory birds caught in the icy weather's grip. At Williamstown, Vermont, the temperature at 5 P.M. on one June day was recorded at 30.5 degrees F.

SSENTIALS

On the shores of Lake Geneva, the gloomy weather prompted Lord Byron to suggest that his houseguests join him in a ghost story–writing contest. Byron and Percy Shelley abandoned their attempts before long, but Shelley's wife, Mary, conjured a story of a ghoul named Frankenstein that made literary history.

The Danville, Vermont, *North Star* described the scene under the headline "Melancholy Weather":

> *On the night of the 7th and morning of the 8th a kind of sleet or exceeding cold snow fell, attended by high wind, and measured in places where it drifted 18 to 20 inches in depth. Saturday morning (8th) the weather was more severe than it generally is in the winter. It was indeed a gloomy and tedious period.*

Things weren't much better in Europe, which was just recuperating from the Napoleonic Wars. In Britain and France, riots broke out as food shortages loomed, and in Switzerland the violence caused the government to declare a state of national emergency.

Forecast: Explosive

After studying eruptions for decades, volcanologists now understand that a volcano's history is one major key in forecasting its future. Volcanoes such as Kilauea in Hawaii erupt on a regular basis and in a predictable manner, and because they don't generally erupt explosively, they can be monitored with sensitive instruments that provide clues to the conditions that exist just before an eruption.

SSENTIALS Volcanoes give many clues before erupting, including underground earthquakes that become more frequent and intense before a blast—activity that scientists call seismicity. Volcanologists can now measure and track the shock waves generated by these temblors with seismometers, which record quakes' magnitude and epicenters as magma flows deep below the surface.

Angle of Attack

Melted rock can also push upward toward the surface until the volcano's "skin" is distorted into a pressure-filled dome. Before Mount St. Helens erupted in 1980, the mountain began to develop a huge bulge on its north face that grew at the rate of more than 5 feet per day. Geologists were able to track the growth of the bulge using a device called a Geodimeter, which can measure very small changes in distance with reflected light. By the day of the eruption, the instruments showed that some parts of the north face had bulged outward more than 450 feet from their original positions.

FACTS Scientists are getting some assistance from space in their continuing quest to accurately predict volcanic outbursts. Earth-observing satellites can spot rising underground pools of magma from orbit. The upwellings, which often precede an eruption, show up as "hot spots" on digital images.

Scientists also employed tiltmeters at St. Helens; as their name implies, they can measure minute changes in the slope angle or tilt of the ground. Tiltmeters work much like a carpenter's level: The movement of a bubble floating in conducting fluid is monitored electronically, and any change in the bubble's position is translated into a degree of tilt and relayed to a base station. Tiltmeters are so sensitive they can measure a change in angle as small as 0.00006 of a degree!

Another tool used in forecasting eruptions is a correlation spectrometer, which measures how much sulfur dioxide is being emitted by a volcano. These emissions tend to increase markedly before an eruption.

Positive Predictions

In 1991, scientists were able to use all these devices to successfully predict the eruption of Mount Pinatubo. It first gave warning by generating a series of earthquakes, followed by an increase in sulfur dioxide emissions. Then, the sides of the volcano began to swell outward. Alarmed authorities evacuated nearby Clark Air Force base and 58,000 residents who lived within 20 miles of the volcano just days before the mountain exploded in one of the most powerful eruptions of the twentieth century.

CHAPTER 14

The Worst of the Worst

The Westerly Wind asserting his sway from the south-west quarter is often like a monarch gone mad, driving forth with wild imprecations the most faithful of his courtiers to shipwreck, disaster, and death.

—Joseph Conrad

N o matter how bad the weather in your neighborhood gets, it has almost certainly been worse at some point in recent history. During the twentieth century, a few disasters forever seared themselves into the public consciousness.

The Johnstown Flood—1889

When the South Fork Fishing and Hunting Club bought 400-acre Lake Conemaugh and 70 acres of land near Johnstown, Pennsylvania, in 1879, the aim was to provide a fishing and vacation retreat for wealthy Pittsburgh industrialists and businessmen such as Andrew Carnegie, Henry Frick, and Andrew Mellon.

The earthen dam that held back the lake's waters had fallen into disrepair, so the club's president, Benjamin Ruff, began reinforcing it with rocks, hay, mud, and tree stumps, and didn't bother to replace the discharge pipes that had been removed by the previous owner. Although plagued by problems, the construction was finally finished in 1881, leaving the new dam 72 feet high and 918 feet wide. The lake was stocked with black bass and the clubhouse was opened soon afterward.

Johnstown lay 14 miles downstream in a flood plain at the fork of the Little Conemaugh River and Stony Creek. Many of the town's 30,000 residents viewed the dam as a menace; no engineer had planned its reconstruction, and the 3-mile-long lake loomed a full 450 feet above the town. Said one worried resident, "No one could see the immense height to which that artificial dam had been built without fearing the tremendous power of the water behind it. . . . People asked why the dam was not strengthened, as it certainly had become weak, but nothing was done, and by and by they talked less and less about it."

Buildup to Disaster

On May 30, 1889, a hard rain began and continued through the night. The U.S. Signal Service estimated that between 6 and 8 inches of rain fell in just twenty-four hours, carrying 10,000 cubic feet of water into Lake Conemaugh each minute—enough to fill an Olympic-sized swimming pool every three and a half minutes. By morning, the club's resident engineer, John Parke Jr., saw that the water level was only 4 feet below the top of the dam, its 20 million gallons putting immense pressure on the earthworks. Repeated attempts to shore up the weakened structure failed, and at 11:30 A.M., Parke jumped on his horse and galloped down to the town of South Fork directly below the dam to warn of the danger. He also sent two men to the South Fork telegraph station to alert Johnstown.

Because Johnstown was located in a floodplain, periodic inundations were nothing new to the residents, and many ignored the warnings. At 3:10 P.M. on May 31, the dam collapsed, and a wall of water 40 feet high swept down the narrow valley, tearing out trees, boulders, and telegraph poles and adding them to its boiling fury. The inhabitants of Johnstown heard a low rumble in the distance that soon turned into "a roar like thunder," as one survivor would later describe it.

First came a violent wind that blew down frame houses, and then the 40-foot wave crashed into the town, pulverizing buildings with huge chunks of debris carried by the raging waters. When the flood smashed through a wire factory, miles of barbed wire were added to the thundering debris. The deluge swept onward, racing through the town until its thousands of tons of wreckage encountered the old stone railroad bridge below the river's fork.

The Bridge to Hell

There, 45 acres of timber, rock, and barbed wire smashed many victims against the bridge, and some of those who escaped being crushed were burned to death as the oily mass caught fire. As rescue workers desperately attempted to reach the victims, some of whom were still trapped in the remains of their homes, the flames spread until they engulfed the entire mass of debris, burning with "all the fury of hell" according to one newspaper account. In all, 2,209 people lost their lives in the flood.

It took Johnstown five years to recover from the disaster, and yet no legislation was enacted to protect residents from future floods. In fact, despite the considerable loss of life, it would take more deaths and forty-seven more years before serious flood control efforts were begun.

The Great Galveston Hurricane—1900

As the residents of Galveston, Texas, opened their morning papers on Saturday, September 8, 1900, many noticed a small news item on page 3 about a tropical storm in the Gulf of Mexico. Due to the lack of effective communication channels, no further information was available. But the Weather Bureau had issued a storm warning the previous day, and sure enough, clouds and gusty winds were blowing over the city as many residents left home to put in the last day of what was for most a typical six-day workweek.

Known by many as the "New York of the South," Galveston in 1900 was a prosperous city of 38,000 people looking forward to the new century. Home of the only deepwater port on the Texas coast, it was also the thriving center of America's cotton export business; the kind of place where millions of dollars could be made by those with the right connections. In short, it was a great place to live.

But the city had an Achilles' heel: It was built on an island of sand some 30 miles long, separated from the mainland by 2-mile-wide Galveston Bay. The island's average height above sea level was only 4.5 feet in 1900, but residents had been assured by meteorologists and geographers alike that the wide, sloping sea bottom that led to the island protected them against incoming storms.

One such meteorologist was local Weather Bureau chief Isaac M. Cline, who had long maintained that the island was not only safe from hurricanes, but that anyone who felt differently was delusional. So far, Cline had been right: Major storms had hit Galveston in the past, but none of them had caused severe damage, and as residents left their homes for work, they were secure in the belief that their city was safe.

A Theory Disproved

But Cline was startled to see the barometer plummeting that Saturday morning, the tide rising steadily against a strong offshore wind that should have kept it at bay. Cline took to his horse-drawn carriage and raced down to the beach, telling everyone he encountered to get to higher ground. Few listened: The waves crashing on the beach were a magnificent spectacle, and many had traveled from the mainland just to see them.

But as the storm approached land, the wind shifted, and with nothing to hold them back, the Gulf waters crashed into beachside homes and other buildings, shattering them to bits. Terrified residents ran inland, but there was nowhere to go: The bridges to the mainland had been destroyed by an errant barge, and rising waters were intruding from Galveston Bay, trapping thousands.

FIGURE 14-1:
Hurricanes launch deadly missiles

(refer to page 281 for more information)

By 3 P.M. the entire island was submerged, and refugees climbed onto roofs and into trees to escape the steadily rising water. At 5:15 the Weather Service anemometer blew away after recording gusts of 100 miles per hour, and at 6:30 a giant storm wave driven ashore by the approaching eye suddenly raised the water level to 15 feet. As the waves crashed through the darkening city, they tore entire buildings from their foundations and swept them into the bay.

Some who tried to make their way to safer shelters at the height of the storm were killed by slate shingles flung from rooftops, while others were bombarded with flying bricks and timber. As floodwaters rose around St. Mary's Orphanage, nuns frantically rushed their young charges to the newly built girls' dormitory. But by nightfall, the winds were screaming at an estimated 150 miles an hour, and after the dormitory's roof collapsed, the nuns cut down a clothesline and lashed the children to them like mountain climbers to keep everyone together. Sadly, the orphanage collapsed in the midst of the gale, sweeping ninety-three children and ten nuns into the black, churning water.

A Staggering Death Toll

The next morning, stunned survivors were met with a scene of utter desolation. Many of those who had ridden out the storm were naked, having been stripped of their clothing by wind and water-driven debris. Galveston Bay was adrift with dead bodies, both human and animal, and as many as 10,000 people were left homeless. The number of deaths was estimated to be between 10,000 and 12,000, but the poor record keeping of the time made it impossible to be sure.

Isaac Cline survived, but sadly, his pregnant wife did not: Her body was later found in a mound of debris. Three boys from St. Mary's Orphanage were found clinging to a tree, bruised and battered but still alive, the only orphan survivors of that fateful night. Many families had been completely wiped out by the storm, which became known as the most deadly natural disaster in the history of the United States.

With rising heat and humidity, disposal of the thousands of bodies became a priority. At first, barges were loaded with bodies and sunk in the Gulf, but when the corpses began washing up on the beaches, burning became the preferred tactic. By the following Tuesday funeral pyres were burning all over the city. The grisly job of stacking and incinerating the bodies fell to laborers, who were plied with whiskey to dull their senses; others were forced to perform the thankless task at gunpoint.

Reconstruction and Remembrance

Once again, Clara Barton arrived to care for the survivors of the hurricane in what would be her last relief mission. The Red Cross founder was now seventy-eight years old, but she was still able to establish an orphanage and help obtain lumber for the rebuilding process, raising money by selling photographs of the devastation. Barton later wrote of the scene, describing it as so horrific that her workers "grew pale and ill" and that even she, who had seen so much heartbreak and devastation in her life, "needed the help of a steadying hand as I walked to the waiting Pullman on the track, courteously tendered free of charge to take us away."

With Galveston's sense of security literally gone with the wind, efforts were begun to construct a 17-foot-high seawall that would run 3 miles along the shoreline. In addition, the entire city was raised as high as seventeen feet by propping buildings up on pilings and pumping fill underneath. In 1915, another hurricane struck Galveston, but only eight people died, proving that the city's efforts to protect itself had been successful.

Disaster planners estimate that it would take forty hours to evacuate the 65,000 people who now live on the island, and plans to close the causeway to the mainland when winds reach 39 miles per hour mean that many could once again be trapped with no place to go. So despite the sea wall and other precautions, Galveston remains a city at risk.

FACTS

At Coney Island in 1902, vacationers could visit a re-creation of the Galveston flood. Entering the Galveston Flood building, visitors saw a miniature model of the city spread out before them. Then viewers watched as a flood of both real and fake water combined with other special effects to simulate the destruction of the real Galveston.

The Tri-State Tornado—1925

If the Weather Channel had been around to broadcast the warning, the great Tri-State Tornado of 1925 might not have gone down in history as the most lethal ever to touch down in the United States. But in that year, Prohibition was still in full swing, television was years away, and radio was still so new that the first World Series broadcast had taken place just four years earlier.

FIGURE 14-2:
A tornado's indiscriminate destruction

(refer to page 281 for more information)

Even if the media had been ready, forecasting was still in its infancy; weather watchers had no way to predict that a severe thunderstorm forming in southeast Missouri on the afternoon of March 18 was about to brew up a monster. The twister formed near the town of Ellington around 1 P.M. and began spiraling toward the northeast. Within minutes, it had leveled the small town of Annapolis, taking the lives of four people, before destroying the town of Biehle and killing four more.

An F5 Freight Train

The storm then sliced across the Mississippi River into Illinois at 60 miles per hour, bearing down on Gorham, where it virtually wiped the town off the map and killed or injured nearly half its 500 residents. Observers later said the twister's base was a mile wide at that point, and some recalled that it looked like a bad thunderstorm approaching, since it lacked the traditional funnel shape. By the time victims recognized the storm's true nature, it was too late; outrunning the fast-moving tornado in a 1920s automobile was simply out of the question.

The monster tornado now drew a bead on the town of Murphysboro, where it leveled three-quarters of the city and killed 234 people. One eyewitness described seeing a house explode like a bomb after being flung into the air by the cyclone. The storm swept into De Soto, destroying 30 percent of the town and bringing death to sixty-nine of its residents, and then plowed on into Parrish, leaving nothing in its wake but foundations.

SSENTIALS An unprecedented combination of factors made the Tri-State Tornado a unique storm. With winds of more than 300 miles per hour and a 62 miles per hour average ground speed, it was the fastest-moving tornado in history—an F5 on the Fujita scale.

As the tornado passed a barometric recording station at West Frankfort, it recorded the lowest air pressure ever—an amazing 28.87 inches of mercury. The tornado crossed the Wabash River into Indiana with a ground speed of 73 miles per hour—more than twice as fast as an average tornado—as it destroyed Griffin and several more towns and farms before dissipating near Princeton.

The Long Run

The Tri-State Tornado stayed on the ground longer than any tornado in history. Most long-lasting tornado outbreaks produce multiple twisters born of cyclical supercells, and they repeatedly disperse and regenerate as the system moves along. As a result, the ground tracks of these on-again/off-again storms tend to stop and start as tornadoes break off and then reform within the supercell.

The unbroken path carved by the Tri-State Tornado underscores the exceptional nature of this storm. Not only did it rage across America's heartland for three and a half hours where most tornadoes last only fifteen minutes or so, but it stayed on the ground so long that it blasted a continuous path of destruction 219 miles long across three states. The storm's death toll reached 695, with property damage estimated at $16.5 million.

The Super Outbreak—1974

Nearly fifty years after the Tri-State storm, another weather event would occur that proved the importance of early warning systems. On April 2, 1974, a cold air mass over the Rocky Mountains was heading directly toward a warmer blanket of humid air flowing northward from the Gulf of Mexico. Forecasters at the National Severe Storms Forecast Center couldn't determine exactly where, but they were certain that severe storms would form within twenty-four hours in the middle or lower Mississippi Valley, and they advised local weather station offices throughout the area to be on the alert.

Some municipalities have contemplated eliminating their tornado siren systems after being spared for a number of years. If your city no longer has a warning system, weather radios that automatically turn themselves on when a warning has been issued are available and recommended.

Around 2 P.M. Central Daylight Time, two tornadoes touched down at nearly the same moment in Gilmer County, Georgia, and Bradley County, Tennessee. For the next sixteen hours, one tornado after another churned to life, slicing through thirteen states from Mississippi to Michigan. The outbreak was unprecedented in U.S. weather history: In less than twenty-four hours, 148 tornadoes churned across America, 6 of which grew into giant F5 twisters with winds as high as 318 miles per hour. The previous year, only one F5 storm was recorded in the United States, and some years there are none at all.

Timely Warnings

One of the cities hardest hit by the outbreak was Xenia, Ohio, where an F5 tornado destroyed half the town in just nine minutes. A local television channel spotted the approaching twister on its radar scope and broadcast the image of its hook echo, and police cruisers took to the streets with loudspeakers, warning residents to take cover immediately.

The massive tornado entered the city around 4:30 in the afternoon, ripping apart a housing development before leveling the downtown business district, leaving a trail of wreckage 2,000 to 3,000 feet wide. The tornado destroyed schools and businesses with equal fury and went on to demolish 85 percent of Central State University. It took out 9 churches and 1,333 homes and businesses, and left thirty-three people dead in the wake of its rampage. After the storm, 200 trucks a day rumbled through Xenia's rubble-strewn streets to clear away the debris, but the process still took more than three months. On a wall at City Hall, a small plaque pays tribute to those who died on that terrible day.

Tragedy and Triumph

In all, the super outbreak took 330 lives and injured 5,550 people in a wide swath from Georgia to Illinois, causing damages totaling $600 million in 1974 dollars. By the time it was over, storm warnings had been issued for nearly half a million square miles, and tornadoes had directly affected more than 600 square miles of countryside.

But few would argue that many more lives would have been lost if not for the warnings issued by the National Weather Service and other agencies. Even without the benefit of modern NEXRAD radar and high-resolution satellite images, the Weather Service saved lives by issuing 150 tornado warnings and 28 severe weather watches during the developing disaster, helping to keep the death toll at less than half that of the Tri-State tornado, even though the affected area was much larger.

Andrew—1992

As a tropical storm, Andrew was something of a bust by the time the first Hurricane Hunter flight reached it on Wednesday, August 19, 1992. Still far out in the Atlantic with no clear center of circulation and rising barometric pressure, Andrew seemed to be a storm looking for a place to die.

FIGURE 14-3:
Evil eye: Andrew approaches

(refer to page 281 for more information)

But meteorologists at the National Hurricane Center in Coral Gables, Florida, knew better than to turn their backs on the storm. Andrew was moving into an area where strengthening was possible, although none of the computer models agreed on just where it might go. In the early hours of Saturday, August 22, Andrew became the first hurricane of the year. With a large dome of high pressure building to the north of the storm, Andrew had picked up speed and was turning farther to the west by evening, with sustained winds blowing at 110 miles per hour.

Residents along Florida's southeast coast awoke the next morning to find themselves under a hurricane watch, and many went in search of canned food, bread, and other staples, while others stripped home improvement warehouses of plywood. By midmorning the sound of hammers could be heard up and down the coast as windows were boarded up and other last-minute preparations were rushed to completion. Some locked up their homes and drove north or west, away from the approaching storm.

The Threat Intensifies

By noon, Andrew's winds had increased dramatically to a sustained speed of 135 miles per hour, gusting to 165. A crew of meteorologists was dispatched from National Hurricane Center in Miami to NOAA headquarters in Washington, D.C., in case the center was disabled, since it now appeared as if Andrew would score a direct hit there. As night fell, Hurricane Center director Dr. Bob Sheets was the man in demand, fielding questions from a team of television reporters and issuing warnings and reports. On a monitor behind him, viewers watched a radar image of Andrew churning toward Florida like a giant red buzz saw.

As midnight approached, forecasters were alarmed to see that Andrew had gained even more strength as it passed over the warm waters of the Gulf Stream. Now screaming at 145 miles per hour, Andrew's winds were gusting to an incredible 175 miles per hour as it bore down on the Florida peninsula. That same day, Hurricane Center meteorologist Stan Goldenberg's wife had borne their first baby girl, and afterward he had rushed home to help his three sons and his sister-in-law's family prepare for the storm.

In the Teeth of the Gale

Just before 5 A.M., the 2,000-pound radar dome on the Hurricane Center's roof came crashing down after a wind gust of 150 miles per hour.

At Goldenberg's home, the winds had ripped plywood shutters from the windows, and flying debris had sent glass shards flying into the house. The family fled to the kitchen, but the roof blew off and the walls began to fall around the frightened group. At the Hurricane Center, the howling winds finally destroyed the anemometer after it recorded its final reading: 164 miles per hour.

As bad as Andrew was, research scientists say that hurricanes could get a lot worse if the earth's atmosphere continues to heat up. They also speculate that in the event of an asteroid or comet impact, which rapidly heats ocean water, the result could be a "hypercane" 20 miles high with winds near the speed of sound.

As dawn arrived the following morning, the winds were finally dying down, and dazed survivors emerged from the wreckage of their homes to a scene many likened to the aftermath of the bombing of Hiroshima. Most trees were completely gone, and those few that remained were nothing but splintered trunks. The devastation stretched on for miles, with a few homes relatively untouched while others nearby were razed to their foundations. With streets covered with debris and landmarks either gone or unrecognizable, rescue workers became lost as they responded to emergency calls. Goldenberg and his family had survived the night after taking refuge at a neighbor's house, but they returned to their home to find it mostly destroyed, one of its concrete-block walls resting on top of the family car.

Andrew's Aftermath

The days to follow would be even more trying for residents, as the heat, humidity, and lack of water and electricity took their toll. In the days following the storm, dazed homeowners picked through the wreckage, trying to salvage what they could while waiting for government relief workers to arrive. As bureaucrats bickered over what to do and when, Dade County Emergency Management Office director Kate Hale angrily asked, "Where the hell is the cavalry on this one?"

FACTS

As residents turned their attention to rebuilding after Andrew, thousands of itinerant construction workers descended on south Florida, some honest and others less so. With housing scarce, many settled in a tent city dubbed Camp Hell by the police, who were forced to constantly patrol the area as stabbings and shootings became common.

On Friday, a full four days after Andrew had ripped Dade County apart, 8,000 National Guard troops finally arrived with portable toilets, ready-to-eat meals, tents, food, and other necessities. Earth-moving equipment was brought in to clear streets of debris, and the business of clearing and rebuilding began.

Good Versus Evil

The aftermath brought out the best and worst in human behavior. Atlanta-based Home Depot set up three tent stores in addition to its twenty-five Dade County locations and sold the basic products for restoring walls and roofs at cost. Members of the Grocery Manufacturers of America distributed food to hurricane victims free of charge, and cities all over Florida and in other states took up donations for relief supplies. The Charleston, South Carolina, Chamber of Commerce sent a team of disaster-resource specialists battle-hardened by Hurricane Hugo. By the weekend, twelve tent cities were taking shape with room for 36,000 people.

As *Miami Herald* reporters investigated the damage, they discovered that many newer homes had been lost due to shoddy construction. Dade County building codes are among the most stringent in the country, but the *Herald* found that overworked inspectors were simply unable to cover all new construction adequately. Significantly, it was also discovered that a fourth of campaign contributions during the past decade had come from the building industry.

The Final Toll

Andrew killed fifty-three and caused $25 billion in damage, making it the costliest storm in U.S. history. One hundred twenty-five thousand homes were partially or totally destroyed by the storm, and 7,800 businesses were affected, putting 120,000 out of work. The advanced state of hurricane prediction and massive evacuations were the main reasons why the death toll wasn't higher.

The *Miami Herald*'s findings indicated that south Florida had actually dodged a bullet: Had Andrew made landfall just 20 miles farther north, the damage would have been three times worse and would have affected five times as many people in south Florida. A more northerly track might have also taken it directly into New Orleans.

There is a common misconception that Andrew was a Category Five storm, but with its officially recorded 145-mile-per-hour sustained winds, it rated only a Four on the Saffir-Simpson scale. Nevertheless, Andrew was a wake-up call, not only for south Florida but for all East Coast residents. The last major hurricane to hit the area had been Betsy in 1965, followed by a lull that lasted an entire generation. Andrew brought that period of calm to a violent end, but it raised the public's awareness of the killer storms and made it much less likely that anyone would be caught unaware by the next one.

The Oklahoma/Kansas Outbreak—1999

It's estimated that an F5 tornado strikes an urban area an average of only once every 100 years. In the twentieth century, it happened just as the millennium was drawing to a close. Ironically, the storm hit very near the NSSL in Norman, Oklahoma, which has the responsibility of providing the entire country with forecasts and warnings of tornadoes and other severe weather. This time, the danger was in its own back yard.

May is the most active time for tornadoes on the Great Plains, and the month was only three days old when giant black thunderstorms began to form over Oklahoma. During the next eleven hours, a total of seventy-six twisters would be born, more than half of them in the Oklahoma City area. That afternoon, forecaster Mike Vescio was alarmed at a series of satellite images showing the rapid growth of several supercells near the city. Doppler radar showed they contained the mesocyclones that often spawn tornadoes, and at 4:30 P.M. Vescio issued a tornado watch for much of the state. Television stations picked up the bulletin and began broadcasting warnings in their coverage areas. All around Oklahoma, residents who were alerted by neighbors, family members, and warning sirens tuned in to watch the developing storms.

The Media Storm

At television station KWTV Channel 9, Oklahoma City's CBS affiliate, meteorologist Gary England was alarmed by the giant red blobs that had appeared on his Doppler screens. "This was bigger, meaner, uglier, nastier than anything I had ever imagined," he remembered. England and his crew watched with horrified fascination as a giant black wedge churned into view of the station's outdoor cameras. England immediately took to the air, warning his viewers: "This is extremely dangerous, so you folks in the path of the tornado, get below ground. If you can't do that, get in the center part of your house."

QUESTIONS?

Does El Niño cause tornado outbreaks?
David Schultz of the NSSL says, "Tornadoes happen every year regardless of whether we're in a La Niña or El Niño. The best studies conducted to date show tenuous evidence for a link between tornadoes and the phase of El Niño."

In the city and its surrounding areas, people heeded England's words and other warnings from the media, running to their storm cellars or hiding in closets, bathrooms, and hallways as the twister approached. Others burrowed under pillows and mattresses. One man hid his family in a walk-in closet in their master bedroom, pulling a mattress over them for good measure. When the tornado struck the house like a barreling freight train, it tore away the closet's walls and ceiling but left the family with only minor injuries.

As it became clear the tornado would miss the station, England was able to give street-by-street reports on the twister's position as it thundered through the city. The giant cyclone stayed on the ground for an hour and a half—bad news for the residents of Oklahoma City—but it allowed tornado researchers a relatively long time to gather observations that might aid in future storm prediction.

Scientific Convergence

As luck would have it, a team from the NSSL and the University of Oklahoma had picked May 3 to begin VORTEX-99, a follow-up to the original tornado research project of 1994 and 1995. VORTEX-99's three teams encountered one of the first tornadoes in the outbreak near Elgin, Oklahoma, and were able to surround it and several other tornadoes with their mobile mesonet vehicles, watching the birth and death of the funnels with high-tech instruments.

In addition to the WSR-88D radar that had proven so effective at peering into the guts of previous tornadoes, a new fine-scale radar was used in the Oklahoma outbreak, slicing into the twisters like a CAT scan to show details of their internal structure. The images clearly showed for the first time that a tornado's inner funnel is not round, but contains distortions along the walls that may be caused by internal vortices.

The outbreak took forty-eight lives, but according to Harold Brooks, head of the Mesoscale Applications Group at the NSSL, perhaps as many as 700 might have died if not for the early and widespread warnings made possible by technological innovations and forecasters' hard work. "The National Weather Service modernization effort was designed to provide forecasters with a superior level of technology to make it easier for them to issue very accurate warnings, which is exactly what happened during this event," said James Belville, Director of the NEXRAD Operational Support Facility.

CHAPTER 15

Playing It Safe

In difficult and hopeless situations the boldest plans are the safest.

—Titus Livy, Roman historian

Staying safe from hazardous weather is a lot like playing chess: The farther ahead you plan, the more likely you are to win. With lightning, floods, hurricanes, and tornadoes wreaking havoc all over the globe, it sometimes seems the weather is out to get you, but planning for every possible scenario can pay off when disaster strikes.

Dodging Thunderbolts

A powerful thunderstorm is one of nature's most awesome shows, and a vivid lightning display can often send the curious outside to watch. But lightning can travel great distances from its source, and there's really no safe outdoor location when a thunderstorm's around. Research by the National Lightning Safety Institute has shown that there are some places you just don't want to be in or near during an electrical storm:

- In large open spaces or high spots
- In unprotected outdoor structures such as gazebos
- Near any high objects such as telephone poles or flagpoles
- Near any metal objects such as bleachers or fences
- Near bodies of water
- Under trees

Safer places include fully enclosed vehicles such as cars, trucks, and buses, as long as the windows are rolled up and you stay away from any metal parts such as window handles or gearshifts. You may have been told that the tires on your car protect you from lightning because rubber is a good insulator. Yet air has great insulating properties as well, but lightning blasts right through it. If a bolt of lightning has traveled many miles to reach your car, a couple of inches of rubber aren't even going to slow it down.

SSENTIALS

The reason cars make safer havens in a storm was discovered by Michael Faraday, a nineteenth-century British scientist who found that electromagnetic fields would not penetrate a metal grid. When lightning strikes a metal vehicle, the car protects its occupants by carrying its current through the frame, leaving passengers unharmed.

If you're in a car when a severe thunderstorm strikes, the best thing to do is simply to pull off to the side of the road, taking care to leave plenty of room between you and the highway if possible. Then turn off the engine, turn on your emergency blinkers, and wait for the bad weather to pass. If you're in a car with a body made of fiberglass or composite plastics, you should seek shelter in a safer place such as a metal automobile or a building. Although a metal car's frame may protect you, the car itself may not be so lucky: Police reports show that lightning can blow out tires, destroy an automobile's electrical system, and, not surprisingly, completely ruin the paint job.

Staying Safe, Inside and Out

The best place to be in a thunderstorm is indoors, preferably in a large building. If the delay between seeing a lightning strike and hearing the thunder is less than thirty seconds, it's time to get away from the windows and find an interior room. Other indoor tips:

- Avoid bathing or using water until the storm passes.
- Stay off the telephone (cordless and cell phones are okay).
- Turn off and unplug appliances, computers, TVs, and power tools.

FACTS

A single lightning strike can kill several people if they're close together. If you're in an outdoor group when lightning threatens and there's no shelter nearby, make sure everyone spreads out so there are several body lengths between each person. If you're at a sporting event or concert, get up and make your way to an exit.

If you're caught outdoors with no immediate shelter, get to the safest location you can, away from trees, water, and metal. If you feel your hair suddenly standing on end or your skin begins to tingle, there's a good chance a lightning bolt is coming. To make a smaller target, put your feet together and crouch as low as you can. Tuck your head down and cover your ears. When the immediate threat passes, get to a safer place as quickly as possible.

What if, despite your best efforts, someone in your group is hit? Call 911 immediately. The victim may not be breathing, since lightning can cause cardiac and respiratory arrest, so it's vital to maintain brain oxygen levels with cardiopulmonary resuscitation (CPR) and mouth-to-mouth ventilation while waiting for emergency services to arrive. Don't be afraid to touch the victim; no residual electrical charge remains in a person's body after a lightning strike. If you're outside in an active thunderstorm, consider moving the victim to a safer location.

Avoid These Charges

Lightning kills 20 percent of its victims on the spot, and the survivors often suffer long-term effects such as seizures, confusion, weakness, paral-ysis, and depression. According to a study by the National Weather Service and the Severe Storms Laboratory, males account for around 84 percent of lightning fatalities and 82 percent of injuries. Between 1959 and 1994, there were 3,239 deaths and 9,818 injuries caused by strikes, making light-ning the second-worst weather-related killer after floods.

A lightning bolt lasts only a fraction of a second, but in that time it can pump 300 kilovolts (300,000 volts) of electricity through a victim. Compare that to the 120 volts carried by your home electrical system, and you can see that there are very good reasons to take cover when the next thunderstorm hits your area.

Don't Go with the Flow

The best precaution you can take against being in a flood is to determine a prospective home's flood history before moving in. But even if you've been in your current location for some time, finding out if you're in a flood-prone area allows you to take precautions you might otherwise forego. Many residents of eastern North Carolina didn't realize they were living in a 100-year floodplain until after Hurricane Floyd ravaged the region in 2000, washing many homes away and making even more unlivable with its muddy floodwaters.

Homeowner's insurance doesn't cover flood damage, so ask your insurance agent how to apply for separate coverage. You could be eligible for insurance via the National Flood Insurance Program, but only if your community has decided to participate. To join, a municipality must agree to adopt and enforce ordinances that restrict construction in floodplains, which helps reduce both flooding damage and insurance rates.

FACTS

To find out if you're in a potential flood zone, contact your local Red Cross chapter, emergency management agency, or National Weather Service office. FEMA also maintains a list of areas that are prone to flooding. The agency's Flood Risk Maps help identify whether a specific location falls in or near a Special Flood Hazard Area (SFHA), subject to inundation by 100-year floods.

First Steps

Once you know your flooding risk, you're in a much better position to take action when a flood is imminent. If it looks like your area is in for an extended period of rain, filling your car's gas tank is a good first step; when the power goes off, most gas pumps won't operate. Water service may be affected, too, so fill up clean jugs and other containers with water and store them tightly capped. It's good to have at least 3 gallons of water per person on hand. Buy food that doesn't need refrigeration or cooking, and store it in sealable plastic bins on the higher shelves in your pantry. Most important, make sure you have first-aid supplies available.

A good rule of thumb is to keep at least three days' worth of necessities on hand for emergency situations. You can keep all the necessary items in a disaster kit, which should include:

- Extra car keys, cash, and credit cards
- A first-aid kit and extra prescription medications
- A cell phone, battery-powered radio, flashlight, and extra batteries
- Two changes of clothing for each person
- Blankets and sleeping bags
- Towels and rubber gloves
- Any special items needed for infants or the elderly

This is where the rest of the family comes in. Before the first storm cloud appears on the horizon, sit down and discuss what each person's responsibility will be in case of an emergency. Pay special attention to family members with special needs, as well as your pets. The more you have settled calmly in advance, the less you'll have to worry about when the time comes.

Write down all the steps to be taken. Select a relative or friend as a contact person, and post that person's phone number, as well as emergency numbers, in a prominent location. If you don't already know, learn how to turn off gas and electric services, and explain the process to the rest of the family. Teach children how to dial 911, and explain when it's okay to call and when it's not.

When It's Not a Drill

When a flood is possible, the National Weather Service will issue a flood or flash-flood watch. This means that conditions that can cause flooding are developing in your area, and it's a good time to review your flood plan and be prepared to evacuate if instructed to do so. Move valuables to the higher floors of your house or into the attic.

If you're outdoors when a flood threatens, get to higher ground and stay there until the risk has passed. Get as far away from rivers, storm drains, streams, and creeks as you can. Do not attempt to cross a flowing stream if the water is more than ankle-high.

When a flood or flash flood has actually been reported or is imminent, the Weather Service issues a flood warning. Stay tuned to television or radio broadcasts, and be ready to move at a moment's notice. Have your disaster kit readily available. If told to evacuate, don't delay—get out as fast as you can. Flash floods often leave little time for escape, and evacuation routes can quickly be blocked by rising waters.

Cars Make Lousy Boats

If you're driving, avoid areas that are already flooded or where water is flowing. Below the water's surface, the roadway could be damaged or washed away, and it's often impossible to determine how deep the water is, especially at night.

Nearly half of all deaths caused by flooding happen in automobiles. Because water weighs 62.4 pounds per cubic foot, it exerts tremendous pressure on anything in its way. Every foot that floodwaters rise below a car displaces 1,500 pounds, in effect making the car weigh that much less. Unless a car is already flooded, 2 feet of water can turn it into a floating death trap, so if your car stalls during a flood, get out immediately.

ESSENTIALS

If you find that stored food has been in contact with floodwaters, dispose of it. If you have a well, have it pumped out and get the water tested before assuming it's safe to drink. If you're on city water, boil it before use until you're notified that the water supply is safe.

After a flood, most evacuees understandably want to return to their homes as soon as possible. Although the water may have receded, entering a flooded building may still be hazardous. Electrical wiring may have developed dangerous short circuits and should be inspected and repaired before the power is restored. Floods can also destabilize a building's internal structure, so be cautious until it has been inspected and declared sound. Wearing a hard hat or other protective headgear is always a good idea.

Floods are the number one cause of weather-related deaths in the United States, killing an average of 139 people each year. However, armed with knowledge of your area's flood history and a solid disaster plan, you and your family can avoid the danger when the hard rains come.

Tornado Survival 101

If you live on the Great Plains, you're no doubt aware that your area catches the brunt of tornado action each spring. But the Midwest has no exclusive contract with the atmospheric funnel factory; tornadoes can occur just about anywhere, at any time of the day. Tornadoes generally travel from southwest to northeast, but their movement depends on local upper-level winds, and they've been spotted heading in just about all directions.

The giant funnels are not only the most violent storms on Earth but also the most unpredictable, underscoring the need for thorough preparation before tornado warnings flash across your TV screen. The erratic nature of tornadoes means that they can form without warning, so if you see a funnel in the distance, alert the police, a local television station, or a disaster management office immediately; it could help save many lives.

FACTS

If you see ragged clouds rotating around the base of a thunderstorm, it's evidence of a mesocyclone that can give birth to a funnel cloud. Sometimes there will be dust and debris being kicked up under a storm, even though there's no funnel; that just means the vortex hasn't sucked up enough material to become visible—yet.

Of course, if you see a tornado forming near you, your own safety should be your main concern. Knowing what to look for is important, because a tornado doesn't always form in a neat Wizard-of-Oz shape, and can even be totally hidden by curtains of rain. Falling hail can be a cautionary sign if your area is under a tornado watch or warning, although it also falls in severe thunderstorms. Perhaps the most obvious indication is a rumbling or roaring sound that increases in volume; many have said an approaching tornado sounds like a freight train or jet.

As with other types of severe weather, a disaster plan is a must. Know where you'll take cover when a tornado threatens, and practice getting to safety with your family until the process becomes automatic. One of the safest places in your home is a corner of your basement. If you don't have a basement, the next best place is a windowless interior space such as a closet or bathroom on the lowest floor of the house. If there is a siren warning system in your area, make sure your family understands what each type of tone indicates. Show everyone where the first-aid kit, fire extinguishers, and emergency numbers are kept. Pick a nearby meeting area for the family to gather in the event the house is destroyed. Select a contact person in another part of town as a check-in point if family members are separated during a storm.

When a tornado watch is issued by the National Weather Service, it means that conditions are ripe for a twister to form in or near the watch area. This is the time to locate your disaster kit and have it handy. Turn on the TV or a radio and stay tuned to a local station for current information.

A tornado warning means that a twister has been spotted on the ground in your area, or is indicated by weather radar. This is when you should activate your family disaster plan. Most importantly, get away from all windows immediately. Most tornado injuries are caused by flying debris, and glass shards are at the top of the list. There's no need to partially open a window to reduce the pressure; if a tornado hits your house, it will take care of that for you!

Taking Shelter

FIGURE 15-1:
Tornadoes can form suddenly

(refer to page 281 for more information)

When you get to your prearranged safety area, get under something sturdy like a heavy table or work-bench, or cover yourself with a mattress, several layers of blankets, or a sleeping bag to protect yourself from flying objects. If you're in the basement, make sure there's nothing heavy such as a piano or refrigerator on the floor directly above you; it could come crashing down if the tornado hits your home.

Mobile home residents should leave as soon as a tornado watch is issued and go to a neighbor's house or other safe place. Although today's manufactured homes are much more well constructed than they used to be, they're still no safe haven in a tornado. Even if a mobile home is tied down, it is likely to be destroyed by the 200- to 300-miles-per-hour winds a tornado can generate.

Following the Plan

Most schools and businesses have disaster plans and hold drills from time to time, so follow the prearranged plan when a tornado warning comes. You'll no doubt be instructed to get away from windows and take cover in an interior room in the center of the building. Stairwells also make good refuges, since they're built to support heavy weight and provide a means of exit. When you get to a sheltered place, crouch down and protect the back of your head with your arms.

If you must go into a damaged building, don't use a lighter or matches; the twister could have broken gas lines. And watch out for downed electric lines, glass, nails, and other sharp objects; one study showed that 50 percent of injuries from a tornado happen after the fact.

Cars and trucks are not safe refuges in a tornado; if you've ever seen footage of a huge twister tossing vehicles around like toys, you already know that. Although it's possible to outrun a tornado in a car if the roads are clear, there's good visibility, and there happens to be an escape route away from the twister, it's much more likely that rain will block your view and you'll end up in a traffic jam with other fleeing motorists. The best thing to do is pull off the road and seek shelter in a sturdy building. If you're driving in the countryside when a tornado threatens, quickly park the car and run to low ground, away from any object that could fall onto you. Lie facedown and protect your head with your arms.

Take a Pass on the Overpass

You may have seen the dramatic 1991 footage of a television crew taking refuge under a highway overpass as a tornado roared overhead, leaving them unharmed. This has led to a widespread misconception that overpasses are safe hiding places from a tornado. The fact is, the people in the video are extremely lucky to be alive; their tornado was a relatively weak one and didn't score a direct hit on the overpass where they had taken cover.

When a tornado strikes, an overpass becomes a wind tunnel, concentrating and funneling wind and debris like air through a jet engine. They have no handholds, and as the tornado passes, victims can be suddenly exposed to violent winds from the opposite direction.

On May 3, 1999, seventeen people took shelter under an overpass on I-35 in Oklahoma as an F5 tornado approached. When the tornado hit, only one person was able to hang on; the rest were blown out of the underpass and one was killed.

Once a tornado has passed, get your family together and wait for emergency crews to arrive; your first-aid kit will be useful if there are any minor injuries. If your house has been heavily damaged, it's best to stay out of it due to the danger of collapse.

Making a Shelter

Years ago, storm cellars were common in tornado-prone areas, but many newly constructed homes lack them due to the additional cost. Today many homeowners are creating a different type of refuge, either during or after construction of their homes. They're called safe rooms, strengthened areas within a house with extra fortification to withstand the extreme conditions that come with tornadoes and hurricanes. Additional information about building a safe room is available from FEMA, which has created a guide to building such a shelter. It's available online or by contacting FEMA directly.

If you don't live in a flood-prone area, a good place to put a safe room is in the basement, but a cellar shelter must have its own reinforced roof, separate from the basement ceiling. Think of a storm shelter as a self-contained shell with a roof and walls that are isolated from your home's structure. That way, if the outside walls of your home are blown away by a hurricane or tornado's winds, they won't take the walls of your safe room with them.

ESSENTIALS

A safe room must be anchored to your home's foundation, with strong connections between all of its components to resist being torn apart. It must be readily accessible from all parts of the house, and should be solid enough to withstand the impact of flying wind-driven objects.

If you have no basement, an interior space such as a closet can be retrofitted as a shelter, as long as you have enough room to add walls and a ceiling that isolate it from the rest of the house. The materials used in shelter construction are readily available from building supply stores, so whether you build a safe room yourself or hire a contractor, finding construction materials shouldn't be a problem. Take extra care selecting a door for your shelter; it's usually the weakest point in a safe room.

FACTS

If you live in a hurricane zone, the best time to review your disaster plan is before the season starts in June. Your insurance policy probably covers damage from wind and rain but may carry a special hurricane deductible. Make sure you carry enough coverage to rebuild your home if it's demolished by a storm.

Handling Hurricane Hazards

Many homeowners would much rather confront a hurricane than a tornado. For one thing, today's advanced forecasting methods and a hurricane's relatively slow forward motion give you some time to prepare, which is more than you can say for flash floods and tornadoes. Still, it's never too early to begin preparations before these tropical behemoths come beating on your door.

During hurricane Andrew, many homes' roofs were ripped off and flung through the air like Frisbees. Later it was discovered that some roofs weren't even attached to the frame; builders had relied on gravity to keep them in place. You can inspect your home for this oversight by climbing into the attic and looking for metal straps holding the roof trusses to the walls. Hurricane straps attached firmly to wall studs are a must if you live in a hurricane-prone area. Bracing trusses with two-by-fours running the length of the roof is also a good idea; each stud should overlap across two trusses.

FIGURE 15-2:
Hurricanes often spawn tornadoes

(refer to page 281 for more information)

Long before a hurricane's outer bands begin to sweep across your neighborhood, you should have all your important papers tucked away in a safety deposit box or other secure place, and give copies to a friend or relative, preferably one in another town or state. Items to stash away: insurance policies, birth certificates, passports, identification cards, irre-placeable photographs and heirlooms, and removable computer disks containing backups of your valuable data. Take "before" pictures of your home and any valuable items and store them safely as well.

Should You Stay or Should You Go?

It's important to decide exactly where you and your family will ride out the storm well ahead of time. For most people, except those with mobile homes and anyone in a flood-prone area, riding out the hurricane at home is the preferred course, because hurricane shelters will most likely be jammed with refugees if a major storm threatens.

Some find it easier to buy canned goods, snacks, bottled water, and other necessary items before the hurricane season starts, then consume them after the season is over. Doing this can save you a last-minute, desperate journey to the grocery store, only to find long lines and bare shelves. If you intend to cover your windows with plywood shutters, buy them ahead of time, cut them to size, and install the anchors and bolts you'll need to mount them; then store the panels and hardware in an easily accessible location. If you think groceries disappear quickly when a hurricane's coming, just wait until you see how popular plywood can be.

Authorities don't recommend trying to escape the area by car, because massive traffic jams usually form on all outbound roadways well in advance of a hurricane. If you must drive, leave as far ahead of the storm as possible, and don't leave without a confirmed destination.

If you must go to a Red Cross shelter, make sure you've exhausted all other options first. Shelters can supply only the most basic of needs, and may not have beds or medical care available. Conditions will probably be uncomfortable at best, and if a hurricane stalls, you could be spending a lot of time in close proximity to hundreds of other people. Unless that sounds appealing, you'd be better off finding a friend or relative to stay with if you can.

The Wind Is the Enemy

Most wind damage caused by hurricanes is caused when wind gets into a structure and blows it apart from the inside, so job number one is to keep the wind out of your house. The most vulnerable places for wind to enter your home are the doors and windows, so they need special attention before a storm strikes. New impact-resistant laminated windows are available if expense is no object, but shutters are more affordable and work just as well. Precut plywood panels are even less expensive; make sure they're at least ¾ of an inch thick.

QUESTIONS?

Does taping windows help?
No. Masking tape won't keep windows from breaking, and it takes valuable time away from your other important preparations. Besides, you'll spend many a frustrating hour trying to scrape off the baked-on glue after the sun comes out.

If you own a boat that can't be moved by trailer, secure all deck gear, sails, dinghies, and anything else that could be lost during a storm or damage another vessel. Under no circumstances should you try to ride out a hurricane on a boat, even if it's docked in a marina. After a major storm, it's common to see boats that have sunk, been thrown onto the shore, or been stacked like toys by the wind and storm surge. If your boat is on a trailer in your yard, move it as close to the house as possible, avoiding any trees that might fall when the storm hits. You can do the same thing with your car if you don't have a garage.

If you live in a mobile home, check the straps and anchors that tie it to the ground before you leave for safer shelter. The number of straps required varies by state, but a good rule of thumb is one tie-down at each end and one for every 10 feet of length. Tighten any loose straps to keep the home from shifting during a storm, and make sure the concrete block piers supporting the frame are vertical, not leaning at an angle.

If you live in a multistory apartment building or condominium, be aware that winds are stronger at higher levels. Make sure you know the location of the nearest exit, and if you live in an upper-story apartment, see if you can stay with a neighbor on a lower floor. Many condos are located near the shore and will be evacuated when a hurricane warning is issued. Do yourself a favor and find a safer refuge well before you're forced to leave.

Don't be fooled if the winds suddenly stop and the sun comes out during a hurricane; that just means you're in the eye of the storm. It might be just a few minutes until the winds return from the opposite direction, possibly even stronger. Even when the storm is finally past, the danger is by no means over. As you venture outside, watch for downed power lines and anything touching them. Snakes, insects, and other animals are often driven to higher ground by a storm, so be careful when clearing debris. When you have time, take "after" pictures of your home and possessions for the insurance adjuster.

You can't control the weather, but by being prepared to act at the first sign of trouble, you and your family can stay one step ahead of whatever the atmosphere has in store.

CHAPTER 16

Under the Weather

Hark how the chairs and tables crack!
Old Betty's joints are on the rack;
Her corns with shooting-pains torment her
And to her bed untimely sent her; . . .
'Twill surely rain,—I see with sorrow
Our jaunt must be put off to-morrow.

—Edward Jenner,
eighteenth-century discoverer of vaccination

As if tornadoes and hurricanes aren't bad enough, the weather can be dangerous in less obvious ways, affecting not only life and limb but also your health and well-being.

Allergies: Nothing to Sneeze At

Your eyes are red and swollen, your nose is runny, and you've got the mother of all sinus headaches. They seem like classic cold symptoms but could just as easily be an allergic reaction. It's been estimated that up to 20 percent of the population suffers from seasonal allergies, a collection of maladies that doctors call *allergic rhinitis*. This so-called hay fever usually strikes in spring and can last all the way through summer into fall, generating an estimated 10 million doctor's office visits in the United States each year.

Allergic rhinitis can be traced to airborne pollen and mold spores, allergens that come from a wide variety of sources. Tree pollen accounts for only about 10 percent of allergies in the United States, striking mainly in late winter through spring. You may have awakened one morning to see a thick layer of yellow or green pollen on your car; it's caused by pine trees and doesn't generally trigger allergy attacks. The real culprits are particles of pollen from deciduous trees such as oak, maple, and elm.

FACTS

Grasses cause 30 percent of pollen problems from spring through fall, but the primary offenders are weeds, which account for 60 percent of seasonal allergies. Ragweed is one of the worst: A single ragweed plant can produce a billion grains of pollen, each one smaller than the diameter of a human hair.

Airborne pollen can travel for hundreds of miles, so pulling up all the suspect plants in your neighborhood may not solve the problem. Ragweed is so tenacious and bent on self-preservation that a dry summer will cause it to stop growing and put all of its energy into the production of pollen. If you suffer from seasonal allergies, use your air conditioner, which filters out pollen; dry your laundry in the dryer, not outside on the clothesline; spend your time outside in the morning, when pollen counts are lowest.

Respiratory Rebellion

An even bigger menace is asthma, which affects nearly 12 million Americans and kills around 5,000 annually. The most common type is allergic asthma, which is triggered by many of the same environmental factors as allergies. There is also exercise-induced asthma, thought to be caused by dry bronchial tubes, and infectious asthma, which begins after a viral chest infection. The fourth kind is occupational asthma, contracted when workers come in contact with an asthma-inducing substance on the job. Predictably, their symptoms are worse during the week but improve on the weekends.

ESSENTIALS

Pollen and mold spores can also create problems for emphysema and chronic bronchitis patients by irritating bronchial tubes, worsening symptoms. A sudden drop in temperatures can also bring on respiratory distress, causing bronchial spasms, congestion, and coughing fits. The twin threats of emphysema and chronic bronchitis are collectively known as chronic obstructive pulmonary disease (COPD).

Emphysema is caused by a swelling of the lung's air sacs, or alveoli, and once it occurs, the damage is irreversible. Chronic bronchitis is caused by irritation of the bronchial tubes over a long period of time, thickening their linings and creating shortness of breath and a predisposition to infections. Weather doesn't directly cause COPD—smoking is the usual suspect—but cold air can cause symptoms to worsen.

Forecast: Aches and Pains

On the old television show *Sanford and Son,* curmudgeonly patriarch Fred Sanford insisted his aching joints could predict a change in the weather. You probably know one of these "human barometers," but scientists pooh-poohed the whole idea of humans as weather predictors until fairly recently. In the 1960s, Dr. Joseph Hollander, emeritus professor of medicine at the University of Pennsylvania, conducted the first controlled study of the weather's effects on people with joint and bone problems. He built a barometric chamber where atmospheric pressure could be controlled, and moved in eight patients with rheumatoid arthritis and four with osteoarthritis. The twelve subjects lived in the climate-controlled chamber for two weeks, and during that time, only one person failed to respond to any weather changes. Seven other subjects found that their symptoms worsened 73 percent of the time when the chamber's humidity was increased and the barometric pressure lowered, establishing a clear link between weather conditions and human discomfort.

Many doctors still pooh-pooh the idea of weather-related pain. But others say that since arthritis increases pressure in the joints due to increased joint fluid, lowering the barometric pressure causes the inflamed joint to swell, stretching the inflamed joint lining and capsule and causing discomfort.

Once the link between weather and pain was established, physicians and biometeorologists got to work on finding the causes. Robert N. Jamison, Ph.D., of Brigham and Women's Hospital and Harvard Medical School in Boston, Massachusetts, explains that there are many possible mechanisms: "Because tendons, muscles, bones, and scar tissue are of various densities, cold and damp may expand or contract them in different ways. Sites of microtrauma may also be sensitive to expansions and contractions due to atmospheric changes. Changes in barometric pressure and temperature may increase stiffness in the joints and trigger subtle movements that heighten a nociceptive [injury-caused] response."

Jamison's research, reported in the "Influence of Weather on Report of Pain" (IASP newsletter, July/August 1996), also notes that changes in barometric pressure may cause a "disequilibrium" in body pressure that could sensitize nerve endings and account for increased pain preceding changes in temperature or humidity. Because the weather can also affect mood, it's possible that it could increase the perception of pain in those affected. According to Jamison, moving to a different area won't help, because the body can quickly adapt to new climatic conditions. It's the change in temperature, humidity, and air pressure that causes joint and bone problems, not prevailing conditions.

The Cold Truth

A cold snap may cause some aches and pains, but extremes of hot and cold weather can really do some damage. When the temperature plummets, your body's systems are stressed as they struggle to maintain a sufficient internal temperature. Your body's first reaction to cold is the constriction of blood vessels in the skin to reduce the amount of heat lost and to detour blood to your vital organs. You may start to shiver, which produces heat through involuntary muscular contractions, and your body releases hormones designed to stimulate heat production. When the length of your exposure to the cold is prolonged, however, your body's core temperature begins to decline and hypothermia results.

When Frost Bites

Frostbite is another very real danger when cold weather hits, and it can also be accompanied by hypothermia. Frostbite has four distinct phases: In the first stage, blood vessels constrict, leaving the affected tissue starved for oxygen. When the tissue temperature drops below 24.8 degrees F, the second stage is marked by the growth of ice crystals in the skin, which damage the tissue's cellular structure. During the third stage, fluid leaks from blood vessels into the damaged tissue, and in stage four the blood vessels clot, cutting off all blood supply and causing massive cell death in the affected area.

Untreated, hypothermia can kill. Early signs include numbness in the extremities and a noticeable loss of coordination. The victim will often shake uncontrollably and show signs of mental confusion or apathy. In advanced stages, the patient can become incoherent and unable to walk or stand.

Frostbite symptoms are similar to those of hypothermia: The victim feels extremely chilly, with increasing numbness and decreasing coordination. As the damage progresses, fluid-filled blisters form, and in severe frostbite, the blisters are deeper and permeated with a purplish fluid. When the tissue is warmed up again, it will often swell and turn darker.

First Aid and Prevention

The best treatment for frostbite or hypothermia is to get the victim to an emergency room or doctor's office as soon as possible. If help is more than two hours away, a frostbite victim's affected body part should be slowly brought back toward normal temperature in water at 100 to 105 degrees F, and care should be taken not to allow it to refreeze, since permanent tissue damage would almost certainly occur. For cases of mild hypothermia, try to get the victim moving; exercise generates warmth. Build a fire or get the person near a source of heat. For more severe cases, wrap the patient in as many layers of dry blankets or wool clothing as possible, and then add a layer of plastic. Try to keep the victim out of direct contact with the ground.

FACTS

To prevent cold-related injuries, wear layered clothing to insulate your body against the elements. Avoid getting wet: Water conducts heat away from the body twenty-five times faster than air, especially when evaporation is enhanced by a stiff wind. If exercising or hiking outdoors, stop whatever you're doing and warm the area immediately if you see or feel evidence of a cold injury.

It's Not the Heat, It's the Hyperthermia

The opposite of hypothermia is hyperthermia, when your body can't keep itself cool enough to maintain normal function. An early stage of hyperthermia is called heat exhaustion, when an excessive loss of water causes the body's internal temperature to rise. Someone suffering from heat exhaustion will appear pale and sweaty, and can often be dizzy and experience nausea or vomiting. A victim's skin will sometimes be cold and clammy. The person should be moved to an air-conditioned building and given water or a sports beverage and watched for improvement; if none is seen in thirty minutes, an emergency room should be your next destination.

Heatstroke is hyperthermia gone berserk. With heatstroke, the victim's internal thermostat, or heat-regulating system, has broken down. Symptoms include complete disorientation, difficulty walking, cessation of sweating, fainting, and unconsciousness. The victim's skin will be hot and dry, and his pulse rate may rise as high as 160 beats per minute. Because heatstroke can be fatal, a victim should be cooled down as quickly as possible, using ice packs or cool water splashed on the skin. The person's legs should be elevated, and plenty of fluid should be given. If no medical facilities are nearby, the victim should be wrapped in wet clothing or bedding before transport to the nearest hospital.

Cramping Your Style

Less severe than heatstroke or heat exhaustion are heat cramps, but they can still ruin a perfectly good day outdoors. Heat cramps feel like a severe muscle pull in the calves or other muscles, and are usually brought on by exercising in hot weather before you've built up enough conditioning; a lack of fluids can also play a part. The best remedy is rest in a cool place.

Preventing heat-related illnesses requires listening to your body; it usually gives warning signs before succumbing to heat exhaustion or heatstroke. If you know ahead of time that you'll be exposed to heat and humidity for long periods, try to acclimate yourself by spending some time in those conditions beforehand. When you're working or playing in the heat, take frequent breaks and drink plenty of fluids. Don't wait until you're thirsty; replace lost fluids on a preventative basis. And stay away from alcohol; it makes your body work harder to stay cool.

Shun the Sun

Sunlight is essential for human survival; it aids in the production of vitamin D, which prevents a disease called rickets, and is a potent mood elevator. But even limited exposure to the Sun's rays can cause sunburn in fair-skinned people and children, and long-term exposure can create wrinkles and leathery skin as well as a very dangerous form of cancer called melanoma.

Your skin contains melanin, a pigment that gives skin its color and provides some protection from UV solar radiation. The more melanin in the skin, the longer it will take to burn, so light-skinned people may burn in as little as fifteen minutes in the noonday sun, while the darker-skinned can stay out for hours. But eventually even the most UV-resistant skin will suffer damage from prolonged exposure, and unlike a burn caused by a match or hot stove, a sunburn tends to sneak up on you. The pain may not peak until six to forty-eight hours after exposure, and then your skin can swell, blister, and peel for days.

Just one bad sunburn doubles your chances of eventually contracting malignant melanoma, the most deadly form of skin cancer known. Scientists now think there may be a link between repeated sunburns in childhood and the development of melanoma later in life.

Doctors recommend wearing a sunscreen with an SPF factor of no less than 15 (about the same protection as a cotton T-shirt) when you're planning to spend time outside. Studies indicate that most people apply only half as much sunscreen as researchers do when they're assigning SPF numbers, so be sure to apply the lotion liberally and reapply it after swimming or heavy perspiration.

Umbrellas, hats, and clothing are other good ways to prevent sunburn, and it's a good idea to avoid the beach between 11 A.M. and 1 P.M.—that's the time when the Sun's UV bombardment is at its daily peak. Unfortunately, the effects of solar radiation are cumulative, so the more time you spend in the sun, the more likely it is you'll eventually have skin problems.

Cooler Heads Don't Always Prevail

Too much sun can give you a bad sunburn, but just trying to survive in the heat can strain some people's coping skills to the breaking point. If you've ever been stuck in a traffic jam when the temperature is flirting with the 100-degree mark, you know firsthand that it's hard to stay cool, both physically and emotionally. Some scientists now theorize that hot, sticky weather can cause aggressive behavior, something you've probably always suspected.

People become more aggressive when it's hot, say these astute researchers, because the heat makes them cranky. Being physically uncomfortable changes the way people perceive their environment, and even a minor insult or slight could be taken as a major one, inviting a negative response. According to scientists, heat induces a pattern of aggressive thoughts and hostile feelings that needs only a small push to become active. Think of a small summer fender-bender that escalates into a name-calling session, or an accidental bump in a hot, crowded bar that leads to a fist-fight. Scientists also point to statistics showing that violent crime increases in years with above-average temperatures, and is also higher overall during the summer.

Depressed or Just SAD?

If too much sun can cause crankiness and antisocial behavior, too little can be just as harmful in its own way. The link between heat and aggression remains unproven, but there is now little doubt that long periods of gray, gloomy weather can bring on a crushing case of the blahs. It even has a name: seasonal affective disorder, or SAD for short.

FACTS

SAD is a mood disorder that brings on periods of depression, but unlike other types of depression, these episodes happen only at certain times of the year, usually in fall and winter. According to the National Mental Health Association, SAD was first noted as far back as 1845, but it took nearly 150 years for the mental health industry to label it as an illness.

SAD Symptoms

Symptoms of SAD include carbohydrate craving, weight gain, over-sleeping, and other depressive symptoms such as lethargy and a feeling of hopelessness. The first signs of SAD usually make an appearance in October or November and begin to subside in March or April as spring approaches. Doctors got their first clue into the causes of SAD when some of their patients complained that their depression increased during overcast periods, and they began to look at the effects of different light levels on mood. They found that SAD is more widespread the farther north you go, so people in Seattle are seven times more likely to have it than Miami residents.

ESSENTIALS It's now thought that 4 to 6 out of every 100 people may have SAD, and studies show that it's four times more common in women than in men. The malady doesn't usually begin until after a person's twentieth birthday, and the older you get, the less likely you are to contract the disorder.

Researchers began studies in which SAD patients were exposed to artificial light, and found that thirty to forty-five minutes of fluorescent light therapy a day caused significant improvement in 80 percent of the cases. The treatment, called phototherapy, is now a standard method of care for patients with seasonal depression.

Moods and Melatonin

Scientists now think that the release of the hormone melatonin by the brain's pineal gland, a pea-sized structure just below the brain, has a hand in bringing about the change in brain chemistry that causes the symptoms of SAD. Melatonin causes tiredness and seems to be related to our body's biological cycles—called circadian rhythms—although the exact nature of the link is still unclear. What is known is that SAD patients have more melatonin during a depressive episode than people who are not depressed, and that phototherapy returns their melatonin levels to normal.

It's been known for centuries that animals respond to changes in weather: bears hibernate, geese fly south for the winter, and squirrels gather nuts. But for humans, the weather's effect on mood was often chalked up to crankiness or a generally bad attitude. Now the new science of biometeorology is helping explain how climate can have a very real effect on both physiology and psychology, speeding the development of new treatments for weather-related ills.

CHAPTER 17

Down and Dirty in the Atmosphere

It isn't pollution that's harming the environment. It's the impurities in our air and water that are doing it.
—Former vice president Dan Quayle

Humans have been pouring pollutants into the atmosphere ever since the discovery of fire, but volcanoes, forest fires, and even desert dust can add their particles to the mix, creating atmospheric conditions that are hostile to nearly every form of life on the planet.

What Are You Breathing?

Air pollutants fall into two main categories: primary pollutants, which cause a direct effect on the air, and secondary pollutants, which must first mutate into harmful substances such as acid rain and ozone, following a chemical reaction. Primary pollutants come from smokestacks and auto exhausts, doing their damage immediately on entering the atmosphere.

Approximately 6.6 million tons of pollution are pumped into America's air every year. About 40 percent of it comes from industrial processes, with another 17 percent being emitted by automobile exhaust systems. Particles that can remain suspended in the atmosphere for years are called aerosols. If they're small enough, they can be spread hundreds of miles from their sources by the prevailing winds in the upper atmosphere. The tiniest particles are able to slip right by your lungs' defenses and cause allergic reactions and worse.

FACTS

You may not think of carbon dioxide (CO_2) as a pollutant; after all, your lungs produce it with each breath. But it's also a byproduct of burning fossil fuels such as oil, natural gas, and coal. Aside from being toxic if inhaled in large amounts, carbon dioxide has been identified as one of the major greenhouse gases.

In cities, the major pollution culprit is carbon monoxide (CO), an odorless, colorless toxic gas that results from incomplete combustion of fuel. Motor vehicles account for about ⅔ of carbon monoxide emissions in urban areas, although the figure can rise as high as 90 percent. Carbon monoxide harms humans and animals by reducing the amount of oxygen blood can carry. Since it can bonds more easily with hemoglobin than oxygen, high levels of carbon monoxide in the blood are very difficult for the body's defenses to remove. Low levels of carbon monoxide poisoning create flulike symptoms, while higher levels result in loss of consciousness, convulsions, coma, and finally death.

The Ins and Outs of HAPs and VOCs

The Environmental Protection Agency (EPA) has identified 188 chemicals that can cause serious effects on human health and the environment, and has assigned them the collective name of hazardous air pollutants, or HAPs. Exposure to these compounds can cause serious disabilities and illnesses such as cancer, diseases of the central nervous system, birth defects, and even death by large-scale releases. The major cancer-causing HAPs are 1,3-butadiene, polycyclic organic matter, benzene, carbon tetrachloride, chromium, and formaldehyde.

A major pollution disaster happened in Bhopal, India, in 1984. A release of deadly gasses at a Union Carbide pesticide plant there killed at least 1,700 people and injured several hundred thousand others, many of whom experienced permanent physical disabilities, respiratory ailments, cancers, and multigenerational genetic damage.

Many manufacturing processes, including spray painting, semiconductor manufacturing, dry cleaning, wood finishing, and printing produce volatile organic compounds (VOCs), a class of chemicals that easily forms vapors at normal temperatures and air pressures. Some of these gases are harmful when inhaled, and many of them are carcinogens. Others are readily soluble in water and can pollute not only the air but groundwater supplies as well.

VOCs are indoor hazards as well: They can be found in paints, solvents, household cleansers, and disinfectants, among other common supplies. Limited exposure can cause headaches and irritation of the eyes, nose, and throat. More prolonged contact can result in nausea; loss of coordination; and liver, kidney, and central nervous system damage.

The Good, the Bad, and the Ozone

You'll recall from Chapter 1 that ozone is composed of three atoms of oxygen and forms a layer high in the stratosphere that protects you from the Sun's harmful UV rays. But ozone's benefits are confined to the upper atmosphere; when it's found down in the troposphere, it's a pollutant.

Inhaling ozone can cause several effects on the body, none of them good. Some people report chest pains, throat irritation, coughing, and nausea, and those with pre-existing health problems such as asthma, emphysema, heart disease, and bronchitis find their symptoms can become much worse when ozone is plentiful.

At the surface, nitrogen oxides (NO_x) and VOCs interact to produce ozone, instead of the UV bombardment that causes it to form aloft. But ground-level ozone has the same chemical structure as the higher variety; it's harmful at the surface simply because of its location. Gasoline is one of the most abundant VOCs, and when emitted by car exhausts, it's considered an ozone precursor since it reacts with sunlight to form ozone.

Ozone harms plants by reducing their ability to produce and store food, making them more susceptible to attack by insects and disease.

In cities, up to half the population is exposed to ozone levels well above the EPA standards at some point during the year. In Los Angeles, ozone peaks have exceeded the maximum limit nearly a third of the time in recent years.

Sulfur dioxide can be harmful to the lungs, and some long-term studies have shown that children are especially at risk. According to the research, if exposed to high levels of sulfur dioxide pollution at an early age, children are likely to develop more breathing problems as they get older and may get more respiratory illnesses than they otherwise would.

Sulfur dioxide (SO_2) is a pollutant that can be caused by erupting volcanoes, but is more commonly created as a byproduct of the burning of sulfur-containing fuels such as coal and oil, by the smelting of metal, during paper production, and by other industrial processes. Sulfur dioxide is a colorless gas that is odorless in small concentrations but has a strong smell at higher levels. In water, sulfur dioxide dissolves to form highly toxic sulfuric acid; in the atmosphere, it binds with water molecules and falls as acid rain.

Acid Rain: A Burning Issue

The term "acid rain" is a misnomer in some cases, because pollutants don't always fall to earth in a wet form. The earth's gravity is constantly trying to pull anything in the atmosphere back to the surface, so acidic gases and particles can make their way to the ground without rain in a process called dry deposition. About half of all acidity in the atmosphere returns to earth in a dry form, so a more accurate term for acid rain is "acid deposition."

Acid deposition can happen hundreds of miles from a pollution source, as particles get swept up by the wind and transported across state and national borders, making air pollution a global problem, not just a local one. In the United States, more than 90 billion pounds of sulfur dioxide and nitrogen oxides are released into the air each year. When this acid binds with water droplets and falls as rain, it carries pollutants into the ground, along with particles that have already fallen as dry deposition.

Don't Drink the Water

When acidic water enters streams, lakes, and marshes, it begins to lower their pH levels. Soil and water normally have some capacity to neutralize acid, but where soils have low alkaline levels and precipitation has a high acid content, acidity can quickly overwhelm a watershed's natural buffering capacity. As acid rain flows through soil it liberates aluminum, which is carried into lakes and streams along with polluted water. For fish, low pH and high aluminum levels are a deadly combination.

More than thirty years ago, scientists first became concerned when they noticed that even in remote areas, lakes that were once full of fish had become barren. The U.S. Geological Survey was brought in to determine the reason, and eventually acid rain was pegged as the culprit. The survey established the National Atmospheric Deposition Program/National Trends Network (NADP/NTN), which collects rain and snow samples from across the country and monitors them for acid deposits.

The survey found that rain or snow falling in the eastern United States has a much lower pH level than precipitation elsewhere in the country. In addition, a National Surface Water Survey identified several areas where streams were especially sensitive to acidification, including the mid-Appalachian region, the Adirondack and Catskill Mountains, the upper Midwest, and mountains of the western United States. Acid rain was found to be the cause of acidity in 75 percent of acid lakes and 50 percent of acidic streams.

Acidic Earth

The effects of acid rain aren't limited to bodies of water; the low pH levels it causes in the soil can slow the growth of entire forests, make leaves turn brown and fall off, and even cause trees to die. In the eastern United States, the Shenandoah and Smoky Mountain National Parks have been particularly hard-hit. Atop Clingmans Dome in the Smokies, a once-proud stand of conifers is now a ghost forest, its denuded trees covered with moss and lichen.

Although acid rain doesn't directly kill trees, it weakens them by damaging their leaves and exposing them to toxic compounds in the soil. Just as it does in fish, acidity stresses trees and plants, making them more susceptible to disease or attack by insects, drought, or cold weather. In high forests such as those in the Smoky Mountains, pollution's effects can be magnified and accelerated by the constant presence of acid fog, which acts to deplete essential nutrients in the leaves of plants and trees.

Oh Say, Can You See?

Acid deposition isn't always tangible, but it affects everything it touches, even buildings and automobiles. In our nation's capital, monuments made of seemingly eternal materials such as marble are literally being eaten away by acid in the atmosphere. Marble is composed of calcium carbonate, or calcite, which is easily dissolved by even mild acid. Because many of our national monuments are made of marble or limestone, some are slowly crumbling as acid deposition takes it toll. Some of the buildings particularly affected are the Capitol, the Jefferson Memorial, the Lincoln Memorial, and the Federal Triangle buildings.

Reduced visibility has devalued what was once an exciting outdoor experience for an estimated 280 million annual park visitors. In the East, where the visual range used to be 90 miles, it's now only 15 to 25 miles. The visibility in western states has declined from 140 miles to 35 to 90 miles.

Pollution can also cause problems with visibility, creating transportation hazards on the ground as well as increased collision dangers for aircraft. Haze in the atmosphere is created by tiny particlesof pollution in the air that can either absorb light or scatter it before it reaches an observer. Once-clear vistas in our National Parks are now shrouded in brown or white haze for much of the year.

A Polluted History of the Twentieth Century

Air pollution isn't a recent development; it's been around since the beginning of the Industrial Revolution. One of the worst air pollution disasters occurred in 1948 in the town of Donora, Pennsylvania, which lies in the Monongahela River valley. The town's location isn't normally a problem, except on rare occasions when a temperature inversion forms. As warm air rises, it usually carries particles of pollution up into the atmosphere where they're dispersed by wind. But during an inversion, a warm layer of air forms over a cooler, denser layer, trapping pollution near the ground.

That's what happened in Donora in October 1948. The city of 14,000 was a company town, dominated by the U.S. Steel factory where many of its residents worked. Townspeople were used to a certain level of smog, but on that fateful Thursday morning, residents awoke to a thick gray fog that seeped into homes even with the doors and windows closed. One by one, community members began to succumb to the acrid cloud, filling hospital emergency rooms with choking, wheezing victims. Many attempted to evacuate the city by car, but the dense smog and massive traffic jams soon made driving impossible. By Saturday, the town's three funeral homes had no more room for bodies and a temporary morgue was set up. The deadly haze enshrouded Donora for the better part of five days until a rainstorm finally dispersed it.

When the air cleared, 20 people were dead and nearly 6,000 were ill from the smog's effects. Many blamed the steel and zinc works along the river, which had continued to pump fumes into the saturated atmosphere until four days after the emergency began. The disaster led to the first air pollution conference, convened by President Harry Truman in 1950, which raised public awareness of the problem and set the stage for the Air Pollution Control Act, which was passed in 1956. For the first time, the U.S. government identified air pollution as a national problem and announced its intention to improve the situation.

Clearing the Air

Because of the efforts to purify the air enacted by the EPA and other U.S. governmental bodies, the country's air is measurably cleaner that it was at midcentury, but there is still much work to do. The United Nations and the World Health Organization have set up a program called the Global Environment Measuring System (GEMS); its findings show that as many as 1.2 billion people are being exposed to daily levels of pollution sufficient to endanger their health. In the United States and other developed countries, great strides have been made in cleaning up the air. But in poorer developing nations, dependence on coal and other polluting energy sources continues to endanger millions of people.

In this country, the Clean Air Act of 1963 went a long way toward ridding the air of factory smoke and chemicals by setting emissions standards for polluters such as power plants and steel mills. Later amendments set standards for automobiles and other vehicles, and the Clean Air Act of 1970 applied even more stringent rules, especially for the automotive industry. In 1990, the Act was amended again, reflecting newer scientific findings such as ozone's role in protecting the atmosphere. The 1990 amendment specified that the use of CFCs be reduced to prevent ozone destruction and set a definite timetable for the reduction of automotive emissions.

QUESTIONS?

What is the Kyoto Accord?
It is an international treaty between industrialized nations to reduce carbon dioxide emissions. The United States declined to participate, claiming it would harm the economy.

A Personal Program

Since then, there has been a growing realization that each person in the United States is on the front line of the war on pollution. It's possible for everyone to take steps to curb the amount of pollution generated by every-day activities. The EPA has the following suggestions that individuals can take to reduce pollution:

- Follow gasoline refueling instructions for efficient vapor recovery, being careful not to spill fuel and always tightening your gas cap securely.
- Keep car, boat, and other engines tuned up according to manufacturer's specifications.
- Be sure your tires are properly inflated.
- Carpool, use public transportation, bike, or walk whenever possible.
- Use environmentally safe paints and cleaning products whenever possible.

On days with particularly high ozone levels, try to:

- Choose a cleaner commute—either share a ride to work or use public transportation.
- Combine errands to reduce trips, and walk to errands when possible.
- Avoid excessive idling of your automobile.

- Refuel your car in the evening when it's cooler.
- Conserve electricity, and set air conditioners no lower than 78 degrees.
- Use household, workshop, and garden chemicals in ways that minimize evaporation, or wait until ozone levels are lower.
- Defer lawn and gardening chores that use gasoline-powered equipment, or wait until evening.

Pollution reduction is under way at the community level as well. Some towns located in areas of high risk have installed air quality monitors, and alerts are issued via the local media when particulate pollution is high. Air monitors can also be used to identify the sources of local pollution, and cooperative actions involving municipalities and businesses can help reduce the effects of regional air pollution.

Scrubbing the Air

One particularly interesting air-cleaning solution has been proposed by Melvin Prueitt, a physicist from the Los Alamos National Laboratory in California, who has patented a design for a network of 650-foot "convection towers" he says can pull large amounts of contaminants from the air, including sulfur dioxide, ozone, soot, and other particulate matter. The towers would be made of fiberglass coated with Teflon, and would be supported by ten steel beams around their edges.

In Prueitt's design, a fine mist of electrostatically charged water vapor is sprayed over the opening at the top of each tower. The charged droplets attract particles of pollution, and some noxious gases dissolve into the water as well. As some of the water evaporates, it cools the surrounding air, which becomes denser and falls toward the bottom of the tower, leaving a partial vacuum where more air rushes in. As the process accelerates, a sort of controlled downburst of descending air is created.

Nobody wants to breathe air filled with industrial and automotive waste. Aside from affecting health directly, many scientists point to the buildup of atmospheric pollutants as a factor in sweeping changes now occurring on a planetary scale.

Chapter 18

A Climate of Uncertainty

*If we don't change direction soon, we'll end up where
we're going.*

—Professor Irwin Corey

W ith carbon dioxide and other
pollutants being piped into the
air all over the world, many scientists believe man is causing a slow but
inexorable warming of the entire globe.
Are humans really to blame, or is the
earth just going through another of its natural stages?

A Hot Topic

Climate change has become a media obsession lately, but the earth's climate is variable by nature, and has gone through drastic changes in its history. In fact, just 18,000 years ago (a mere blip in geological time), the North American continent and Europe were in the grip of an ice age, with glaciers extending south as far as New York. So much water was stored in the earth's ice caps that the sea level was up to 400 feet lower than it is now.

FACTS

The earth's climate reflects the balance of energy between the planet and its atmosphere. You've seen how precipitation, condensation, and wind tend to distribute heat from solar radiation around the globe. Evidence is mounting that the earth goes through regular cycles that disrupt its energy balance and produce extremes of heat and cold.

Of course, at that time the nomadic people who inhabited the land that would become America could migrate south to more temperate climates, but if the glaciers began moving in today, the consequences would be catastrophic. Why does the earth experience such dramatic changes in its climate from time to time? And what—or who—is responsible?

You may have come to think of the greenhouse effect as a bad thing, but were it not for greenhouse gases, the planet's average temperature would be about 61 degrees F colder than it is now. It's important that a certain amount of heat be trapped near the surface, or summer would turn to winter, and winter would be—well, you get the idea.

Is the Earth Running a Fever?

During the twentieth century, the earth's average temperature increased by about 1 degree F, with half of that rise taking place between 1975 and 2000. The last few decades have seen the warmest summers in the Northern Hemisphere since about A.D.1000 or perhaps even earlier. In addition, the sea level is rising at the rate of up to a foot per century.

All of these symptoms indicate a warming trend, just as a high thermometer reading indicates that a patient has a fever. But the fact that someone has a temperature doesn't tell the doctor what's causing it, and the same is true of global warming. There's little doubt the earth is getting warmer, but the debates over the cause are hotter still.

Spin Cycles

A Serbian astronomer named Milutin Milankovitch proposed one theory back in the 1930s that involves three components of the earth's position in space. The planet's orbit isn't a perfect circle, but more of an oval, or ellipse. Over a period of 100,000 years, the orbit becomes more and then less elongated, changing the distance the Sun's energy must travel to reach Earth. This process, called eccentricity, reduces and then increases the effect of solar radiation on the surface over time.

Precession, the slow wobble the earth makes as it spins on its axis, is the second part of the theory. Over a period of 23,000 years, the north polar axis describes a narrow circle in the sky, first pointing to Polaris, the North Star, and then Vega. This changes the seasons in which the earth is closest to the Sun, and the theory predicts that a significant seasonal and climatic alteration results.

The third component of Milankovitch's theory is the earth's tilt on its axis, known as obliquity. This degree of tilt changes as well, from 21.5 to 24.5 degrees over a period of 41,000 years. The planet is now in the middle of the cycle, but as the tilt increases or decreases, the difference in warmth between polar and equatorial regions changes, affecting the severity of the seasons.

The Evidence Mounts

The three components are collectively known as Milankovitch cycles. The scientist theorized that when parts of the three variables occur at the same time, their combined effects are responsible for major climate changes. In the 1970s, NOAA's CLIMAP project, which aimed to develop a detailed climatological map of the ancient world using computer modeling, found evidence in deep-sea core samples that substantiated Milankovitch's theory. The samples showed a strong correlation between long-term climate variations and Milankovitch cycles.

Further studies have shown that ice ages reach their peaks every 100,000 years or so—the same amount of time it takes for the earth's orbit to stretch and contract. Examination of ice sheets in Earth's colder regions also indicates that there was about 30 percent less carbon dioxide in the air during ice ages, adding a cooling effect to the atmosphere that could have reinforced and lengthened the colder period.

QUESTIONS?

Will ice ages happen again?

Because recurring ice ages are one of Earth's regular cycles, it's not only possible there'll be another one, it's inevitable. They only happen once every several thousand years, though, so don't break out the parkas just yet.

Positive Feedback and Shifting Plates

Once the earth enters a warming phase, certain atmospheric effects can help sustain the change. If the surface temperature is slowly rising, more and more water will evaporate from the oceans, saturating the atmosphere with tons of extra vapor. With more water vapor in the air, the absorption of infrared radiation speeds up, heating the atmosphere and increasing the rate of evaporation even more. Self-sustaining processes like this are known as positive feedback mechanisms.

FACTS

Positive feedback can help maintain colder periods, too. If the earth is in a cooling stage, more snow will fall and will remain on the ground for a longer period of time. Snow has a very high albedo, or reflective property, so much of the sunlight falling on it would be bounced back into space, which would make the temperature drop even more.

One way that climate changes can take place is through the redistribution of the earth's landmasses. According to the theory of plate tectonics, the planet's continents ride on a layer of molten magma, and although the annual rate of motion is only a few inches, over millions of years continental plates can move considerable distances.

Before the continents broke apart and began drifting, the theory states, they were grouped together in a huge landmass called Pangaea. Some scientists think this large area gathered so much snow in colder periods that it reduced average temperatures over the entire globe. Another factor could be continental uplift, the process that formed the Plateau of Tibet. Newly raised mountains and plateaus could have disrupted prevailing winds and caused other drastic changes in the atmosphere. And as continents broke apart, ocean currents would have shifted, creating deserts in some places and rain forests in others.

ESSENTIALS
Continental drift causes monumental stresses to build up underground, resulting in earthquakes. Many observers have reported strange "earthquake lights" during these events. Some researchers think that seismic stresses may generate high voltages that are then released into the atmosphere, but there is no definitive cause.

Another way that creeping continents can disrupt the atmosphere is through volcanic degassing, which happens when one continental plate meets another. This often takes place deep in the ocean at boundaries called ridges, where molten material from deep in Earth's mantle rises to the surface, spreading out as the plates retreat from each other. If the plates collide, the heavier one will be pushed downward, where it begins to melt. Either way, large quantities of carbon dioxide are produced, enhancing the atmosphere's heat-retaining ability over the long term.

Humans Get into the Act

Nature has been dumping CO_2 and other gases into the atmosphere for eons, but until the beginning of the Industrial Revolution, man's primary contribution was ash and smoke from wood fires and methane emissions from farm animals. In the 1700s, that began to change with the invention of the coal-fired steam engine, steamboats, and locomotives. Suddenly, transportation was faster and more economical, and with the advent of coal-fueled factories, goods could be produced much more efficiently, at lower cost, and in greater quantities.

The downside, of course, was pollution. But there was a seemingly limitless supply of air, and with mankind now the master of nature (or so it was believed), few gave atmospheric contamination a second thought. As a result, much damage was done before the problem was identified.

A rise in the sea level increases the likelihood and severity of coastal flooding, and has harmful effects on marshes and wetlands along the shore. It can destroy animal habitats and cause saltwater intrusion into aquifers, polluting water supplies. The economic effects can be truly disastrous, making beaches and businesses in tourist areas literally disappear.

Within the past two decades, the subject of global warming and climate change has become a priority in many countries. In 1988, the United Nations and the WMO formed the Intergovernmental Panel on Climate Change (IPCC) to monitor the earth's atmosphere and study the effects of man's influence. The IPCC is made up of scientists from all over the world; their job is to assess the possible impacts of climate change and inform national leaders of their findings.

In January 2001, the IPCC released a report that affirmed its previous position: Global warming is real and is changing the earth's climate in ways that natural processes cannot. According to the agency, mankind is now in the midst of a long-term environmental experiment that could have serious negative consequences in the years ahead. The latest report from the IPCC states that "there is new and stronger evidence that most of the warming observed over the last fifty years is attributable to human activities."

Apocalypse: Soon?

Proponents of the global warming theory predict that as the earth continues to heat up and more greenhouse gases are released into the atmosphere, the rate of temperature increase will accelerate. They predict a rise in the average global surface temperature on the order of 1 degree F to 4.5 degrees F over the next fifty years, as compared with the 1 degree F increase during the entire twentieth century. During that time, the sea level rose about 4 to 8 inches, and the EPA estimates it could rise another 12 to 18 inches by 2100. The IPCC's prediction range is between 3.5 and 34.6 inches. Some scientists even think the West Antarctic Ice Sheet could slide into the sea with enough sustained warming, raising ocean levels up to 20 feet.

A Global Hothouse

As temperatures increase, more frequent and intense heat waves could cause heat-related deaths to soar. The heat would also aggravate pollution problems, causing more respiratory distress and other illnesses. Forests and farmland could be swallowed up by expanding deserts, reducing crop output and causing an even greater temperature spike.

The loss of plant life would reduce the earth's ability to remove carbon dioxide from the air, amplifying the greenhouse effect. Higher temperatures and rainfall amounts would also increase deaths from insect-borne diseases such as malaria and the West Nile virus, which first appeared in the United States in 1999. And with vegetation drying up in the hotter regions, wildfires could run amok across the globe.

The amount of heavy precipitation over land has also increased during the past century, a trend that some scientists say will speed up as the earth warms. Their theory: Increased warmth will result in more evaporation, directly generating more rain and snow, causing increased flooding in some areas. With higher sea surface temperatures would come more frequent and much stronger hurricanes, since much more warm water vapor would be available to feed the giant storms.

Is Man to Blame?

The global climate has been in flux throughout recorded history. Could the changes we see happening today be a result of natural processes that have occurred over millennia? Not a chance, say global-warming supporters.

For one thing, they point out, carbon dioxide created from natural sources such as volcanoes still retains a measure of the radioactive element carbon-14, while carbon dioxide released from the burning of fossil fuels does not. In addition, studies performed between the 1950s and the present indicate that levels of this nonradioactive carbon dioxide have risen each year. This evidence, say scientists, can be seen in the decreasing amount of radioactive carbon dioxide captured in tree rings during that time.

Bubbles in ice trapped below the earth's ice caps have produced samples of prehistoric air in core samples brought to the surface, and researchers say they show that atmospheric carbon dioxide was 25 percent less plentiful 10,000 years ago than it is today. The key: That level remained constant over thousands of years instead of showing the steady rise we see today, which some scientists are certain results from the actions of human beings.

The Opposition Weighs In

Balderdash, say critics: Most of these CO_2 emissions would still take place even if there were no humans on Earth at all, and blaming people for global warming is too simplistic a solution for such a complex problem. They argue that the intricate relationships among all the atmosphere's elements make the creation of a truly accurate climate change model impossible. They point to a competing study that examined ice core samples and concluded that CO_2 levels *did* fluctuate during the preceding 10,000 years. Besides, they say, CO_2 accounts for only 10 percent of the greenhouse gases in the atmosphere; the major culprit is water vapor.

Are you confused yet? So is everyone else, but with 6.6 tons of greenhouse gases being emitted for each man, woman, and child in the United States each year, some say the "better safe than sorry" approach of reduction is the best policy. America is the earth's largest source of CO_2 pollution, and the rate is increasing—one reason why Congress established the U.S. Global Change Research Program in 1990.

ESSENTIALS

Some scientists theorize that global warming could actually be beneficial, bringing relief to snow-prone areas in the winter and reducing the number of annual deaths due to hypothermia. Warmer weather would also bring longer growing seasons, increasing crop yields, and more carbon dioxide in the atmosphere would make plants more vigorous.

Creating more bureaucracies is certainly one way to attack the issue, but other ways of reducing carbon dioxide emissions have been proposed. One is carbon sequestration, which the U.S. Department of Energy thinks could be used to cut carbon dioxide emissions by 1 billion tons a year by 2025 and 4 billion tons by 2050. The method proposes to get rid of carbon dioxide by dumping it into the ocean, which is already the earth's major carbon dioxide holding area. The seas contain more than 45 trillion tons of carbon, but scientists say there's room for a lot more.

FACTS

During the last Ice Age, parts of Alaska, Canada, and Siberia were covered with giant sheets of ice up to a mile thick, a change in climate many scientists chalk up to a decline in solar radiation. Even in the early twentieth century, icebergs would often break off the Greenland ice sheet and drift south into North Atlantic shipping lanes.

The process involves pressurizing and chilling carbon dioxide, then pumping it deep into the sea. Sinking to the bottom, it spreads out and thins, eventually dissolving into the seawater. Tests indicate the carbon dioxide dissolves slowly enough to leave sea life unharmed, but fast enough that it doesn't form thick pools that could smother bottom-dwelling plants and fish. Other scientists say it would be easier and just as effective to pump carbon dioxide back into the ground where it came from, and tests are under way to examine that possibility.

Climate Change from Space?

Many scientists say that to better understand why the earth is warming, you have to look at its main source of heat: the Sun. As with any other global warming theory, the effect of the Sun's influence is still being debated, but many researchers feel that solar variability could be responsible for at least a third of the temperature rise seen in the past century.

But isn't the Sun's energy output a constant? Not really. To astronomers, our Sun is known as a variable star, because its production of radiation varies in a cycle that lasts an average of eleven years, a pattern discovered by amateur astronomer Heinrich Schwabe in 1843. That variation is small—only about 0.1 percent—but it's thought that the fluctuation has been greater over longer time scales, changing by as much as 0.5 percent.

The Sun: A Harsh Mistress

Recently, scientists have discovered statistical links to the Sun's energy output and the number of sunspots on its face. Examining historical records, they found that in the period between 1640 and 1720, the number of sunspots fell dramatically, and so did the earth's average temperature, plunging an average of 2 degrees F. The effect was particularly noticeable in Northern Europe, where glaciers advanced southward and winters were especially harsh.

In Chapter 6, you learned that sunspots are relatively cooler areas in the Sun's photosphere, so it would seem that fewer sunspots would mean a hotter Sun and hence a warmer atmosphere here on Earth. Once solar-observing satellites were able to examine sunspots closely, however, the mystery was solved: The bright areas called faculae, which accompany sunspots during the solar cycle, are much hotter than sunspots and more than make up for their cooling effect.

Another possible solar effect on climate could be the fluctuation in the UV part of the spectrum, which is much more wildly variable than visible light. During a peak in the Sun's eleven-year cycle, UV radiation increases by a few percent, compared with the 0.1 percent increase in total radiation. Most of it is blocked by the upper atmosphere, but because all the atmospheric layers are connected, constant UV bombardment can affect the amount of ozone in the stratosphere. That effect eventually propagates down to the surface, so UV radiation could be another component of the climate change riddle.

Twisting in the Solar Wind

The Sun also ejects vast amounts of charged particles and magnetic radiation, also thought to have an effect on Earth's climate. This flood of energy—the solar wind—constantly streams past Earth, flowing around the planet's magnetic field. During periods of solar maximum output, the Sun's magnetic field is stretched past the earth, helping to block cosmic rays from entering the atmosphere. But during quieter phases, more cosmic rays leak through.

Some scientists suggest that an increase in cosmic rays can affect the amount of clouds and rain, having a direct effect on the earth's temperature. It was recently discovered that high levels of cosmic ray activity cause the upper atmosphere to become highly conductive, leading to higher electrical charges in water droplets, causing more rain. The proof, they say, is found in the increased carbon-14 levels caused by cosmic rays that have been recorded in tree rings.

As the Sun passes through its cycles, it's also moving through space at around 486,000 miles per hour, dragging the solar system with it. At that speed, it takes the Sun about 226 million years to complete one revolution around the Milky Way Galaxy. The last time the Sun was at the present spot in its galactic orbit, humans didn't exist yet, and dinosaurs were the dominant species on the planet.

The Cosmic Merry-Go-Round

Interesting, but what's that got to do with global climate change? Well, as the solar system orbits in the galactic plane, the flat disk in which the galaxy's spiral arms are found, it bobs up and down like a cork. So every 30 million years or so, the entire solar system passes through a thicker layer of interstellar dust, gas, and debris. During the passage, it becomes much more likely that the Sun will encounter large bodies like other stars and planets, and when this happens their gravitational effects can have a powerful influence on the solar system.

FIGURE 18-1:
The sun:
Climate
controller

(refer to page
281 for more
information)

As a large body passes near the Oort cloud, the gigantic halo of rock and ice fragments that orbits out past Pluto, some of these objects are slowed or sped up by gravitational attraction, either ejecting them from the solar system or causing them to fall inward toward the Sun. As these celestial missiles enter the inner solar system, they pose an increased danger of collision with Earth. Another effect a passage through the Milky Way's spiral arms might cause is higher-than-normal concentrations of dust falling into the Sun, causing it to burn brighter and hotter, which would increase the amount of solar radiation received by the earth and the average temperature of the atmosphere.

Death Rays

In 1967, another potential source of climate disturbance was discovered when scientists were studying data from satellites looking for

Nuclear Test Ban Treaty violations. Instead of radiation from Earth, they found several sources of intense gamma ray bursts coming from outer space. Gamma rays are the most intense form of energy known. Since then, researchers have been unsure of what causes the bursts—called GRBs for short—but increasing evidence indicates they may be the result of supernovas, which are the explosive deaths of massive stars.

When a giant star collapses, it causes an explosion so violent that for a few moments it becomes the brightest object in the universe. The blast creates an intergalactic shock wave that expands outward in all directions like a giant bubble while the star's interior collapses on itself, often forming a black hole. A new theory states that another, faster jet of material from the dying star moving at nearly the speed of light can overtake that bubble's outer boundary, causing a second explosion, which generates a GRB.

An Uncommon Threat

Although astronomers have located GRBs only in other galaxies, it is thought they were once more common in the Milky Way and could have affected ancient Earth's climate. Be glad they're not common today: GRBs can release more energy in ten seconds than the Sun will generate in its entire 10-billion-year lifetime! Scientists think a GRB in our galaxy could have serious consequences for life on Earth.

One NASA publication describes a GRB's effects: "A gamma ray burst originating in our neck of the Milky Way, within a thousand light-years or so, could lead to mass extinction on Earth. Gamma rays interacting in the earth's atmosphere would burn away the ozone layer, allowing deadly ultraviolet radiation to penetrate through the atmosphere."

Put in that perspective, slow global warming doesn't sound quite so bad. Certainly, much more research is needed to determine whether the changes seen in Earth's climate during the past few decades are a result of natural processes or if man's recent industrialization is lending a hand. Until then, expect the debate to continue unabated.

CHAPTER 19

Meteorology, Media, and Marketing

Forecast for tonight: dark. Continued dark through tonight with scattered light in the morning.

—George Carlin as Al Sleet,
the Hippy-Dippy Weatherman

Interpreting the vast amounts of data being gathered by the National Weather Service and other agencies is a huge job. Most radio and television stations have come to depend on specialized weather products, created by private-sector companies, to help them boost ratings by providing dazzling high-tech graphic displays.

Broadcasting Shenanigans

The very first U.S. weathercast took place in New York City on October 14, 1941, as World War II raged overseas. Consisting of a few lines of text, it was transmitted by experimental television station WNBT-TV, which later became WNBC. The forecast was announced by a cartoon character named Woolly Lamb, and was sponsored by Botany Wrinkle-Proof Ties, establishing a lighthearted approach to TV weathercasting that continues today.

FIGURE 19-1:
Satellites provide instant data

(refer to page 281 for more information)

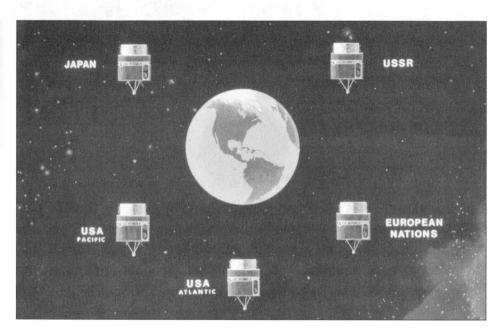

After the war, the weather forecast became a staple of broadcast news. As the new medium gained viewers, competition increased and stations began to hire professional meteorologists and other on-air personalities to handle their forecasting duties. Many of them were discharged veteran Weather Bureau officers, but many more were hired for their personalities or attractiveness, and some were just clowns, dressing in silly costumes on the air. Although they amused war-weary audiences, appalled meteorologists felt their credibility was on the line.

That's why the AMS established its seal of approval in 1957. To earn one, a candidate had to pass a series of rigorous tests and be able to not only adequately explain the processes that create various weather conditions, but also to produce a forecast based on those patterns. The applicants' test results were reviewed by a board of AMS members, performance was graded, and the candidates who received a seal of approval could move from station to station without reapplying.

FACTS

Since the seal was established, the AMS has certified nearly a thousand weathercasters. A seal of approval is also issued by the National Weather Association, which, unlike the AMS, offers skilled weather-people without degrees an equal opportunity for certification.

With no digital 3-D maps or satellite loops yet in sight, early weather broadcasters came up with some ingenious ways of reporting the forecast graphically. In Mark Monmonier's book *Air Apparent: How Meteorologists Learned to Map, Predict, and Dramatize Weather,* Gary England is quoted recalling his first broadcast for an Oklahoma station that used large rotating drums for its maps:

> *The metal weather maps on the large four-sided drums somehow looked larger that night. Each drum weighed 180 pounds but felt much heavier. Every time I turned a drum, some of the letters and numbers would fall off or would assume a crazy tilt and have to be rearranged. It was frustrating those days, the norm.*

Some weathercasters drew a series of weather maps on large paper charts and flipped through them one by one during their broadcasts, while others developed sliding panels to display their charts. Meteorologist Don Noe of Miami's WPLG created animated maps using stop-motion photography long before it was done with digital technology.

Technology Takes Over

In the 1960s, inventor Petro Vlahos developed a system of matting—inserting one picture into parts of another—that was eventually used in movies such as *Mary Poppins*. Vlahos's invention, called Chroma Key, allowed a television station to insert their on-air meteorologist into a weather map or other background in a process called compositing, and it soon became a standard part of most weather broadcasts during the 1970s and 1980s. Vlahos continued to refine the process, and today his company Ultimatte provides digital compositing products for both television and motion pictures.

FACTS

In the late 1980s and early 1990s, advances in computer technology allowed companies like Earthwatch Communications to develop detailed, high-resolution 3-D weather maps and other high-tech products. Some stations that were still producing their own graphics were dismayed to see their competitors adopting these third-party offerings, as viewers came to expect dazzling eye candy with their daily dose of weather news.

Today, visuals are king in the world of television weathercasting. Technically advanced graphics quickly and easily explain complex climatic events to viewers, while radar loops and animated satellite images give them immediate feedback on what's going on in the atmosphere.

The Local Connection

One station that uses Weather Services International Corporation's WeatherProducer system is WNCN, the NBC affiliate in Raleigh, North Carolina. Meteorologist Emily Byrd and her fellow weathercasters use information from WSI to create detailed local forecasts, but personal observations are often just as important in predicting what the weather will bring to Raleigh.

"The first thing I do when I get up in the morning is look out the window," Byrd explains, "checking to see if my forecast from the night before was right. If it wasn't, I have to figure out why." Arriving at the station, Byrd checks the current numerical models and their associated graphics, since they don't always agree. Then it's time to sort through the models to find the ones that have best predicted the current conditions.

Some Models Are Smarter Than Others

Byrd says, "We check out those models to see if they're behaving, to see if there are any we can throw out because they're, say, telling you it's going to snow tomorrow but it's 70 degrees outside. You compare them to yesterday's forecast, because you want some degree of consistency. You don't want to just spit out a forecast, because the models will give a wide variation the further out you go in time."

Byrd notes that human experience and intuition still beat numerical models' accuracy for the first twenty-four hours, while the models outperform humans after that. The effects of terrain and unusual current conditions like floods or drought can be particularly important, Byrd explains, and models that don't account for them will often produce erroneous results. "So after a few days of watching the models underperform, we can take those factors into account and tweak out what all of the models have gotten wrong," she notes.

Weather Services International Corporation offers Intellicast.com, a Web site that provides twenty-four-hour weather coverage and a multitude of graphic, color-coded maps, charts, and satellite images. In 2000, WSI was purchased by Landmark Communications, the same company that owns the Weather Channel.

Homework Pays

When it comes time to go before the cameras, Byrd works without a script. "We use the maps to cue us," she explains, "and then we just tell the story." Viewers often call to request a forecast for the next nine or ten days, and Byrd's answer is always the same: The accuracy of forecast models doesn't extend out that far yet, and much can change in that time. "But I'm really impressed that they have that much faith in our skill," she laughs.

For those who might be considering broadcast meteorology as a career, Byrd has this advice: Get the best education you can. "Don't be afraid of the math and science," she says. "People don't wake up knowing how to do calculus—they have to learn it." Once the educational requirements are taken care of, the key to getting a job is persistence, says Byrd: "It's a very competitive field, and you really have to be able to sell yourself to the person who's doing the hiring."

FACTS

Although television probably comes to mind when you think of meteorologists, the U.S. government is by far the largest employer of weather professionals in this country. NOAA, NASA, and the Department of Defense are just some of the agencies that employ meteorologists.

Conquering Cable

Now a household name, the Weather Channel was the brainchild of John Coleman, the first weathercaster for ABC's *Good Morning America* program. In the late 1970s, Coleman became frustrated with the short time he was allotted for each broadcast—usually only two or three minutes—to convey weather information for the entire United States.

FIGURE 19-2:
Weather
Channel
briefing

(refer to page
281 for more
information)

Encouraged by a public survey showing that there was a great interest in weather among viewers, Coleman noted that cable television was making rapid inroads in the broadcast industry. Coleman began approaching potential backers, using products like WSI's SuperRadar to prove that the technology was in place to provide twenty-four-hour weather information for cable TV.

SSENTIALS Like CNN, the Weather Channel is based in Atlanta, Georgia, giving the company a central location and access to a variety of satellite facilities. It boasts a staff of more than 120 professional meteorologists, and its signal now reaches more than 80 million U.S. households.

Virginia-based Landmark Communications, a privately held media firm that owns several newspapers, television stations, and other information outlets, agreed with Coleman, and on May 2, 1982, the Weather Channel was launched. It wasn't exactly an auspicious debut: Only four advertisers were on board to pay the fledgling channel's expenses, and the company narrowly avoided disaster in its first year, when it reported a loss of $10 million.

Turning the Corner

In 1983, the company revamped its offerings and began to be picked up by more cable operations. It finally turned a profit in the late 1980s, and has since become the country's leading source of broadcast weather information.

With the availability of twenty-four-hour weather TV came the emergence of a new kind of viewer: the weather addict. According to the Weather Channel, people with a deeper interest in climate and weather comprise 41 percent of the American public, and that curiosity isn't easily satisfied. A Weather Channel press release put it this way:

Seemingly, the more TWC viewers learn, the more they want to know; some of these people look to the all-weather network with the same interest and enthusiasm some television viewers devote to watching movies. According to Jim Alexander, vice president of research for TWC, "A segment of the TWC audience is particularly interested in understanding the mechanisms that influence weather patterns and the meteorological background behind a tornado or hurricane."

Web Weather

Weather fans were granted even faster access to their favorite subject when the Weather Channel launched its Web site, ✍*www.weather.com,* in April 1995. The site allows viewers to design a custom Web page featuring their local information, and offers specialized weather tips on the topics of health, driving, gardening, golf, and travel, among others. A new module lets computer users download weather data to a Weather Channel interface on their computer desktops, and personal digital assistant users can transfer weather information directly into the units.

QUESTIONS?

Are there any famous weather fans?
Bill Cosby, Bill Murray, violinist Gil Shaham, and columnist Russell Baker all have the bug, according to the Weather Channel. No doubt there are many more lurking in anonymity.

The Weather Channel now has a radio network that reaches 84 percent of U.S. radio markets, and a service that provides customized weather packages to newspapers across the United States. The channel's Web presence has expanded to include the United Kingdom, Brazil, Portugal, Spain, and the U.S. Hispanic market. The Weather Channel also broadcasts severe weather alerts to cell phone and pager users. For a company once on the verge of bankruptcy, it's come a long way.

CHAPTER 20

Changing the Weather

Any party which takes credit for the rain must not be surprised if its opponents blame it for the draught.
—W. Somerset Maugham

In the past, there have been many attempts to change the weather, most of which were failures because of humans' limited power and the atmosphere's sheer size. But some recent developments might finally make large-scale weather modification a reality—for better or for worse.

Rainmen

In the 1956 film *The Rainmaker,* Burt Lancaster stars as Bill Starbuck, a con artist working his way from town to town through the drought-ridden Southwest, promising to bring rain to parched communities for a flat fee of $100. The movie is no weather primer: Its main theme is how Starbuck helps transform Katherine Hepburn's plain-Jane character into a ravishing beauty. The con man is just as surprised as anyone when he seems to conjure up a cloudburst in the movie's finale. But it does raise the question of how—and if—humans can really affect weather conditions.

The science of weather modification was barely a decade old when *The Rainmaker* was released, but humankind's attempts to change the weather have been ongoing for centuries. The Mayans of the ancient Yucatan offered up human sacrifices to the weather god Chac, hoping to ensure plentiful rain during the growing season. In the eighteenth century, the ringing of church bells was thought to dissipate storm clouds, but the theory took its toll on the unlucky souls who rang them. In just thirty-three years, 103 bell ringers died in lightning hits on 386 European church towers.

But the most famous rainmaker in history must be Charles Mallory Hatfield, a sewing-machine salesman who developed an interest in meteorology around the turn of the twentieth century. By December 1904, Mallory was so confident of his rainmaking abilities that he promised the city of Los Angeles relief from its drought within four months for the paltry sum of $1,000. In that time, Hatfield promised that a foot and a half of rain would fall on the bone-dry city, and set to work building wooden towers where he sent his foul-smelling chemical compounds wafting skyward.

To everyone's surprise, 18 inches of rain fell on the City of Angels in only three months, bringing Hatfield instant fame and more job offers from all over the country. His price went up, too, and by 1915 he was demanding $10,000 to fill the Moreno Dam reservoir near San Diego with rainwater. After making the deal, Hatfield went to work, and soon a flood of major proportions was under way, killing fifty people and destroying houses and railways.

Hatfield was working under a verbal contract, and with the rain came the blame. Hatfield left town empty-handed, but it didn't slow him down; through the years he was credited with more than 500 rainmaking successes. Today meteorologists doubt that Hatfield had some now-forgotten secret formula for rainfall, and insist that the rainmaker just had extraordinary luck and good timing. But his story was still intriguing enough to inspire the filming of *The Rainmaker.*

Letting It Snow

In 1946, an experiment performed by Vincent Schaefer, a research assistant at the General Electric Laboratory in Schenectady, New York, showed that making rain and even snow in a scientific way just might be possible. For weeks, Schaefer had been trying to produce artificial precipitation by various methods using a cloud chamber—basically a 4-foot-square freezer—but nothing seemed to work.

July 13 was a particularly hot day, so Schaefer left the lid off his chamber while he went to lunch, hoping it would help cool the laboratory. When he returned, the open cooler gave Schaefer an idea. He found a chunk of dry ice—frozen carbon dioxide—and put it into the cloud box. Instantly the chamber filled with a miniature snowstorm as tiny ice crystals fed off water vapor and turned into snowflakes.

Later that year, Schaefer and pilot Curtis Talbot repeated the experiment in an airplane. On November 13, while flying above "an unsuspecting cloud over the Adirondacks," as he put it, Schaefer dumped a few pounds of dry ice overboard, and ground observers saw snow streamers begin falling from the cloud. Schaefer realized that if he seeded a supercooled cloud, snow would fall even if few condensation nuclei were present.

Trouble was, dry ice was difficult to work with: It is bulky and hard to handle, with the dismaying tendency not only to stick to bare skin but to disappear into thin air if not tightly contained. Something was needed that would have a similar chemical structure, but without the drawbacks of dry ice.

The Silver Solution

Bernard Vonnegut, another GE researcher, studied the structure of a number of natural crystals and finally found a compound that fit the bill. It was silver iodide, a compound of iodine and silver that turned out to have an internal structure nearly identical to ice crystals'. Vonnegut tried the compound in Schaefer's freezer box and was rewarded with another tiny blizzard.

For postwar America, the thought that weather control was possible was heady stuff. The United States had already proved it could control atomic energy, and now it looked as though control of the weather was just around the corner. From those first early experiments, interest in rainmaking and weather modification mushroomed.

The Air Force got involved in 1947, offering aircraft and manpower to continue the experiment, which Schaefer called Project Cirrus. Working with the Army Signal Corps and the Office of Naval Research, B-17 bombers were soon crisscrossing the skies of New Mexico, dumping huge quantities of silver iodide and dry ice into prospective thunderclouds.

Project Cirrus proved that cloud seeding worked, although scientists argued over the effect's magnitude. As research continued, it became evident that seeding only worked under certain conditions, with certain types of clouds. And when no clouds were present, seeding the atmosphere with silver iodide or any other substance turned out to be a waste of time.

Core Strategies

Since then, two main types of cloud seeding have been developed, depending on whether a cloud is a warm-core or cold-core type. In cold-cloud seeding, silver iodide or other compounds injected into the cloud cause supercooled liquid water droplets to freeze. These ice seeds grow as they pull vapor from the surrounding air in a process called sublimation, eventually becoming snowflakes. The flakes fall to the ground intact if the air at the surface is cold enough, or melt into raindrops if it isn't.

If the cloud's temperature is above freezing, bits of material such as salt particles are introduced to provide additional condensation nuclei. Increasing amounts of water vapor are attracted to the particles, which grow larger as they encounter more of the tiny droplets. Warm-cloud seeding, of course, produces rain.

In cold-core systems, proponents say that reducing the size of hailstones is possible using silver iodide. As the theory goes, there is only so much supercooled water in a cloud, and introducing more particles causes the production of more, but smaller, hailstones. If the hailstones are small enough, they will often melt before reaching the surface, but those that survive the drop will still cause much less damage.

Seeds of Controversy

As usual, the scientific community is sharply divided on the subject of cloud seeding. Because the atmosphere is so complex and dynamic, detractors contend there is no real way to know how much rainfall would have occurred if clouds hadn't been seeded. And they argue that during a drought there are often no clouds at all to seed, and there is no way to form them artificially at present.

Some fear that increasing rain in one area might reduce it in another, depriving downwind farmers of the water needed to sustain their crops. Others object to weather manipulation on the general principle that humans shouldn't be involved in trying to change natural processes, at least until the long-term consequences of altering rainfall are known.

QUESTIONS?

Are there any other substances used in cloud seeding?
Liquid propane is sometimes used in the Northeast and Alaska to clear fog from airport runways. Dry ice crystals are sometimes used for seeding instead of silver iodide.

Commercial cloud-seeding companies remain confident that the process is effective and safe. They point to studies backed by the California-based Weather Modification Association that they say prove that cloud seeding provides a significant increase in rain or snow under the right circumstances. And they insist that no significant environmental effects have been observed due to their actions.

On the question of whether cloud seeding can rob moisture from other areas, proponents claim that seeding actually removes less than

20 percent of the moisture from the air in a given region, and that it's quickly replaced by natural processes. Scientists are still worried about the possible unintended consequences of meddling with the atmosphere, however, arguing that the process is still experimental and much more research is needed.

ESSENTIALS

Using the scientific method requires a comparison between the object being modified (a cloud) and another identical object that isn't being changed (another cloud), but no two clouds are alike. All of this natural variability makes it extremely difficult to tell how the effects of cloud seeding differ from Mother Nature's own processes.

Another problem, some say, is the tendency of rainfall to create downdrafts that destroy the cloud that produced it. So, cloud seeding could actually hasten the death of a cloud rather than squeeze more rain out of it. In addition, studies have shown that even silver iodide and other compounds that can act to increase precipitation don't work unless a cloud is on the verge of producing rainfall on its own.

Scrambling Ions

The Department of Defense is conducting another large-scale atmospheric experiment that some say could have truly frightening consequences. It's called the High-Frequency Active Auroral Research Program (HAARP), and it is based near Gokona, Alaska. A series of large radio antennas, the array is designed to transmit huge amounts of microwave radiation into the ionosphere, where the aurora borealis is found. Much of HAARP's technology is based on the work of Dr. Bernard J. Eastlund, physicist and former oil industry consultant.

According to the Department of Defense, the purpose of HAARP is to learn more about the nature of long-range radio communications and surveillance by employing the reflective nature of the ionosphere. But an internal document obtained by *Popular Science* in 1990 shows that HAARP's real mission is to "control ionospheric processes in such a way as to greatly improve the performance of military command, control, and communications systems."

To that end, HAARP is designed to use microwave radiation to distort the upper atmosphere into virtual lenses and mirrors that can detect stealth aircraft and other flying weapons at great distances over the horizon. Extremely low frequency (ELF) waves generated by HAARP will be able to peer beneath the earth's surface to locate buried munitions stores and other enemy installations. Those waves will also be used to communicate with submarines, eliminating the miles-long antennae that are now required.

The Department of Defense insists that HAARP poses no threat to the surface environment or the atmosphere, and even scientific luminary Dr. James Van Allen, professor of physics at the University of Iowa and the discoverer of the radiation belts that bear his name, contends that any effects would be confined to local disturbances in communications.

Harmful HAARP?

Other scientists are worried about so much radiation saturating the ionosphere, because no project on such a grand scale has ever been attempted. They cite the concept of "nonlinear processes," in which a relatively small input of energy can be magnified into a much larger transmission of power. As professor Gordon J. F. MacDonald put it when he was a member of the President's Council on Environmental Quality, "The key to geophysical warfare is the identification of environmental instabilities to which the addition of a small amount of energy would release vastly greater amounts of energy." This leads many analysts to believe that HAARP's ultimate purpose will be as a long-range particle beam weapon of mass destruction. Eventually HAARP's output will top 4.7 billion watts, which could potentially be directed to destabilize the agricultural and environmental systems of entire countries, scientists say.

HAARP is only one part of a long-term, large-scale military program that aims to control and manipulate the weather for tactical and strategic advantages. In a report entitled "Weather As a Force Multiplier: Owning the Weather in 2025," the benefits of military weather modification are detailed by the government. By manipulating fog and precipitation over an enemy's location, the report says, visibility could be degraded in the target area while enhanced over friendly forces. The growth of developing storms over enemy strongholds could be accelerated, and triggering more lightning strikes on enemy targets would provide a natural kind of firepower.

ALERT

In its study entitled "Spacecast 2020," the Air Force predicts that the National Weather Service will be absorbed by the Department of Defense. According to the report, weather service personnel would become paramilitary operatives, "supporting the military mission as a civilian during peacetime, becoming active duty military personnel during war, contingency (and) national emergency."

One of the first steps in any military campaign is to obtain air superiority over a battlefield, but the report goes one step further, asserting that space superiority will be essential in future wars. That includes the HAARP concept of manipulating the ionosphere to produce lensing effects, which would not only enhance communications between friendly forces but could be used to disrupt the enemy's capabilities.

But these artificial electromagnetic fields can have a more insidious effect, as one Air Force report relates:

> *The potential applications of artificial electromagnetic fields are wide-ranging and can be used in many military or quasimilitary situations . . . Some of these potential uses include dealing with terrorist groups, crowd control, controlling breaches of security at military installations, and antipersonnel techniques in tactical warfare. In all of these cases the EM [electromagnetic] systems would be used to produce mild to severe physiological disruption or perceptual distortion or disorientation. In addition, the ability of individuals to function could be degraded to such a point that they would be combat ineffective.*

Source: *www.au.af.mil/au/aul/school/sncoa/low.html*

FIGURE 20-1:
An Alaskan
HAARP array

(refer to page
281 for more
information)

In other words, the same kind of focused electromagnetic energy created by HAARP is capable of disrupting mental processes. It may sound like the stuff of science fiction, but all indications are that HAARP is currently fully operational.

Until recently, mankind's attempts to manipulate the weather have shown very little success, but new technological tools may be changing that. As with any experiment involving multiple unknown variables, the results will be unpredictable. Let's hope they're not detrimental to the earth and her inhabitants as well.

Whither Weather?

Mankind may or may not learn to manipulate the weather at will, but it's certain that the next few years will bring significant changes to the world of meteorology. Technological advances will drive most of the improvements in areas such as radar, satellites, and supercomputers.

As radar continues its evolution, new technology will improve its resolution as well as its ability to gather data that are not currently available from NEXRAD. NSSL is currently developing polarimetric technology to upgrade the National Weather Service's current Doppler radar. Known as dual-polarization radar, the technology transmits radio wave pulses in both vertical and horizontal orientations, providing a much more detailed look at precipitation and cloud formation.

Satellite technology also continues to improve, and that trend is expected to accelerate. Not only will resolution increase, but future Earth-observing platforms will be able to view the atmosphere in many more parts of the spectrum, allowing them to peer through clouds and smoke and image the internal structures of hurricanes and supercells. A technique called satellite interferometry will give early warnings of volcano eruptions and earthquakes, as well as tracking ocean currents and the movement of ice floes.

Fortunately, computing power is expected to keep pace with the exponential increase in weather data, making numerical models much more accurate. As supercomputers become more powerful, grid spacing will decrease while the data contained in each grid block increase, markedly improving predictions. NOAA and NASA recently established the Joint Center for Data Assimilation to expedite this process.

In the longer term, instantaneous weather data will become available to the public through a number of channels, including direct satellite transmission. Motor vehicles will sport weather alarm systems capable of routing drivers around severe weather, while many homes will feature inexpensive weather stations tied to their climate control systems. Three-day forecasts will become virtually flawless, while seven-day predictions will be about as accurate as three-day outlooks are today.

Technology is now advancing faster than at any other time in history, and the future of climate and weather prediction is bright. Even Ben Franklin, who once said, "'Tis easy to see, hard to foresee," would be amazed at how far the science of meteorology has come in such a short time. For weather buffs, it's a great time to be alive.

Appendix A
Resources

Books

- Burroughs, William J., Bob Crowder, Ted Robertson, Eleanor Vallier-Talbot, and Richard Whitaker. *The Nature Company Guides: Weather* (McMahons Point, NSW, Australia: Weldon Owen Pty Limited, 2000).

- Larson, Erik. *Isaac's Storm* (New York: Crown Publishing Group, 1999).

- Laskin, David. *Braving the Elements: The Stormy History of American Weather* (Garden City, NJ: Anchor Books, 1997).

- Lewis, John S. *Rain of Iron and Ice: The Very Real Threat of Comet and Asteroid Bombardment* (Reading, MA: Addison-Wesley, 1996).

- Lockhart, Gary. *The Weather Companion* (New York: John Wiley & Sons, Inc., 1988).

- Ludlum, David M. *The National Audubon Society Field Guide to North American Weather* (New York: Alfred A. Knopf, 1996).

- Lyons, Walter A., Ph.D. *The Handy Weather Answer Book* (Detroit, MI: Visible Ink Press, 1997).

- Porter, Henry F. *Forecast: Disaster—The Future of El Niño* (New York: Dell, 1998).

- Sheets, Bob, and Jack Williams. *Hurricane Watch* (New York: Vintage Books, 2001).

- Thompson, Dick. *Volcano Cowboys: The Rocky Evolution of a Dangerous Science* (New York: St. Martin's Press, 2000).

- Walker, Paul Robert. *Head for the Hills!: The Amazing True Story of the Johnstown Flood* (New York: Random House, 1993).

- Watts, Alan. *The Weather Handbook* (Dobbs Ferry, NY: Sheridan House, 1999).

- Williams, Jack. *The USA Today Weather Book* (New York: Vintage Books, 1997).

Organizations

- **American Meteorological Society**
  45 Beacon Street
  Boston, MA 02108
  www.ametsoc.org

- **Federal Emergency Management Agency**
  500 C Street, SW
  Washington, DC 20472
  www.fema.gov

- **National Climatic Data Center**
  Federal Building
  151 Patton Avenue
  Asheville, NC 28801
  http://lwf.ncdc.noaa.gov

- **National Hurricane Center**
  11691 S.W. 17th Street
  Miami, FL 33165
  www.nhc.noaa.gov

- **National Oceanic and Atmospheric Administration**
  U.S. Department of Commerce
  14th Street & Constitution Avenue, NW, Room 6013
  Washington, DC 20230
  www.noaa.gov

- **National Severe Storms Laboratory**
  1313 Halley Circle
  Norman, Oklahoma 73069
  www.nssl.noaa.gov

- **National Weather Association**
  1697 Capri Way
  Charlottesville, VA 22911
  www.nwas.org

- **National Weather Service**
  1325 East-West Highway
  Silver Spring, MD 20910
  www.nws.noaa.gov

- **World Meteorological Organization**
  7 bis, Avenue de la Paix

CH 1211 Geneva 2
Switzerland
www.wmo.ch/index-en.html

Storm Chasing

❧ Cloud 9 Tours: *www.cloud9tours.com*

❧ Severewx.com: *www.severewx.com*

❧ Silver Lining Tours:
www.silverlining.pair.com

❧ Storm Track: *www.stormtrack.org*

❧ Tempest Tours: *www.tempesttours.com*

❧ Warren Faidley: *www.stormchaser.com*

Weather Companies

☁ **AccuWeather, Inc.**
385 Science Park Road
State College, PA 16803
www.accuweather.com

☁ **EarthWatch Communications**
5125 County Road 101, Suite 300
Minnetonka, MN 55345
www.earthwatch.com

☁ **WeatherBank, Inc.**
1015 Waterwood Parkway, Suite J
Edmond, OK 73034
www.weatherbank.com

☁ **The Weather Channel**
300 Interstate North Parkway
Atlanta, GA 30339
www.weather.com

☁ **Weatherwise Magazine**
1319 18th Street NW
Washington, DC 20036
www.weatherwise.org

☁ **WSI Corporation**
4 Federal Street
Billerica, MA 01821-3569
www.wsi.com
www.intellicast.com

Web Sites

▱ CNN Weather Page: *www.cnn.com/weather*

▱ Skywarn: *www.skywarn.com*

▱ TVWeather.com: *www.tvweather.com*

▱ Unisys: *www.weather.unisys.com*

▱ USA Today Weather Page:
www.usatoday.com/weather/wfront.htm

▱ WeatherMatrix: *www.wxmatrix.com*

▱ WeatherSage: *www.weathersage.com*

▱ The Weather Underground:
www.wunderground.com

▱ WxUSA: *www.wxusa.com*

Appendix B
Glossary

absolute zero—The temperature at which there is no longer any thermal motion. Unreachable under real-world conditions.

acid deposition—Acidic pollutants deposited from the atmosphere to the earth's surface in wet and dry forms.

acid rain—See *acid deposition.*

aurora borealis—A glowing display caused by electrically charged particles ejected from the Sun that are guided into the upper atmosphere by Earth's magnetic field.

backdoor front—A front that moves east to west in direction rather than the normal west to east movement.

blizzard—A winter storm with sustained or frequent winds of 35 miles per hour or higher. In a blizzard, snow is falling or blowing so fast it can reduce visibility to one-quarter of a mile or less.

chaos theory—A hypothesis that states that a tiny change can have a huge effect.

chlorofluorocarbons (CFCs)—Organic compounds composed of carbon, fluorine, chlorine, and hydrogen. CFCs released into the atmosphere accumulate in the stratosphere where they destroy ozone molecules.

cold front—The front edge of a cold air mass where it intrudes on a warmer air mass.

condensation nuclei—Tiny particles that allow water vapor to condense into rain and other types of precipitation. They include sulfur compounds, dust, and organic molecules.

Coriolis effect—The tendency for any moving body on or above the earth's surface to be deflected sideways from a straight course due to the earth's rotation.

coronal mass ejection (CME)—Massive bursts of plasma ejected from the Sun that can damage satellites and electrical grids.

cyclone—An area of low pressure. Winds blow in a counterclockwise direction in the Northern Hemisphere and in a clockwise direction in the Southern Hemisphere.

dew point—The temperature to which air must be cooled for it to be saturated with water vapor.

downburst—A strong downward blast of air that causes damaging wind at the surface.

drizzle—Small drops of liquid precipitation that fall at a slower rate than rain.

dryline—A boundary that separates warm, dry air from warm, moist air.

dust devil—A small, relatively weak cyclone that often picks up leaves and other debris from the ground.

earthquake lights—Eerie flashes of light reported to emanate from the ground during earthquakes.

El Niño Southern Oscillation (ENSO)—A regular, large-scale fluctuation of ocean temperatures, rainfall, atmospheric circulation, vertical motion, and air pressure across the tropical Pacific.

equinox—The point in the year when the Sun's rays are striking the equator vertically. In the Northern Hemisphere the spring equinox occurs around March 21, and the autumnal equinox around September 22.

faculae—Bright granular structures on the Sun's surface that are slightly hotter or cooler than the surrounding photosphere.

flash flood—A flood caused by extremely heavy rainfall in a short period of time. Flash floods are very dangerous in hilly or mountainous areas. A flash flood can also be caused by the failure of a dam or from ice jams on rivers and streams.

flood—An inundation of water caused by the overflowing of a stream, river, or other body of water.

fog—A cloud at ground level. Dense fog reduces visibility to a ¼ mile or less.

freeze—A condition caused by low temperatures (32 degrees F or less) over a wide area for an extended period of time.

freezing rain—Liquid rain that freezes when it hits the ground or an object with a temperature of 32 degrees F or less. Freezing rain makes driving treacherous and can pull down power lines and tree branches.

friction layer—The lowest layer of the earth's atmosphere, from the surface up to around 3,300 feet. In this layer, wind speed is slowed by surface features such as mountains.

frost—A thin crust of ice that forms on exposed surfaces when their temperature falls below the freezing point.

Fujita Tornado Damage Scale—A scale that correlates the scope and type of tornado damage with its wind speed.

funnel cloud—A vortex of rotating air beneath a cumulonimbus cloud that does not reach the ground.

gamma ray burst (GRB)—Incredibly powerful blast of radiation thought to be caused by the explosion of a massive star.

Global Climate Observing System (GCOS)—International weather organization established to monitor global climate change.

Global Environment Monitoring System (GEMS)—A worldwide collective effort coordinated by the United Nations to improve environmental data resources.

gyre—Large circular ocean currents bounded by continental landmasses.

hail—Balls or lumps of ice that form in thunderstorms and build up layer by layer.

heat budget—The amount of heat Earth radiates into space versus the amount it absorbs. The planet always tries to keep the two in balance.

heat index—A measurement of how hot it feels when the relative humidity is added to the actual air temperature.

hook echo—Hook-shaped echo return on a radar screen indicating rotation within a thunderstorm and possible tornado formation.

hypercane—A theoretical superhurricane caused by extreme heating of the oceans.

ice age—A period when large areas of the earth are covered with large continental glaciers.

ice crystals—Tiny ice particles that form when water vapor freezes. Cirrus and other high clouds are composed of ice crystals.

ice storm—An accumulation of ¼ inch or more of freezing rain. Makes driving or even walking virtually impossible.

instability—An atmospheric condition caused by sudden temperature changes between levels, often leading to severe weather.

Intertropical Convergence Zone (ITCZ)—A globe-circling band of clouds and showers near the equator where hurricanes tend to form in the summer and early fall in the Northern Hemisphere.

inversion—An atmospheric condition where temperatures increase with height. Also called a negative lapse rate.

isobar—A line on a weather map that connects points of equal pressure. Isobars are often depicted as closed, concentric rings around areas of high and low pressure.

jet streak—A localized area of wind within a jet stream moving faster than the stream's average speed.

jet stream—A narrow current of high winds in the upper atmosphere. They are usually found between 6 and 10 miles above the surface.

landspout—A weak tornado not associated with a supercell or wall cloud.

lapse rate—The rate of change of heat and other meteorological elements with height.

Mesonet—A system of sensors and other weather instruments designed to measure atmospheric conditions on a mesoscale of up to several hundred miles.

microburst—A narrow but violent downdraft of air. Microbursts are extremely dangerous to aircraft.

National Severe Storms Laboratory (NSSL)—A NOAA agency responsible for improving severe-weather forecasting capabilities by advancing the understanding of weather processes. Based in Norman, Oklahoma.

NEXt-generation RADar (NEXRAD)—High-resolution Doppler radar system.

numerical models—Computer programs that are capable of forecasting temperature, pressure, moisture, rainfall, and winds.

obliquity—The tilt of the earth's axis.

occluded front—A blending of a cold front and a warm front when the former overtakes the latter.

orographic lifting—The rise of an air mass as it encounters sloping terrain such as mountains and hills.

Pacific Decadel Oscillation (PDO)—Long-range changes in the warm and cold regions of the Pacific Ocean.

precession—The cyclic wobbling of the earth's axis of rotation.

pressure gradient—A difference in atmospheric pressure between two adjacent areas. Winds always flow from high pressure to low.

pyroclastic flow—High-density volcanic flows of hot, dry rock fragments and gases that surge away from the eruption vent at high speeds.

rain—Drops of liquid precipitation at least $1/50$ of an inch wide.

relative humidity—The amount of water vapor in the air versus the amount of moisture it can hold at that particular pressure and temperature.

ridge—An area of anticyclonic winds around an elongated area of high pressure. See *Trough*.

right front quadrant (RFQ)—The most dangerous section of a hurricane, since the storm's forward speed combines with its wind speed there.

Rossby waves—Large-scale meanders in the midlatitude jet streams. Similar waves form in ocean currents.

scud—Small, ragged cloud fragments often seen moving rapidly below a larger cloud base.

Severe Clear-Air Turbulence Colliding with Aircraft Traffic (SCATCAT)—NOAA project investigating the nature and causes of air turbulence.

severe thunderstorm—A thunderstorm with winds of 58 miles per hour or greater and/or hail $3/4$ of an inch or larger in diameter.

shower—Rain that falls intermittently and for a short time.

sleet—Small ice pellets that form when snow falls through a warm layer of air, melts, and then refreezes.

snow—Geometric ice crystals that form in clouds when water vapor freezes into ice.

snowflake—Large, flat ice crystals with a complex hexagonal form.

snow flurries—Snow that falls intermittently and for a short time.

solstice—The point in time when the Sun's rays are striking the tropic of Cancer or tropic of Capricorn vertically. In the Northern Hemisphere, the summer solstice occurs around June 21, and the winter solstice around December 22.

squall line—A long line of thunderstorms or gusts.

stability—An atmospheric condition in which there are no sudden temperature changes between levels.

stepped leader—An initial discharge of lightning that moves toward the ground in a series of steps.

sublimation—The transition of water or another substance from a solid to a vapor without passing through a liquid phase.

supercell—A large, severe thunderstorm that often produces large hail and tornados.

synoptic scale—A weather map scale that shows highs, lows, and fronts over a continent-sized area.

tornado—A rapidly rotating vortex that extends to the ground under a thunderstorm.

trough—An area of cyclonic winds around an elongated area of low pressure. See *Ridge*.

virga—Rain or snow that evaporates before reaching the ground.

vortex—Any rotating parcel of air. Usually applied to areas of low pressure.

wall cloud—A large rotating area of clouds below a storm that indicates a mesocyclone. Often precedes a tornado.

warm front—The front edge of a warm air mass where it encounters and rides over the top of a cooler air mass.

waterspout—A rapidly rotating vortex that extends from a cloud to the surface of a body of water.

whiteout—A condition caused by heavy, blowing snow that obscures landmarks and leads to disorientation.

wind-chill factor—The temperature it feels like to someone exposed to a combination of low temperature and wind.

PHOTOGRAPHY CAPTIONS

FIGURE 1-1: First-ever tornado photo.
The oldest known photograph of a tornado. Humans have always been at the mercy of severe weather, but new technology means earlier warnings.

FIGURE 1-2: Altocumulus clouds.
Learning about cloud types can keep you one step ahead of the weather. Rows of altocumulus clouds like this often predict a dose of rain.

FIGURE 2-1: D-Day troops wade ashore.
Even the military is no match for bad weather. The Allied invasion of Europe had to wait until the conditions were right.

FIGURE 2-2: German V-2 Rocket.
Although the German V-2 rocket was a weapon of mass destruction, it led directly to the space vehicles that now launch weather satellites.

FIGURE 3-1: Ocean thunderstorms.
Cumulus clouds can rapidly grow into cumulonimbus thunderheads when conditions are right.

FIGURE 3-2: San Francisco fog.
Advection fog often hides the Golden Gate bridge from view.

FIGURE 3-3: Hailstone or ice bomb?
Nature's mortar shells: Hailstones caught in thunderstorm updrafts can grow to deadly dimensions.

FIGURE 3-4: Too much snow.
Let it stop! The aftermath of a 1966 North Dakota snowstorm.

FIGURE 4-1: High winds at sea.
Nor'easters can be nearly as strong as hurricanes.

FIGURE 5-1: Oceans harbor undersea rivers.
Hidden under every ocean are meandering streams of faster-moving water that have a great impact on regional climates.

FIGURE 5-2: Ocean mapping from space.
Satellites like TOPEX/Poseidon and Jason can measure wave height to within millimeters.

FIGURE 5-3: El Niño forecasts help fisherman.
The ENSO cycle can be a fisherman's best friend or his worst enemy, but satellite technology provides an early warning of developing El Niños.

FIGURE 6-1: The sun's angle determines temperature.
Not only does the Sun create the Earth's seasons, it has seasons of its own: Eleven-year cycles of increasing and decreasing activity.

FIGURE 7-1: A windrose.
A Wind Rose was an early device used to determine wind direction.

FIGURE 7-2: Aerovanes measure wind speed.
An aerovane combines an anemometer and wind vane into one sleek unit.

FIGURE 7-3: A doppler radar facility.
The development of Doppler radar caused a revolution in the science of weather forecasting.

FIGURE 8-1: Inside TIROS.
The TIROS series of satellites gave forecasters a bird's-eye view of developing weather systems.

FIGURE 8-2: TIROS prelaunch checkout.
TIROS' technology was crude by today's standards, but was the forerunner of today's sophisticated weather satellites.

FIGURE 8-3: Computers are improving forecasts.
High-speed computers help make weather predictions more accurate, but long-range forecasts are still dicey due to chaos.

FIGURE 10-1: Floods: perennial hazards.
Floods have always been a part of Earth's water cycle, but people still tend to get in their way.

PHOTOGRAPHY CAPTIONS

FIGURE 11-1: Tornado and wall cloud.
Although tornadoes usually last only a short time, their ferocity and unpredictability make them one of nature's most deadly threats.

FIGURE 11-2: Waterspouts: Wet tornadoes.
Waterspouts are generally thinner and slower-moving than tornadoes, and tend to form over very warm water.

FIGURE 11-3: Tornado vs. airplane: Aftermath.
Like mobile homes, aircraft are especially susceptible to tornado damage because of their light weight.

FIGURE 11-4: Doppler on wheels.
Multiple mobile Doppler radar units deployed around tornadoes have provided unprecedented views of their mysterious cores.

FIGURE 12-1: Hugo decimated Charleston.
Hugo was one of the largest hurricanes ever recorded, and its extreme storm surge and violent winds played havoc with the city of Charleston, South Carolina.

FIGURE 12-2: Severe hurricanes: They're coming.
Decades of destruction on the way? The long-range forecast is for increased hurricane activity.

FIGURE 12-3: Which way will they go?
Computers do their best to predict the paths of hurricanes, but when steering currents are weak, forecast models begin to disagree and meteorologists stay up way past their bedtimes.

FIGURE 14-1: Hurricanes launch deadly missiles.
In Category Four and Five hurricanes such as Camille and Andrew, common objects can become deadly projectiles.

FIGURE 14-2: A tornado's indiscriminate destruction.
Twisters like the Tri-state Tornado leave little standing in their wake.

FIGURE 14-3: Evil eye: Andrew approaches.
Ironically, Andrew took dead aim on the National Hurricane Center in Coral Gables, Florida.

FIGURE 15-1: Tornadoes can form suddenly.
Don't be fooled: The early stages of a tornado can look like a dust storm.

FIGURE 15-2: Hurricanes often spawn tornadoes.
Nearly all hurricanes that make landfall in the United States spawn at least one tornado, and the driving rain often makes them difficult to see.

FIGURE 18-1: The sun: Climate controller.
The Sun's cycles affect long-term climatic conditions.

FIGURE 19-1: Satellites provide instant data.
With constellations of weather and communication satellites orbiting overhead, access to complex weather data is now nearly instantaneous.

FIGURE 19-2: Weather Channel briefing.
The Weather Channel provides twenty-four-hour national weather forecasts. Local weather is "on the 8's."

FIGURE 20-1: An Alaskan HAARP array.
As with any uncontrolled experiment, the ultimate effects of HAARP's radiation on Earth's atmosphere is unknown

Index

THE EVERYTHING ASTRONOMY BOOK

By Dr. Cynthia Phillips and Shana Priwer

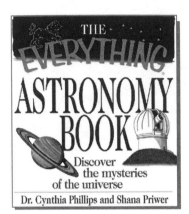

THE EVERYTHING ASTRONOMY BOOK

Discover the mysteries of the universe

Dr. Cynthia Phillips and Shana Priwer

Trade paperback, $14.95
1-58062-723-4, 304 pages

For stargazers of all ages and levels, *The Everything® Astronomy Book* makes understanding the stars, the planets, the galaxies, and the solar system as simple as a peek through a telescope. Noted scientist Dr. Cynthia Phillips does away with complicated astro-jargon and, in plain English, explains a universe of fascinating topics, such as the differences between a *meteor*, *meteorite*, and *meteoroid*; how astronomy was practiced in many ancient cultures; and all about the sophisticated instruments used by today's professional astronomers.

OTHER *EVERYTHING®* BOOKS BY ADAMS MEDIA CORPORATION

Everything® **After College Book**
$12.95, 1-55850-847-3

Everything® **American History Book**
$12.95, 1-58062-531-2

Everything® **Angels Book**
$12.95, 1-58062-398-0

Everything® **Anti-Aging Book**
$12.95, 1-58062-565-7

Everything® **Astrology Book**
$12.95, 1-58062-062-0

Everything® **Astronomy Book**
$14.95, 1-58062-723-4

Everything® **Baby Names Book**
$12.95, 1-55850-655-1

Everything® **Baby Shower Book**
$12.95, 1-58062-305-0

Everything® **Baby's First Food Book**
$12.95, 1-58062-512-6

Everything® **Baby's First Year Book**
$12.95, 1-58062-581-9

Everything® **Barbecue Cookbook**
$14.95, 1-58062-316-6

Everything® **Bartender's Book**
$9.95, 1-55850-536-9

Everything® **Bedtime Story Book**
$12.95, 1-58062-147-3

Everything® **Bible Stories Book**
$14.95, 1-58062-547-9

Everything® **Bicycle Book**
$12.00, 1-55850-706-X

Everything® **Breastfeeding Book**
$12.95, 1-58062-582-7

Everything® **Budgeting Book**
$14.95, 1-58062-786-2

Everything® **Build Your Own Home Page Book**
$12.95, 1-58062-339-5

Everything® **Business Planning Book**
$12.95, 1-58062-491-X

Everything® **Candlemaking Book**
$12.95, 1-58062-623-8

Everything® **Car Care Book**
$14.95, 1-58062-732-3

Everything® **Casino Gambling Book**
$12.95, 1-55850-762-0

Everything® **Cat Book**
$12.95, 1-55850-710-8

Everything® **Chocolate Cookbook**
$12.95, 1-58062-405-7

Everything® **Christmas Book**
$15.00, 1-55850-697-7

Everything® **Civil War Book**
$12.95, 1-58062-366-2

Everything® **Classical Mythology Book**
$12.95, 1-58062-653-X

Everything® **Coaching & Mentoring Book**
$14.95, 1-58062-730-7

Everything® **Collectibles Book**
$12.95, 1-58062-645-9

Everything® **College Survival Book**
$12.95, 1-55850-720-5

Everything® **Computer Book**
$12.95, 1-58062-401-4

Everything® **Cookbook**
$14.95, 1-58062-400-6

Everything® **Cover Letter Book**
$12.95, 1-58062-312-3

Everything® **Creative Writing Book**
$12.95, 1-58062-647-5

Everything® **Crossword and Puzzle Book**
$12.95, 1-55850-764-7

Everything® **Dating Book**
$12.95, 1-58062-185-6

Everything® **Pregnancy Organizer**
$15.00, 1-58062-336-0

Everything® **Project Management Book**
$12.95, 1-58062-583-5

Everything® **Puppy Book**
$12.95, 1-58062-576-2

Everything® **Quick Meals Cookbook**
$14.95, 1-58062-488-X

Everything® **Resume Book**
$12.95, 1-58062-311-5

Everything® **Romance Book**
$12.95, 1-58062-566-5

Everything® **Running Book**
$12.95, 1-58062-618-1

Everything® **Sailing Book, 2nd Ed.**
$12.95, 1-58062-671-8

Everything® **Saints Book**
$12.95, 1-58062-534-7

Everything® **Scrapbooking Book**
$14.95, 1-58062-729-3

Everything® **Selling Book**
$12.95, 1-58062-319-0

Everything® **Shakespeare Book**
$12.95, 1-58062-591-6

Everything® **Slow Cooker Cookbook**
$14.95, 1-58062-667-X

Everything® **Soup Cookbook**
$14.95, 1-58062-556-8

Everything® **Spells and Charms Book**
$12.95, 1-58062-532-0

Everything® **Start Your Own Business Book**
$12.95, 1-58062-650-5

Everything® **Stress Management Book**
$14.95, 1-58062-578-9

Everything® **Study Book**
$12.95, 1-55850-615-2

Everything® **T'ai Chi and QiGong Book**
$12.95, 1-58062-646-7

Everything® **Tall Tales, Legends, and Other Outrageous Lies Book**
$12.95, 1-58062-514-2

Everything® **Tarot Book**
$12.95, 1-58062-191-0

Everything® **Thai Cookbook**
$14.95, 1-58062-733-1

Everything® **Time Management Book**
$12.95, 1-58062-492-8

Everything® **Toasts Book**
$12.95, 1-58062-189-9

Everything® **Toddler Book**
$12.95, 1-58062-592-4

Everything® **Total Fitness Book**
$12.95, 1-58062-318-2

Everything® **Trivia Book**
$12.95, 1-58062-143-0

Everything® **Tropical Fish Book**
$12.95, 1-58062-343-3

Everything® **Vegetarian Cookbook**
$12.95, 1-58062-640-8

Everything® **Vitamins, Minerals, and Nutritional Supplements Book**
$12.95, 1-58062-496-0

Everything® **Weather Book**
$14.95, 1-58062-668-8

Everything® **Wedding Book, 2nd Ed.**
$14.95, 1-58062-190-2

Everything® **Wedding Checklist**
$7.95, 1-58062-456-1

Everything® **Wedding Etiquette Book**
$7.95, 1-58062-454-5

Everything® **Wedding Organizer**
$15.00, 1-55850-828-7

Everything® **Wedding Shower Book**
$7.95, 1-58062-188-0

Everything® **Wedding Vows Book**
$7.95, 1-58062-455-3

Everything® **Weddings on a Budget Book**
$9.95, 1-58062-782-X

Everything® **Weight Training Book**
$12.95, 1-58062-593-2

Everything® **Wicca and Witchcraft Book**
$14.95, 1-58062-725-0

Everything® **Wine Book**
$12.95, 1-55850-808-2

Everything® **World War II Book**
$12.95, 1-58062-572-X

Everything® **World's Religions Book**
$12.95, 1-58062-648-3

Everything® **Yoga Book**
$12.95, 1-58062-594-0

*Prices subject to change without notice.

EVERYTHING  SERIES!

Everything® **Kids' Baseball Book, 2nd Ed.**
$6.95, 1-58062-688-2

Everything® **Kids' Cookbook**
$6.95, 1-58062-658-0

Everything® **Kids' Joke Book**
$6.95, 1-58062-686-6

Everything® **Kids' Mazes Book**
$6.95, 1-58062-558-4

Everything® **Kids' Money Book**
$6.95, 1-58062-685-8

Everything® **Kids' Monsters Book**
$6.95, 1-58062-657-2

Everything® **Kids' Nature Book**
$6.95, 1-58062-684-X

Everything® **Kids' Puzzle Book**
$6.95, 1-58062-687-4

Everything® **Kids' Science Experiments Book**
$6.95, 1-58062-557-6

Everything® **Kids' Soccer Book**
$6.95, 1-58062-642-4

Everything® **Travel Activity Book**
$6.95, 1-58062-641-6

Available wherever books are sold!
To order, call 800-872-5627, or visit us at everything.com

Everything® is a registered trademark of Adams Media Corporation.